World Economic Forum
Geneva, Switzerland

Global Competitiveness Pr[
General Editors:

Klaus Schwab
President, World Economic Forum

Jeffrey D. Sachs
Director, Center for International Development
Harvard University

The European Competitiveness and Transition Report 2001–2002

Ratings of Accession Progress, Competitiveness, and Economic Restructuring of European and Transition Economies

Editor:

Andrew M. Warner
Center for International Development
Harvard University

Project Coordinator:

Peter K. Cornelius
World Economic Forum

New York • Oxford

Oxford University Press

2002

The European Competitiveness and Transition Report 2001–2002: Ratings of Accession Progress, Competitiveness, and Economic Restructuring of European and Transition Economies is published by the World Economic Forum, where it is a special project within the framework of The Global Competitiveness Program.

At the World Economic Forum:

Professor Klaus Schwab
President

Dr. Peter K. Cornelius
Director

Yong Zhang
Economist

Fiona J. Paua
Economist

At Harvard University:

Dr. Andrew M. Warner
Research Fellow, Center for International Development at Harvard University

Professor Jeffrey D. Sachs
Director, Center for International Development at Harvard University

The term *country* as used in this report does not in all cases refer to a territorial entity that is a state as understood by international law and practice. The term covers well-defined, geo-graphically self-contained economic areas that are not states but for which statistical data are maintained on a separate and independent basis.

Oxford University Press

Oxford New York
Athens Auckland Bangkok Bogotá
Buenos Aires Cape Town Chennai
Dar es Salaam Delhi Florence Hong Kong
Istanbul Karachi Kolkata Kuala Lumpur
Madrid Melbourne Mexico City Mumbai
Nairobi Paris São Paulo Shanghai
Singapore Taipei Tokyo Toronto Warsaw

and associated companies in
Berlin Ibadan

Published by
Oxford University Press, Inc.
198 Madison Avenue
New York, New York 10016
http://www.oup-usa.org

Oxford is a registered trademark of
Oxford University Press

ISBN 0-19-515257-3

Printing (last digit): 9 8 7 6 5 4 3 2 1

Printed in the United States of America
on acid-free paper

Contents

Preface

KLAUS SCHWAB

President, World Economic Forum

For over a decade, central and eastern Europe has been at the center of one of the most profound economic and political transformations in history. At the start of the 1990s, the region embarked on an ambitious reform program to depart from central planning toward more market-based economies. A decade later and amid significant difficulties, the region has achieved remarkable accomplishments, with several countries becoming increasingly integrated into the global economy. Despite the absence of a blueprint, dramatic changes have occurred: the liberalization of industries, the growth of private enterprises, and to a more limited extent, the development of capital markets. Political structures have been transformed and new institutions have emerged. Indeed, the progress in structural reforms achieved in the region has been so substantial that several countries are now at the threshold to membership in the European Union.

Yet the transition process has further to go. Although the region has made great strides in implementing reforms, the results have been mixed and vary widely across countries. Difficult social and political conditions prevail and many obstacles to growth remain. Institutional capacity building has lagged, while legal and regulatory frameworks remain weak in many sectors. Moreover, the transition process has been further compounded by the impact of external economic upheavals, financial crises, and, more recently, tremendous uncertainties in the global economy.

Aware of the significance of the successful integration of central and eastern Europe into the global economy, the World Economic Forum is proud to introduce the first *European Competitiveness and Transition Report 2001–2002*, a thorough review of the transition process that has unfolded in the last decade. Through an in-depth evaluation of regional trends and detailed analyses of country competitiveness, the *Report* is policy oriented and highlights the impediments to, and prospects for, further growth. It is our intention that this *Report* support the advancement of the transition process and the successful accession to the European Union by current candidates from the region.

This *Report* is a product of a fruitful collaboration between the World Economic Forum and the Center for International Development at Harvard University. I wish to thank Professor Jeffrey D. Sachs, Director of the Center for International Development, and especially Dr. Andrew Warner, who, apart from his own important contributions, has also edited the *Report*. At the World Economic Forum, my appreciation goes to Dr. Peter K. Cornelius, who, as the Director of the Global Competitiveness Program, has coordinated the project. The *Report* complements a family of research studies, which include the *Global Competitiveness Report 2001–2002* and reports on other regions. Together, they reflect the substantial integration of the world economy of which the transition economies of central and eastern Europe have become part.

Finally, we extend very special thanks to Troika Dialog Investment Company for their support. Troika Dialog has been an important collaborator in the Forum's initiative of *Changing Corporate Governance in Russia*, a key challenge not only in the largest transition economy but also in virtually all other countries in central and eastern Europe. I remain very grateful for Troika Dialog's outstanding engagement.

That we launch our very first *European Competitiveness and Transition Report* amid tremendous uncertainty arising from the recent terrorist attacks in the United States mirrors our conviction that, in an intertwined world economy, no country will be isolated from the adverse short-term effects these events will no doubt bring about. It is therefore more timely and imperative than ever to assess the longer-term prospects of the region and the challenges that lie ahead on the further path to market economies.

Introduction

ANDREW M. WARNER, Center for International Development
at Harvard University

From Communism to the European Union

As soon as negotiations over European enlargement are
completed, Europe's future will be integrally connected
with that of transition countries. For this reason we have
prepared a report on the competitiveness of Europe and
the transition regions together. The *Report* presents new
data that we use to rank countries according to their
growth potential, new data on structural change in transition countries, and fact-driven articles by independent
experts to help you understand better the real issues
behind European enlargement. A number of issues that
were once exclusively transition issues are fast becoming
pan-European issues.

The first major issue is further economic growth of
transition countries and Europe. What has proven to be
effective in promoting growth? Will transition countries
grow fast enough to reach the levels of income of western
Europe in the coming decades? Are there preconditions
to growth that some countries have not met? The reason
that growth of transition countries is important for
enlargement is that virtually all of the frictions in the
enlargement process ultimately derive from the large
income gaps that still prevail between East and West.
The single exception to this statement is the dispute over
voting rights in an enlarged Union. These and other issues
connected with enlargement are discussed in an excellent
article by Jan Fidrmuc, Susanne Mundschenk, Iulia
Traistaru, and Jürgen von Hagen.

The first article in this *Report* presents rankings of
75 countries on the basis of 20 engines of growth. Within
these rankings one can see the relative standing of the ten
candidate countries for accession to the European Union
and other European countries. We also show evidence on
which of these factors have been correlated in the past ten
years with growth rates, both within the group of transition countries and for a wider set of countries.

One important finding to emerge from recent work
is the special role played by start-up conditions in growth
in transition countries. The article by Daniel Berkowitz
and David DeJong shows new evidence that across regions
of Russia, regions with better start-up conditions have

had faster growth. The chapter on growth engines in
the beginning of the *Report* shows that across Asian and
European transition countries, there has also been a
positive association between growth rates and start-up
conditions. These findings make sense, since new
enterprise formation is an important facilitator for
restructuring. Restructuring in turn is crucial for sustained
growth. These findings can help to provide a focus for
a second generation of reform efforts in transition
countries, moving away from macroeconomic issues to
the microeconomic institutions that promote long-term
sustainable growth.

Many have recognized that one key to unlocking
the growth equation in transition countries is structural
change—the ability of an economy to move economic
resources from old activities to new ones. This *Report* also
shows results from a new enterprise survey conducted in
17 regions of transition countries. This survey is designed
to collect facts about structural change not available in the
traditional economic statistics. One finding to emerge
from this is that, although transfers of labor between state
industries and new private industries has been large in all
transition regions, the transfer of capital has been limited.
Most new private firms report that relatively little of their
useful capital was once in the hands of state entities. Most
of the capital they have acquired has therefore come from
new investments. Much of the transfer of capital from the
state to the private sector has therefore come in the form
of "instant transfers" achieved through privatization.

A second aspect of structural change is the
re-orientation of international trade in transition
countries from the east toward Europe. The geographic
re-orientation of trade is documented in an excellent
article by Peter K. Cornelius, Friedrich von Kirchbach,
and Yong Zhang. They show that for some countries in
central Europe, trade re-orientation has actually gone
beyond the long-run estimates made at the start of
the 1990s. They also document the relatively slow
re-orientation of trade in former Soviet countries.

A potential barrier to structural change that is relevant for larger enterprises attempting to enter international markets is the cost of financing large investments. This is where a country's international credit rating can come into play and affect growth. Peter K. Cornelius, Thomas Hall, Joel A. Kurtzman, and Fiona J. Paua discuss what affects a country's external credit rating and, in particular, the role of lack of transparency in regulations, policy, and legal matters. They argue that the cost of capital is raised by lack of transparency. The chain of causality that runs from lack of transparency to higher costs of international borrowing to lower growth is an important impediment to structural change for large internationally oriented enterprises in transition countries.

The enlargement of Europe is the second major issue in this report. It is not hard to understand why many are ambivalent about the prospect of an ever-larger European Union. After all, what is being proposed is a union between a group of western European countries with established institutions and productive and reasonably well-functioning economies with another group of countries with nascent, fragile institutions and poorly functioning economies. However, this trepidation is probably not warranted. Jan Fidrmuc, Susanne Mundschenk, Iulia Traistaru, and Jürgen von Hagen present evidence and argue why the balance for Europe will probably be positive. They argue that enlargement will have important effects in three areas: European institutions, labor markets, and structural policies (regional fiscal transfers). But they argue, based on interesting evidence from Russian migration to Israel as well as evidence from other countries, that effects on the local economy and wages will be smaller than feared by many Europeans.

What about the consequences of enlargement from the perspective of eastern Europe? The article by Wiltold Orłowski provides a detailed analysis of accession from the perspective of Poland. For those wondering what an integrated Europe will look like, Orłowski provides an interesting forecast of the likely outcome of the current negotiations. This includes a discussion of sensitive points such as how the Common Agricultural Policy will be applied to Poland, and how Poland will be treated by the so-called structural funds (regional aid to relatively poorer regions of Europe). He also discusses how the elements of the *acquis communautaire* may affect Polish growth, and uses the contrast between Greece and Ireland to draw conclusions about the role of European aid versus national policies in promoting growth. The Greek example is an object lesson for anyone who thinks that European regional aid alone can raise incomes of poorer member countries.

One of the big unanswered questions about European enlargement is simply "What next?" or "When will the process end?" There is no doubt that some have dreamed of a harmonious Europe extending from Ireland to the Urals, but is this realistic? One frontier region close to the heart of Europe is the Balkans. Vladimir Gligorov provides a thoughtful article on European integration from the perspective of southeastern Europe. He points out that the EU is on a path to encircle the Balkans without actually integrating with it. By force of geography, the countries of the region will be eventually economically integrated with Europe. Whether, in addition, the countries will qualify to have sufficiently European cultural and political institutions is still an open question. Gligorov discusses what this means in practice and how the EU is dealing with it so far.

The final really big issue on the horizon for European enlargement is the potential inclusion of Russia. This may become a serious issue for discussion in Brussels if Russia continues growing at the rates seen in the past 2 years. Thierry Malleret, Fiona J. Paua, and Peter K. Cornelius discuss the extent to which this growth is temporary by looking at Russia's ranking on long-term competitiveness issues. They conclude with a list of priorities for action to put Russia on the path to long-term rapid growth.

7

Part 1

Growth and Competitiveness of Europe and Transition Countries

Twenty Growth Engines for European Transition Countries

ANDREW M. WARNER, Center for International Development at Harvard University

Introduction

After 10 years, the transition counties of central Europe and the former Soviet Union have not yet achieved rapid economic growth at a level that would permit fast convergence of living standards with the European Union (EU). For fast convergence, growth on the order of 5 or 6 percent would be required on a sustainable basis. Only a few countries have achieved this level, and even then only for a few years.

Rapid growth in the East has taken on added importance with negotiations over accession to the EU. This is because most of the potential frictions in the accession process from the European perspective are ultimately connected to the large differences in income between Europe and the accession countries. The incentive for East-West migration is greater the greater the difference in wages and incomes. The concerns that European firms will shift operations to the East or will shift investments to the East are linked to the incentives created by differing wages, lower tax rates, and poorer enforcement of costly regulations. Since better public institutions and improved enforcement of regulations cost money, these too are linked to income differences. In addition, the greater the income differences, the greater the need to revise the current European system of regional aid.

For both of these reasons, rapid growth is an important objective. This paper attempts a summary of what we know about growth in the transition countries, looking backward in time at the recent evidence and looking forward in time at the ways in which the determinants of growth in transition countries are likely to change. We first review what has been correlated with growth during the first 10 years of transition, and then we examine how the transition countries rank today on factors that have been correlated with growth in the rest of the world. We do this by developing a list of 20 growth engines and comparing the ranking of transition countries and the EU on each of these growth engines.

Any attempt to make sense of growth in transition countries is complicated by the fact that these are countries in the midst of large structural changes. The major structural change is, of course, the transfer of labor, capital, and other productive resources from the state sector to the private sector. The occurrence of structural change has three main implications for studying growth. One is that the determinants of growth during structural change can be different from the determinants of growth once the structural change has finished. If this is true, the experience of the recent past in transition countries may not be a good guide to their future growth. This is why we look at evidence not only from the transition countries themselves, but also from other countries that are not undergoing structural change on such a large scale. The evidence from what determines growth in the rest of the world, and how transition countries now rank on these factors, may be a better guide for the future of transition countries than their own recent past.

The second implication for growth of large structural change is that the relation between reform and growth involves several effects. When countries are in the process of transferring resources from sector A to sector B, growth depends on three things: the growth of the expanding sector, the growth of the declining sector, and the rate of transfer between the two sectors. The essence of the reforms in transition countries during the early years of transition has been precisely this kind of structural change between the older state sector and the new private sector. The simplest way to think of reforms and growth during this process is that the reforms boost growth in the private sector, accelerate the decline of the state sector (which contributes negatively to growth), and accelerate the transfer of resources. This transfer of resources eventually makes a positive contribution to growth as long as the resources are more productive in the new sector than the old sector, as they most certainly are. However, since the resources are not immediately employed in new activities, this transfer is also a drag on growth to the extent that resources are left idle. Hence one can see right away that the full effect of the reforms on growth rates will be a combination of effects that offset one another to some degree.

The fact that large transfers of resources are involved and that some of these have negative effects on growth means that countries with deeper reforms may actually have lower growth than nonreforming countries. A second point is that, when looking at the growth of the entire economy, the apparent success of reform will vary over time: reforms will appear ineffective at first, yet appear to be more efficacious as the weight of the declining sector falls over time. This changing impact of reform on the growth path of the economy as time progresses will occur even if the intensity of reform stays constant over the period.

The third point to bear in mind about structural change and growth is that once the resource transfers stop, growth of the economy depends on growth of the two sectors, period. Moreover, if one believes that the state sector in post-socialist economies will not expand significantly, then future growth prospects really essentially depend on the growth prospects only of the private sector in these economies.

In light of these considerations, this paper has two main sections. First, we review the traditional evidence from the first 10 years of transition, treating the European transition countries as a self-contained group and showing evidence on what has been correlated with economic growth during the first 10 years of transition. We show that, despite the fact that fast reform has offsetting effects on growth, the evidence is that faster-reform countries

grew during the first 10 years of transition. Second, we widen the perspective to bring in two other post-communist countries, China and Vietnam, and show evidence on what has been correlated with economic growth in this slightly larger group of post-communist countries. These countries are also undergoing rapid structural change and the evidence shows that factors that are likely to be important for structural change—enterprise startups, financial system, and rule of law—have been positively correlated with growth in this group of countries.

Since we have seen that the past is not necessarily a good guide to the future in periods of restructuring, however, this evidence does not necessarily answer the extent to which these countries are well positioned for sustained growth in the future. What we do instead is to rely on the body of accumulated experience and analysis of long-term growth. This includes cross-country empirical studies on the determinants of growth rates over long periods of time in other countries, as well as more analytical or theoretical works on long-term growth. Based on this work we draw up a list of 20 engines of growth. This list of 20 engines is designed to include everything that has been put forward either in empirical or theoretical studies as a determinant of long-term growth. One can include a large fraction of what analysts have argued for in this list. Then we rank 75 countries on each of these 20 engines. We focus attention especially on the transition countries and the EU in these rankings in order to see whether transition countries achieve higher rankings than EU ones. We do this to assess the evidence for whether these countries are likely to grow faster than the EU.

Income gaps between transition countries and the European Union in 2000

To start with the most basic facts, Table 1 shows real GDP per inhabitant, on a purchasing power parity basis for the transition countries and the EU (except Luxembourg). Five countries were listed as candidates for accession in 1998: the Czech Republic, Poland, Hungary, Estonia, and Slovenia. The table shows that these five countries had an average GDP that was 53 percent of the EU average in the year 2000. A further five countries were listed as accession candidates in the year 2000: Bulgaria, Romania, Latvia, Lithuania, and the Slovak Republic. This group had an average GDP that was only 32 percent of the EU average. Turning to recent growth rates, the 14 EU countries grew by an average of 3.4 percent over the 3-year period 1996 to 1999. The two groups of accession candidate countries grew by an average of 3.9 percent and 2.5 percent, respectively, over the period 1996 to 2000. It is clear that these growth rates are not substantially above those of the EU, so that on average the region is not catching up with Europe very quickly.

Table 1: GDP per person and recent economic growth in Europe and European transition countries

	GDP PER CAPITA PPP, current $			GDP PER CAPITA percent of EU-14 average			GROWTH RATES %
	1996	1998	2000	1996	1998	2000	1996–2000
Albania	3,023	2,974	3,372	15	14	15	2.8
Armenia	2,065	2,304	2,541	10	11	11	5.3
Azerbaijan	2,016	2,310	2,720	10	11	12	7.8
Belarus	5,423	6,544	7,175	27	31	32	7.2
Bulgaria	5,235	5,103	5,590	26	24	25	1.7
Croatia	6,595	7,190	7,409	33	34	33	3.0
Czech Republic	13,341	13,109	13,450	66	62	60	0.2
Estonia	6,975	8,273	8,942	35	39	40	6.4
Georgia	2,199	2,558	2,726	11	12	12	5.5
Hungary	9,786	10,791	11,914	48	51	53	5.0
Kazakhstan	4,544	4,549	5,134	22	21	23	3.1
Kyrgyzstan	2,206	2,474	2,666	11	12	12	4.9
Latvia	5,303	6,173	6,832	26	29	31	6.5
Lithuania	6,034	6,872	6,880	30	32	31	3.3
Macedonia, FYR	4,377	4,466	4,651	22	21	21	1.5
Moldova	2,205	2,095	2,059	11	10	9	−1.7
Poland	7,227	8,090	8,766	36	38	39	4.9
Romania	6,923	6,224	6,212	34	29	28	−2.7
Russian Federation	7,077	6,832	7,848	35	32	35	2.6
Slovak Republic	9,319	10,276	10,689	46	48	48	3.5
Slovenia	13,864	15,067	16,646	69	71	75	4.7
Tajikistan	—	—	—	—	—	—	—
Turkmenistan	3,116	2,809	3,712	15	13	17	4.5
Ukraine	3,490	3,353	3,586	17	16	16	0.7
Uzbekistan	2,104	2,189	2,312	10	10	10	2.4
Group 1998 average	**10,238**	**11,066**	**11,944**	**51**	**52**	**53**	**3.9**
Group 2000 average	**6,563**	**6,930**	**7,241**	**32**	**33**	**32**	**2.5**
Others average	**3,603**	**3,760**	**4,136**	**18**	**18**	**19**	**3.5**
	1996	1998	1999	1996	1998	1999	1996–1999
Austria	23,229	23,888	25,089	115	113	112	2.6
Belgium	23,309	24,405	25,443	115	115	114	3.0
Denmark	24,290	25,209	25,869	120	119	116	2.1
Finland	20,006	21,894	23,096	99	103	103	4.9
France	21,404	21,927	22,897	106	103	103	2.3
Germany	22,390	22,921	23,742	111	108	106	2.0
Greece	13,878	14,575	15,414	69	69	69	3.6
Ireland	19,159	22,730	25,918	95	107	116	10.6
Italy	21,255	21,531	22,172	105	101	99	1.4
Luxembourg	33,419	39,506	42,769	165	186	191	8.6
Netherlands	22,081	23,014	24,215	109	108	108	3.1
Portugal	14,502	15,326	16,064	72	72	72	3.5
Spain	16,011	17,041	18,079	79	80	81	4.1
Sweden	20,927	21,371	22,636	104	101	101	2.7
United Kingdom	20,498	21,159	22,093	101	100	99	2.5
EU-14	**20,210**	**21,214**	**22,338**	**100**	**100**	**100**	**3.4**

The picture for individual counties does not differ greatly from that of these groups. Some individual countries appear to be catching up, but not many, and with a few exceptions, not very fast. Table 2 shows that of the 28 transition countries listed, only 12 had growth rates that exceeded the EU average during the four years 1996 to 2000. If these 12 countries continued on the path exhibited during these years, the number of years it would take to reach 90 percent of EU income levels can be calculated to range between 10 and a century (Table 2). Only three countries would be projected to reach this level within 30 years.

Table 2: Number of years to close to within 90 percent of EU-14 income (based on 1996–2000 or 1996–1999 growth rates)

	Current gap (2000)	Growth 1996–2000	Growth of EU-14 1996–1999	Years to close to 90%, at 1996–2000 growth rates
1998 ACCESSION CANDIDATES				
Czech Republic	60%	0.2%	3.4%	
Hungary	53%	5.0%	3.4%	32
Poland	39%	4.9%	3.4%	53
Slovenia	75%	4.7%	3.4%	15
Estonia	40%	6.4%	3.4%	27
2000 ACCESSION CANDIDATES				
Bulgaria	25%	1.7%	3.4%	
Latvia	31%	6.5%	3.4%	34
Lithuania	31%	3.3%	3.4%	
Romania	28%	–2.7%	3.4%	
Slovak Republic	48%	3.5%	3.4%	671
OTHER COUNTRIES				
Albania	15%	2.8%	3.4%	
Armenia	11%	5.3%	3.4%	107
Azerbaijan	12%	7.8%	3.4%	46
Belarus	32%	7.2%	3.4%	27
Croatia	33%	3.0%	3.4%	
Georgia	12%	5.5%	3.4%	94
Kazakhstan	23%	3.1%	3.4%	
Kyrgyzstan	12%	4.9%	3.4%	139
Macedonia	21%	1.5%	3.4%	
Moldova, Rep. of	9%	–1.7%	3.4%	
Russian Federation	35%	2.6%	3.4%	
Tajikistan				
Turkmenistan	17%	4.5%	3.4%	156
Ukraine	16%	0.7%	3.4%	
Uzbekistan	10%	2.4%	3.4%	

Source: Author's estimates

Reforms during the first 10 years: Did they boost growth?

The essential objective of the economic reform programs in transition countries during the first 10 years of transition was to lay the foundations for and to promote structural change. As mentioned earlier, restructuring involves shifts of resources to new sectors. Since the employment of these resources in new sectors is not immediate, this process can retard income growth. In addition, since the restructuring process often requires shutting down old sectors, there is a further negative effect on growth while this occurs. Offsetting these two negative effects are the positive effects of reforms in accelerating growth of newer sectors and the additional positive effect resulting from shifting resources from low-productive sectors to higher productive sectors.

The net effect of all this is that reforms may not have a positive effect on growth in the short run, but as the retracting sectors disappear, the effect of reforms on growth should improve over time. The evidence, however, shows that despite these offsetting effects of reforms on growth, countries that pursued faster and deeper reform paths did indeed grow more rapidly during the first decade of reform in transition countries.

The evidence of a positive correlation is shown in Figure 1. What we have done here is to rate the reform stance of each country using two things: the sources cited for Table 3, and our own judgment of when each country started on its dominant policy path of the 1990s. As is well known, economic policy was not implemented or delayed in some transition countries due to war or due to the fact that political stalemate delayed effective implementation of any policy. In Table 3 we list each transition country along with data on the year in which that country's dominant reform position was first implemented. The third column provides a short description of the decisive political event that led us to the precise dating. In the final column we show a measure of the reform intensity adopted by each country. The typical pattern in transition countries was that we did not see sharp fluctuations over time in each country between fast and slow reform. Instead, most countries stuck to a particular reform stance and kept it in place over a number of years. We measure the reform stance at the start of the reform period so that, when we correlate this with subsequent growth below, we avoid the possibility of causality running from growth to the reform stance.

Figure 1: In transition countries, economic growth between 1992 and 2000 has been positively correlated with the intensity of market-oriented reforms adopted at the start of the transition period

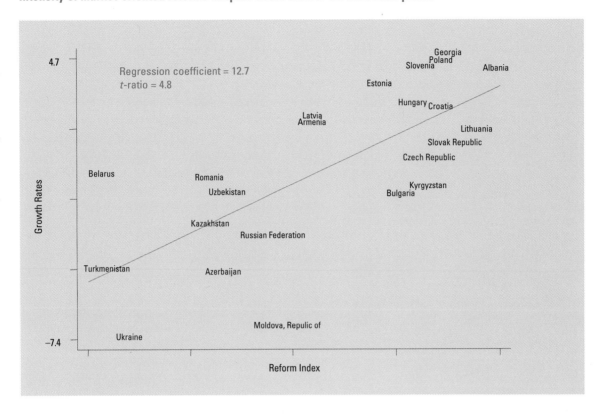

Table 3: Reform indexes at the start of the transition (1 = maximum reform)

	Year in which dominant policy path was first implemented	Reason for choosing that year	Reform Index in that year (1 = max reform)	Reform Index in 1992
Albania	1993	Democrats won elections in 1992	0.70	0.66
Armenia	1992	Year after independence	0.39	0.39
Azerbaijan	1992	Year after independence	0.25	0.25
Belarus	1992	Year after Minsk accords dissolved the Soviet Union	0.20	0.20
Bulgaria	1993	Elections in October 1991, but elected government lost power one year later. 1993 policy decisions set the precedent for the next five years	0.66	0.86
Croatia	1992	Year after Secession from Yugoslavia	0.72	0.72
Czech Republic	1991	Year after June 1990 elections in which Civic Union and Public Against Violence won elections	0.79	0.86
Estonia	1992	Year after independence	0.64	0.64
Georgia	1996	Year after Sheverdnaze won elections under new constitution ending civil war	0.61	0.32
Hungary	1991	Year after free elections	0.74	0.78
Kazakhstan	1992	Year after presidential election	0.35	0.35
Kyrgyzstan	1993	Year after Akayev started to implement reform program	0.60	0.33
Latvia	1992	Year after independence	0.51	0.51
Lithuania	1993	Year after 1992 free elections ended political and constitutional deadlock	0.78	0.55
Macedonia	1992	Independence declared in January 1992	0.68	0.68
Moldova, Rep. of	1992	Year reforms implemented after December 1991 elections	0.38	0.38
Poland	1990	Year of reforms under Mazowiecki government	0.72	0.82
Romania	1991	Year after anti-Ceausescu communists consolidated power	0.36	0.45
Russian Federation	1992	Year after failed 1991 coup	0.49	0.49
Slovak Republic	1991	Year after June 1990 elections in which Civic Union and Public Against Violence won elections	0.79	0.86
Slovenia	1992	Year after Secession from Yugoslavia	0.78	0.78
Tajikistan	1992	Year after independence	0.20	0.20
Turkmenistan	1992	Year after independence	0.13	0.13
Ukraine	1992	Year after independence	0.23	0.23
Uzbekistan	1992	Year after independence	0.26	0.26

Source: Reform index is taken from data in Havrylyshyn, Izvorski, and van Rooden (1998), who in turn rely on de Melo, Denizer, and Gelb (1996) for the years 1990–1993 and the indicators in the EBRD's transition reports thereafter.

Figure 2: Countries closer to the European Union tended to adopt deeper reforms. The exceptions are the Kyrgyzstan (long way from Europe, high reform) and the Belarus and Ukraine (relatively short distance from Europe, low reform).

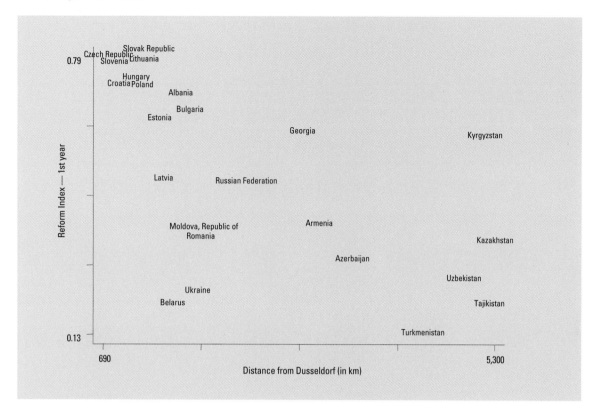

Figure 1 graphs the average annual growth for each country from the date listed in Table 3 to the year 2000. On the horizontal axis, we show the reform index (column 4 in Table 3). One can see that, on average, it has been the case that faster-reform countries have grown faster. Some countries, such as Belarus, have achieved relatively high growth despite slow reforms; on the other hand, Moldova has grown much more slowly for its level of reform. Overall, however, the cross-country relationship is indeed statistically significant.

The lesson from this is not, as some have argued, that reforms have failed. On average, reforms have been correlated with faster, not slower, growth. The reforms may have been disappointing in not providing for faster growth, but one cannot argue based on this evidence that countries would have been better off without reforms.

It is also sometimes argued along a different track that reforms have been a sideshow in the transition process. This line of argument often claims that factors beyond the control of economic policy—such as proximity to the EU, cultural status, or previous experience with markets—can account for the growth performance across transition countries.

What we find, however, when we look at regression evidence is that the countries that are further from the EU did not reform as deeply as those close to the EU. The causality appears to be the following: countries that were closer to the EU reformed faster and therefore grew faster. There is no evidence that remote distance from the EU can account for slower growth after controlling for the country's reform stance. In other words, distance from the EU appears to affect growth by influencing the propensity to adopt reforms, not through an effect independent of reform. This issue is important to the extent that one tries to argue that countries do not have free will over their growth prospects. The evidence does not support this brand of fatalism.

The empirical relation that greater distance from the EU was associated with slower reforms is in Figure 2. In this figure, the reform stance is displayed on the vertical axis and the distance in kilometers from Dusseldorf is displayed on the vertical axis. Note that reforms have tended to be faster and more extensive in counties close to Europe. There are three exceptions to this tendency. Kyrgystan is a fast-reform country that is a long way from Europe; and on the other hand, Belarus and Ukraine are slow reformers that are relatively close to Europe.

Figure 3: In ten post-communist countries, growth between 1990 and 2000 is positively associated with low administrative barriers to start-up enterprises. The regression also controls for the starting level of income.

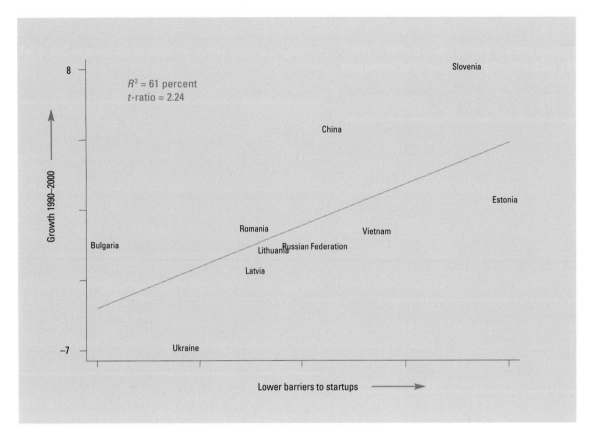

Post-communist countries: China and Vietnam

Another perspective on the growth prospects of the post-communist countries is found by widening the net a little further to include countries of Asia such as China and Vietnam. The differences between China and the former Soviet countries have been extensively analyzed. There are suggestions that a number of elements were at work; the large agricultural labor force in China—ready and eager to move to the cities—was an important structural difference. The Chinese government encouraged rural-urban migration that allowed industry to draw on surplus labor in the countryside for industrialization. In constant, in former Soviet countries key political groups benefited from subsidized credit to the old industries. This had the by-product of not providing large incentives for labor and capital to move to new sectors, and thus retarded structural change.

The reform indicators used in Figure 1 are not available for China and Vietnam. We rely instead on reform indicators from the *Global Competitiveness Report 2001–2002* for this larger sample of countries.

A key indicator of the ability to achieve successful structural change is the ability of an economy to generate new start-up enterprises. We have found that the data on ease of startups tends to correlate with recent growth of a broader sample of Euro-Asian transition counties, including China and Vietnam, in addition to the European transition countries. In Figure 3 we show representative evidence. The figure shows that transition countries with improved start-up conditions have tended to grow more rapidly than other transition countries during the period 1990 to 2000. This kind of evidence makes sense when one thinks about the structural change that must take place in the transition process. Essentially this requires a massive shift of resources from the state sector to the private sector. A country can frustrate growth either by stopping the release from the state sector or frustrating the growth of the private sector. Stopping the release of

resources is something that countries can accomplish through industrial subsides, by restrictive labor market policies that create disincentives to transfer out of the state sector, or by slow privatization or poor bankruptcy laws. In post-Soviet countries, the subsidies were closely tied to inflationary monetary policies that subsidized credit to the state sector. A by-product of these policies was high inflation (because the credits were financed by creation of money) and, of course, slow growth (because the subsidy side of these policies failed to create incentives for workers to leave the state sector). Countries can also block the formation of new enterprises in a number of ways. These include direct administrative barriers to startups and financial practices that are not receptive to credit for small and medium-sized enterprises (SMEs). In addition, poor anti-monopoly policies may fail to prevent predatory practices by incumbent firms bent on frustrating new entry.

All of the evidence presented so far relies on the recent past. However, after the state sectors shrink to a sustainable level such as 10 to 20 percent of the economy, the resource transfers from state to private sectors will slow down and the factors that propel continued growth might well change. Therefore, to examine whether transition countries are likely to grow fast in the future, and in particular whether they are likely to grow faster than EU countries, we turn to a broad list of factors that can arguably play a role in the growth process.

The interesting question is the following: If transition countries today were rated on the basis of how they perform on a broad list of growth engines, would there be evidence that they will achieve rapid growth in future decades?

20 engines of growth

In Table 4, we list 20 facts about economies that have been argued, in some forum or other, to affect economic growth rates. The idea is to avoid taking a stand on exactly which of these facts will be most strongly related to growth in the future, and to see if there are any of these on which the transition counties perform relatively well.

Table 4: Twenty growth engines (see data tables at the end of this paper)

1. MACROECONOMIC STABILITY

Low Government Deficits
Low Inflation
Exchange rate stability
Solvency of Financial System

2. START-UP CONDITIONS

Low Administrative Barriers to Start-ups
Venture Capital Available
Loans available with low collateral

3. FINANCIAL SYSTEM

Low interest rate spreads
High banking sector assets as percent of GDP
High financial risk rating
High perceived sophistication of financial system
Developed equity markets

4. OPENNESS TO INTERNATIONAL TRADE

Low import tariffs
Low hidden import barriers
Low premiums on obtaining foreign exchange
Low export taxes

5. QUALITY OF GOVERNMENT

Public expenditures not wasteful
Subsidies improve productivity
Highly competent personnel in public sector

6. CAPITAL ACCUMULATION

High national saving rates
High investment rates

7. LOW TAXES

Low VAT tax rate
Low top income tax rate
Low corporate profits tax
Tax system perceived to improve competitiveness

8. INNOVATION

Highly rated research institutions
Businesses make R&D
Close collaboration between universities and businesses
Government supports Research
High expenditures on R&D

9. TECHNOLOGY TRANSFER

Foreign Direct investment brings new technology
Licensing pursued to obtain foreign technology

10. NEW ECONOMY

Internet hosts
Computers per-capita
Development of Internet Service Providers
Telephone density
Level of Public Support for Internet
Development of Laws in support of new Economy
Perceived Quality of Local Internet Service Providers

11. EDUCATION

High years of Schooling in Population
High perceived quality of Education
Companies Invest in Training

12. INFRASTRUCTURE

High Road Quality
Efficient Electrical Generation
Fast International Mail
High Level of Competition in provision of basic Infrastructure

13. RULE OF LAW

Independent Judiciary
Ability to Successfully Litigate Against Government
Low Legal Costs
Governments Honor Commitments of Previous Governments

14. RED TAPE

Senior Management Spends Little time Dealing with Government Officials
Administrative Regulations are not Burdensome

15. CORRUPTION

Low corruption in Provision of Trade Permits
Low corruption in Provision of Utility Connections
Low corruption in Award of Public Contracts
Low Corruption Connected with Tax Payments
Low Corruption Connected to Loan Applications

16. COMPETITION

Competition is Perceived to be Intense
Entry of New Competitors is Common
Low Perceived Concentration of Corporate Activity

17. LOCAL SUPPLIER DEPTH

Perceived Quantity of Local Suppliers
Perceived Quality of Local Suppliers
Existence of Local Suppliers of Components and Parts
Existence of Local Suppliers of Process Machinery
Existence of Local Suppliers of Specialized Research and Training
Existence of Local Suppliers of Specialized Information Technology

18. WORKPLACE INCENTIVES

Pay is Connected to Productivity
Management Positions go only to Professionals
Compensation of Managers Includes Incentive Bonuses
Lack of Discrimination Against Females

19. LABOR MARKET FLEXIBILITY

Hiring and Firing Employer-determined
Overtime Regulations not too Expensive
Wage-setting is decentralized

20. CLUSTER DEVELOPMENT

Clusters are Common and Deep

The 20 growth engines listed in the data tables at the end of this paper are based on both hard information, such as investment rates and saving rates, and also the results of the Executive Opinion Survey of the World Economic Forum that we conduct for the *Global Competitiveness Report 2001–2002*. However, when using the Executive Survey, we use a different procedure than has been the practice in the *Global Report*. The *Global Report* takes the simple average of all respondents to a given question. Recall that the typical question asks for a rating on a scale of 1 to 7. Thus the score for Greece, for example, will be the average of all the Greek respondents. There is reason to think that this procedure will contain some bias if there are uninformed respondents. Let us suppose that 50 percent of the respondents were informed and 50 percent were uninformed. How would we expect the uninformed to answer? One possibility is that these respondents simply put down anything. This is equivalent to saying that they would give an entirely random answer. The mean response of this group would then be 4—the middle of the scale of 1 to 7. Now what about the informed group? Since they are informed, after all, they presumably get it right, so the mean of this group would be correct on average. If we then take a simple average of all the respondents, the result would be a weighted average, weighted between the true answer and 4. The weights in this case would be 50-50, but in general we would not know the precise weights unless we knew the proportion of uninformed versus informed respondents. In the language of statisticians, the mean response contains a bias toward 4 in this situation.

Using the mean as in the *Global Report* is not a bad solution to this problem: this would give reasonable results if the proportion of informed respondents in the sample were fairly high. In addition, even though there would be a bias, if the proportion of uninformed in each country were roughly the same, the ranking of countries would be roughly correct since everyone would have similar biases.

Nevertheless, there is probably a better way to handle this situation. Note that in the above example the answers of the uninformed group would be spread evenly between 1 and 7. In contrast, the informed group's answers would be clustered around the correct value. In this case *the most frequent answer given* rather than the average will usually be correct. Statisticians call this the *mode*. What is happening is that we are adding together two distributions: that of the uninformed group, which would be flat across the range of 1 to 7 and that of the informed group, which would be clustered around the true value. The combination of these two distributions would yield a mode that would still be clustered around the correct value. In other words, even with a large group of uninformed or disinterested respondents, the most frequent answer given for each country can still give us an accurate picture of the correct situation in that country.

It is possible to show this in a more technical way with what are called *Monte Carlo experiments*. Our analysis with this technique indicates that the informed group can be as low as 20 percent of the sample for the mode to give us an answer that will be correct on average. Based on these results, we use the mode rather than the mean when analyzing results from the Executive Opinion Survey.

In 20 tables included at the end of this paper, we show the rankings of 75 countries according to each growth engine. In these tables we show the scores for individual countries and scores for the averages of the following three groups: the Countries of the EU (with the exception of Luxembourg, which is too small to be included in the *Report*); the first five accession candidates of the EU (the Czech Republic, Estonia, Hungary, Poland, and Slovenia) and the second five accession candidates of the EU (Bulgaria, Latvia, Lithuania, Romania, and the Slovak Republic). The averages for these groups of countries are shown in bold; the list of individual countries is shown in normal print.

Macroeconomic stability

We turn first to the macroeconomic stability index. Macroeconomic stability is often deemed essential to growth, and it should be ranked as a necessary rather than a sufficient condition for growth. A macroeconomic crisis can surely stop growth, but macroeconomic stability by itself cannot guarantee growth. An additional issue connected to this index is that it is especially difficult fully to separate the past from the future. Traditional predictive variables for a macroeconomic crisis would include the following factors. The first would be high deficits (fiscal or current account), because high deficits always carry with them a question mark regarding financing. Further traditional indicators would be an overvalued exchange rate, which would suggest imminent devaluation, or high inflation, which would be a symptom of a number of unstable situations. A final indicator of an imminent crisis would be a vulnerable banking system, since banks are susceptible to creditor panics. The general point, however, is that all of these indicators can also be high in countries that are coming out of a macroeconomic crisis. For this reason, when observing countries at the bottom of such rankings, one should make an effort to discount countries that have just had a recent crisis. The rankings are potentially informative for countries that are at the bottom of the list yet which have not been through a recent crisis.

Start-up conditions

The next index rates start-up conditions. The information in this index has been discussed earlier as a predictor of growth in transition countries especially. In the data table (at the end of this paper) one sees that transition and EU countries are not especially highly ranked on start-up conditions when compared with the rest of the world. This is possibly important for growth prospects in the region. Going further in the analysis, one may also argue that unreceptive conditions for SMEs can explain sluggish innovation and slow structural change even in advanced countries, because many innovations are observed to be accompanied or promoted by new enterprises. To the extent to which this is true, the results on this index suggest that neither the EU nor the transition countries are especially well placed for fast, sustainable growth.

Financial system

The finance index is constructed using hard data and Survey data on interest rate spreads, Survey data on sophistication of financial markets and adequacy of financial regulation, ratings of financial risk by institutional investor, and Survey data on the ease of raising money through the local equity market. The hard data and Survey data on interest rates spreads are averaged together, and then this index in turn is averaged together with the average of the other measures to form the final index.

Openness to international trade

This index is an average of hard data on average tariff rates and Survey data on the complete costs of importing, together with Survey data on the premium above the official exchange rate (if any) that needs to be paid to acquire foreign currency. It is designed to capture three important aspects of trade closure: tariffs, other related charges, and implicit additional charges on obtaining foreign currency.

Quality of government

This index is an average of Survey data on the quality of public expenditures (whether they are oriented toward necessary public goods or wasted), Survey data on whether subsides improve enterprise productivity or sustain unproductive enterprises, and Survey data on the overall competence of personnel in the public sector as compared with those in the private sector.

Capital accumulation

This index is a simple average of the national saving rate and gross fixed capital accumulation, both in percent of GDP (using data from 2000).

Low taxes

This index is an average of indexes of the level of four taxes: the most common value added tax rate, the marginal income tax rate paid by the average income-earner, the top marginal income tax rate, and the average tax rate on corporate income. In addition, we give some weight to Survey data on whether taxes are perceived to improve or worsen competitiveness. All of these are scaled to a 1-to-7 index and then a simple average is taken.

Innovation

This index is an average of Survey data on the following: the level of technological sophistication, the level of innovation versus imitation of national enterprises, the extent of business collaboration with local universities, the extent of legal protection for intellectual property, the average level of business R&D, and the extent and nature of government support for R&D.

Technology transfer

This index is based on Survey data on the extent to which foreign direct investment in the local market is a vehicle for transfer of technology, as well as Survey data on the extent to which licensing of foreign products is practiced in the local market as a means to obtain and work with foreign technologies.

New economy

This is an average of several new economy indicators. There are two indexes, one based on hard data and the other on Survey data (following the procedure in the *Global Competitiveness Report 2001–2002*). The hard data used include the number of Internet hosts per 1,000 persons, the number of Internet service providers per person, mobile telephone usage, telephone density, and personal computer use per inhabitant. The Survey data rely on indicators of whether information and communication technologies (ICT) are a priority of the government, the level of success of government ICT programs, the development of legal support for ICT, and the quality of local Internet service providers. The final index is an average of these two indexes.

Education

The education index is based on number of school years attained in the population weighted by the average return to education of those schooling levels. These data are then averaged together with Survey data on the quality of education in the local schools. (This is to modify the quantity of schooling data with quality data.) These are then averaged together with Survey data on the extent to which firms support on the job training. The intent is to bring together three elements of education: raw schooling years, quality of schooling, and on-the-job education.

Infrastructure

The infrastructure index is based on the idea that the three most important areas for economic activity are energy, transportation, and water. For transportation, we use a Survey question that asks respondents to estimate the average driving speed they can make between the two major cities in their countries. This question was asked because driving speed is likely to reflect road quality, both in terms of pavement width and extent of highways, and also traffic congestion. As such it is an overall measure of road quality. For energy, we rely on Survey questions on the quality and price of electricity generation, and take an average of the two. Sufficient market competition is also important for infrastructure quality. The final index is an average of the road quality indicator, an indicator of electricity quality and price, and indicators of the level of competition in key infrastructure sectors such as electricity, water, and transportation.

Rule of law

The rule of law index attempts to measure the classical concept of law, namely the existence and respect for a body of statutes and precedents that limit the behavior of those with power in the society, principally the government. The economic context of this is primarily between the interface between enterprises and the government. For this index, we rely on Survey data on the extent of judicial independence, the existence of a legal framework that enables firms to challenge the decisions of governments, the extent to which new governments regard their actions as limited by the commitments of previous governments, and the costs of litigation.

Red tape

This index relies on Survey data on the perceived burden of administrative regulations and Survey estimates of the amount of time senior management spends with government officials.

Corruption

This index measures corruption on five dimensions: corruption in the issuance of import and export permits, obtaining physical connections to water or electricity utilities, award of public contracts, tax payments, and loan applications.

Competition

This index measures three dimensions of competition: perceptions of the overall intensity of competition, the extent of entry of new enterprises as a measure of competitive pressure, and perceptions on the degree of concentration of corporate activity.

Local supplier depth

This index uses Survey data on the quantity and quality of local suppliers to industry. It also uses data on the extent to which companies rely on local sources for the following: components and parts, process machinery, research and training services, and information technology services.

Workplace incentives

This index is a measure of the degree to which incentives are used for motivation in the labor market. This measurement includes Survey data on the connection between pay and productivity, on lack of gender discrimination, on the existence and extent of management bonuses, on the extent to which senior management positions are awarded on merit rather than nepotism, and the willingness to delegate authority.

Labor market flexibility or job security regulations

This index is based on Survey information on the degree to which hiring and firing practices are determined by regulations or employers, on the extent to which hours are flexible, and on the degree of decentralized wage setting.

Cluster development

This index is based exclusively on Survey data on whether industry clusters are well developed and active in each country.

Table 5: Summary of rankings on twenty growth engines

	European Union Average	1998 Accession Group	2000 Accession Group
1. Macroeconomic Stability	18	35	52
2. Start-up Conditions	21	35	65
3. Financial System	17	42	61
4. Openness to International Trade	29	32	43
5. Quality of Government	18	40	41
6. Capital Accumulation	39	22	48
7. Low Taxes	59	28	55
8. Innovation	17	32	57
9. Technology Transfer	33	30	52
10. New Economy	19	31	45
11. Education	21	26	39
12. Infrastructure	16	31	56
13. Rule of Law	14	37	60
14. Red Tape	16	30	60
15. Corruption	22	40	36
16. Competition	12	28	43
17. Local Supplier Depth	17	27	44
18. Workplace Incentives	23	27	49
19. Labor Market Flexibility	62	38	32
20. Cluster Development	20	51	44

Table 7: Which of the twenty growth engines are correlated with economic growth during 1990–2000?

	10 Transition Countries	All Other Countries	
	Simple Regression	Simple Regression	Multiple Regressions
1. Macroeconomic Stability	no	yes	
2. Start-up Conditions	yes	no	
3. Financial System	yes	yes	no
4. Openness to International Trade	no	yes	yes
5. Quality of Government	no	yes	no
6. Capital Accumulation	no	yes	yes
7. Low Taxes	no	yes	yes
8. Innovation	no	no	
9. Technology Transfer	no	yes	yes
10. New Economy	no	yes	yes
11. Education	no	yes	no
12. Infrastructure	no	no	
13. Rule of Law	yes	no	
14. Red Tape	no	no	
15. Corruption	no	no	
16. Competition	no	no	
17. Local Supplier Depth	no	no	
18. Workplace Incentives	no	no	
19. Labor Market Flexibility	no	no	
20. Cluster Development	no	yes	yes

Note: Based on ordinary least squares regressions of real economic growth per-capita between 1990 and 2000 on the log of GDP per-capita in 1992 and each of the growth engines listed in this paper. The simple regressions were estimated first, and then the variables that were significant were retained for the second-stage multiple regressions. Multiple regressions were not estimated for the 10 transition countries because the sample was too small.

Table 6: Comparison of European Union and transition country rankings

	European Union Average	1998 Accession Group	Difference	European Union Average	2000 Accession Group	Difference
1. Macroeconomic Stability	5.8	5.1	−0.7	5.8	4.7	−1.1
2. Start-up Conditions	4.8	3.9	−0.9	4.8	2.3	−2.5
3. Financial System	4.8	3.8	−1.0	4.8	3.0	−1.8
4. Openness to International Trade	6.7	6.5	−0.2	6.7	6.1	−0.6
5. Quality of Government	3.8	3.1	−0.7	3.8	3.0	−0.8
6. Capital Accumulation	3.2	3.7	0.5	3.2	3.0	−0.2
7. Low Taxes	2.6	3.3	0.7	2.6	2.7	0.1
8. Innovation	5.1	4.0	−1.1	5.1	3.3	−1.8
9. Technology Transfer	5.2	5.3	0.1	5.2	4.8	−0.4
10. New Economy	5.9	5.4	−0.5	5.9	4.7	−1.2
11. Education	5.4	5.1	−0.3	5.4	4.3	−1.1
12. Infrastructure	6.1	5.4	−0.7	6.1	4.2	−1.9
13. Rule of Law	6.3	5.3	−1.0	6.3	3.7	−2.6
14. Red Tape	5.1	4.8	−0.3	5.1	3.9	−1.2
15. Corruption	5.9	4.8	−1.1	5.9	4.9	−1.0
16. Competition	5.7	5.4	−0.3	5.7	4.8	−0.9
17. Local Supplier Depth	5.2	4.7	−0.5	5.2	4.3	−0.9
18. Workplace Incentives	5.1	4.9	−0.2	5.1	4.3	−0.8
19. Labor Market Flexibility	2.9	4.1	1.2	2.9	4.6	1.7
20. Cluster Development	4.1	2.0	−2.1	4.1	2.6	−1.5

How do the transition countries and the European Union rank on the growth engines?

Now we turn to the question asked at the outset. Based on the rankings of the EU and transition countries on each of these growth engines, to what extent are such countries well placed to grow rapidly in coming years? The average rankings for the following three groups—14 EU countries, 1998 accession candidates, and 2000 accession candidates—are shown in Table 5.

The first and most basic point from the tables that list the rankings of the 20 growth engines is that the European transition countries do not currently excel on any one of these rankings. Although there is naturally some dispute about precisely which of these growth engines are more important for growth, the evidence shown in the tables indicates that there is no single growth engine on which the transition countries achieve an extremely high ranking. In this sense, we can say that economic policy in these countries is not obviously oriented toward fast growth.

The five countries in the 1998 accession group achieve a relatively high ranking on capital accumulation, low taxes, education, the intensity of competition, local supplier networks, and workplace incentives. However, notice that the rankings of this group are really quite close to each other on all of the growth engines. The five countries in the 2000 accession group do worse, on average, than the 1998 group. These countries, however, achieve a relatively high ranking on labor market flexibility and education.

When we look at the comparison with the EU to assess whether European transition counties may catch up to the EU, Table 6 shows that the 1998 group ranks higher than the EU on labor market flexibility, low taxes, and capital accumulation, and by a very small margin, on transfer of technology. Whether catch-up occurs depends in part on whether these factors turn out to be especially important for future growth. The 1998 accession group ranks above the EU only on labor market flexibility and, by a very small margin, low taxes.

A separate question is whether accession to the EU will improve the growth prospects of the transition countries. On this score, the evidence is because on most of the growth engines, average European practice ranks above that of the transition countries. Therefore, on current evidence, transition countries are likely to see their growth improved in an absolute sense by adopting EU standards. Accession to the European Union will therefore be a positive development, even though it alone probably will not guarantee fast convergence to European income levels.

Although accession will help, it must also be said that EU standards are not extremely high on many of the growth engines, so transition countries probably will need to make a deeper effort than EU standards to achieve very fast growth.

Which of the 20 engines have been most strongly related to growth during the 1990s?

In Table 7 we list the 20 growth engines and summarize statistical evidence on which of these have been correlated with growth rates during the period 1990 to 2000. Given that transition countries have been undergoing structural change during this period, we perform this analysis separately for the ten post-communist countries and the other 65 countries on the list.

The results confirm that growth during the 1990s in transition countries was driven by a different force than it was in other counties, justifying their separate treatment in the analysis. For the ten transition countries, the evidence shows that start-up conditions, the financial system, and the rule of law all correlated with growth rates in simple regressions. The number of countries (10) is too small to choose between these and suggest which are more important. Nevertheless, all three exhibit significant simple correlations with growth rates.

This result makes sense if new enterprises and the development of new sectors are the keys to growth in transition counties. All of these variables have a bearing in some way on the start-up process. The start-up index measures administrative and financial conditions for start-ups directly. Similarly, the financial system is important as the provider of credit for start-ups and finally, the legal system is important in providing intellectual property protection, clear legal ownership rules, and bankruptcy procedures, and in supporting contracts that are important for new enterprises. Therefore an argument can be made that these indicators are all pointing toward the importance of development of new enterprises and restructuring in growth of transition counties. In emphasizing the formation of new enterprises, these regression results provide similar evidence, as Figure 3 showed earlier.

The evidence for the other counties suggests that ten variables have positive simple associations with growth in the 1990s, but, of these, only six are statistically significant when the others are controlled for. The nine variables that show some relation to growth rates are the financial system, openness to international trade, quality of government, capital accumulation, low taxes, technology transfer, new economy indicators, education, and cluster conditions. To assess which of these are correlated with growth after controlling for each other, we estimated regressions with the capital accumulation variable and added the other eight indicators one by one. The results showed additional evidence that capital accumulation, openness to international trade, low taxes, technology transfer, new economy indicators, and cluster conditions bear some independent relation to growth rates.

Figure 4: Although Survey data are frequently criticized for being inaccurate, when we can check the Survey data by comparing quantitative data with Survey rankings, we often find high agreement. The figure shows expenditures on R&D (vertical axis) with Survey-based ratings on the intensity of R&D spending from the Global Competitiveness Survey.

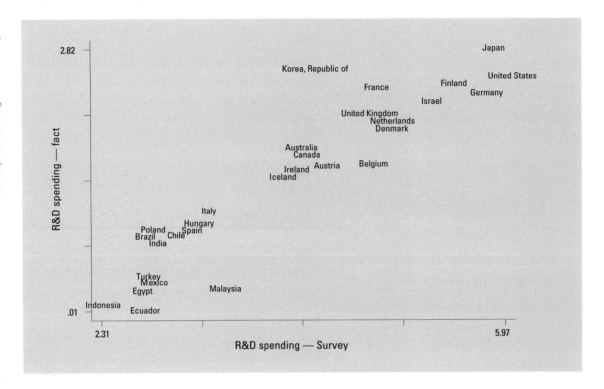

These statistical results are suggestive as to what may currently be important for growth, but they are not definitive, of course. One basic reason is that, as David Hume is famous for saying several centuries ago, the fact that the sun rose yesterday is no guarantee that it will rise tomorrow. It is an empirical regularity that we have come to expect. In the same vein, there is no guarantee that what correlates with growth during the past decade will correlate in the next decade, and even less the next few decades. Nevertheless, it is surely better to be guided by empirical regularities from the past than to walk blindly into the future.

A second reason for caution is that many of the indicators are based on Survey data and there is always some measurement error in this process. The key question however, is not whether *some* error exists but *how much* error. In Figure 4 we show evidence that the error from Survey-based information is not as large as some may believe. In this figure we have plotted the logarithm of expenditures on Research and Development (R&D) as a fraction of total domestic investment on the vertical axis along with Survey-based ratings of the intensity of R&D on the horizontal axis. As one can see, there is a high correlation between the two. Furthermore, as a general matter, the Survey information from the *Global Competitiveness Reports* are available for larger numbers of countries than alternative quantitative data.

Conclusions

Transition countries that have been in the midst of large structural changes, the determinants of growth are probably different from those of economies in more normal circumstances. We would expect that overall growth performance would depend in part on growth of the new emerging sectors particularly. Such growth is probably influenced importantly by start-up conditions and other factors that facilitate the efficient shutdown of older sectors and resource transfers between sectors. The evidence suggests that start-ups, financial conditions, and the rule of law have indeed been correlated with growth performance of transition countries during the first 10 years of transition.

Accession to the EU is now on the horizon for many transition countries. The evidence from looking at 20 growth engines is that accession will improve the growth performance of transition countries, but that accession alone will not guarantee especially rapid growth and fast catch up to the EU.

Data tables of twenty growth engines

1. Macroeconomic Stability Index

RANK	COUNTRY	VALUE
1	Norway	6.6
2	Finland	6.4
3	Denmark	6.3
4	Hong Kong SAR	6.2
5	Belgium	6.1
6	Singapore	6.1
7	Portugal	6.0
8	United States	6.0
9	Trinidad and Tobago	6.0
10	Spain	5.8
11	Ireland	5.8
12	Greece	5.8
13	Switzerland	5.8
14	Austria	5.8
15	Estonia	5.8
16	Canada	5.8
17	Sweden	5.8
	EUROPEAN UNION AVERAGE	**5.8**
18	Israel	5.8
19	Iceland	5.7
20	Netherlands	5.7
21	Argentina	5.7
22	El Salvador	5.7
23	Chile	5.6
24	Germany	5.6
25	France	5.6
26	United Kingdom	5.5
27	Slovenia	5.5
28	Australia	5.4
29	Hungary	5.2
30	Jordan	5.2
31	Malaysia	5.2
32	Brazil	5.2
33	Latvia	5.2
	GROUP 1998 AVERAGE	**5.1**
34	Uruguay	5.1
35	New Zealand	5.1
36	Costa Rica	5.1
37	Poland	5.1
38	Panama	5.1
39	Dominican Republic	5.0
40	South Africa	5.0
41	Peru	4.9
42	Philippines	4.9
43	Mauritius	4.8
44	Venezuela	4.8
45	Italy	4.8
46	Nigeria	4.8
47	Lithuania	4.7
48	Korea	4.7
49	Egypt	4.7
	GROUP 2000 AVERAGE	**4.7**
50	Bolivia	4.6
51	Taiwan	4.6
52	India	4.6
53	Romania	4.5
54	Thailand	4.5
55	Bulgaria	4.4
56	Slovak Republic	4.4
57	China	4.3
58	Russia	4.3
59	Jamaica	4.2
60	Mexico	4.2
61	Vietnam	4.2
62	Czech Republic	4.2
63	Ukraine	4.1
64	Sri Lanka	4.1
65	Bangladesh	3.9
66	Paraguay	3.8
67	Japan	3.8
68	Colombia	3.7
69	Indonesia	3.4
70	Ecuador	3.3
71	Guatemala	3.2
72	Nicaragua	3.0
73	Honduras	2.9
74	Zimbabwe	2.9
75	Turkey	2.8

2. Start-up Conditions

RANK	COUNTRY	VALUE
1	United States	6.8
2	Finland	6.3
3	Switzerland	6.0
4	Hong Kong SAR	6.0
5	Netherlands	5.9
6	United Kingdom	5.8
7	Israel	5.8
8	Iceland	5.6
9	Denmark	5.5
10	Singapore	5.5
11	Canada	5.5
12	New Zealand	5.3
13	Australia	5.3
14	Sweden	5.3
15	Ireland	5.0
16	Norway	5.0
17	Germany	5.0
18	Taiwan	5.0
19	France	4.9
20	Austria	4.9
	EUROPEAN UNION AVERAGE	4.8
21	Portugal	4.8
22	Belgium	4.6
23	Egypt	4.5
24	Brazil	4.5
25	Estonia	4.5
26	Trinidad and Tobago	4.5
27	South Africa	4.3
28	Korea	4.3
29	India	4.3
30	Malaysia	4.3
31	Thailand	4.0
32	Hungary	4.0
33	Spain	4.0
	GROUP 1998 AVERAGE	3.9
34	Poland	3.9
35	Japan	3.8
36	Panama	3.8
37	Indonesia	3.8
38	Nigeria	3.5
39	Jordan	3.5
40	Vietnam	3.5
41	Slovak Republic	3.5
42	Chile	3.5
43	Slovenia	3.5
44	Jamaica	3.5
45	Guatemala	3.5
46	Sri Lanka	3.5
47	Venezuela	3.5
48	Czech Republic	3.5
49	Zimbabwe	3.5
50	China	3.3
51	Philippines	3.3
52	El Salvador	3.3
53	Mauritius	3.0
54	Paraguay	3.0
55	Argentina	3.0
56	Turkey	2.8
57	Costa Rica	2.5
58	Uruguay	2.5
59	Lithuania	2.5
60	Greece	2.5
61	Latvia	2.5
62	Italy	2.5
	GROUP 2000 AVERAGE	2.3
63	Colombia	2.3
64	Russia	2.3
65	Peru	2.0
66	Dominican Republic	2.0
67	Bolivia	2.0
68	Mexico	2.0
69	Romania	2.0
70	Bangladesh	1.5
71	Nicaragua	1.5
72	Ecuador	1.5
73	Ukraine	1.5
74	Honduras	1.3
75	Bulgaria	1.0

3. Financial System

RANK	COUNTRY	VALUE
1	Switzerland	6.0
2	Hong Kong SAR	5.8
3	United Kingdom	5.8
4	Ireland	5.4
5	Netherlands	5.3
6	Japan	5.3
7	Taiwan	5.3
8	Singapore	5.2
9	Canada	5.1
10	United States	5.1
11	Norway	5.0
12	Australia	5.0
13	Sweden	4.9
14	Portugal	4.9
15	Finland	4.9
16	France	4.9
	EUROPEAN UNION AVERAGE	4.8
17	Germany	4.8
18	Malaysia	4.8
19	Israel	4.8
20	Austria	4.8
21	Belgium	4.7
22	Denmark	4.6
23	Spain	4.6
24	Italy	4.5
25	Chile	4.4
26	New Zealand	4.4
27	South Africa	4.4
28	Panama	4.3
29	Korea	4.2
30	Egypt	4.2
31	Jordan	4.2
32	China	4.2
33	Philippines	4.1
34	Trinidad and Tobago	4.0
35	Estonia	4.0
36	Thailand	4.0
37	India	4.0
38	Hungary	3.9
39	Poland	3.9
40	Iceland	3.8
	GROUP 1998 AVERAGE	3.8
41	Indonesia	3.7
42	Vietnam	3.5
43	Slovenia	3.5
44	Jamaica	3.5
45	Greece	3.5
46	Czech Republic	3.5
47	Nigeria	3.4
48	Latvia	3.4
49	El Salvador	3.4
50	Slovak Republic	3.3
51	Brazil	3.2
52	Argentina	3.2
53	Paraguay	3.2
54	Lithuania	3.2
55	Mauritius	3.2
56	Sri Lanka	3.1
57	Uruguay	3.1
58	Mexico	3.1
	GROUP 2000 AVERAGE	3.0
59	Costa Rica	2.9
60	Turkey	2.8
61	Venezuela	2.8
62	Romania	2.8
63	Zimbabwe	2.7
64	Bulgaria	2.6
65	Colombia	2.6
66	Russia	2.5
67	Bangladesh	2.5
68	Peru	2.4
69	Dominican Republic	2.3
70	Bolivia	2.2
71	Ukraine	2.0
72	Guatemala	1.8
73	Honduras	1.5
74	Ecuador	1.5
75	Nicaragua	1.3

4. Openness to International Trade

RANK	COUNTRY	VALUE
1	Hong Kong SAR	7.0
2	Estonia	7.0
3	Switzerland	6.9
4	Singapore	6.9
5	Latvia	6.9
6	Canada	6.9
7	Iceland	6.9
8	United States	6.9
9	Czech Republic	6.8
10	Japan	6.8
11	Slovak Republic	6.8
12	Australia	6.8
13	Taiwan	6.8
14	Greece	6.8
15	Sweden	6.8
16	Spain	6.8
17	Finland	6.8
18	Austria	6.8
19	Denmark	6.8
20	Portugal	6.8
21	Italy	6.8
22	France	6.8
23	New Zealand	6.8
24	Netherlands	6.8
25	Germany	6.8
26	Belgium	6.8
27	Ireland	6.8
28	Hungary	6.8
	EUROPEAN UNION AVERAGE	6.7
29	Israel	6.6
30	Turkey	6.6
	GROUP 1998 AVERAGE	6.5
31	Mexico	6.4
32	Slovenia	6.4
33	Trinidad and Tobago	6.4
34	Malaysia	6.3
35	Lithuania	6.3
36	El Salvador	6.2
37	Jamaica	6.2
38	Norway	6.2
39	South Africa	6.2
40	Mauritius	6.1
	GROUP 2000 AVERAGE	6.1
41	United Kingdom	6.1
42	Thailand	6.1
43	Chile	6.0
44	Argentina	6.0
45	Peru	5.9
46	Ukraine	5.8
47	Uruguay	5.8
48	Poland	5.7
49	Korea	5.7
50	Venezuela	5.7
51	Nicaragua	5.7
52	Romania	5.6
53	Indonesia	5.6
54	Costa Rica	5.5
55	Colombia	5.5
56	Bangladesh	5.4
57	Paraguay	5.3
58	Jordan	5.3
59	Sri Lanka	5.3
60	Philippines	5.3
61	Panama	5.2
62	Ecuador	5.1
63	Honduras	4.9
64	Guatemala	4.9
65	Bulgaria	4.9
66	China	4.7
67	Vietnam	4.6
68	Bolivia	4.5
69	Brazil	4.5
70	Dominican Republic	4.5
71	Russia	4.4
72	Egypt	4.0
73	India	3.6
74	Zimbabwe	2.9
75	Nigeria	2.8

5. Quality of Government

RANK	COUNTRY	VALUE
1	Singapore	5.7
2	Finland	5.3
3	Hong Kong SAR	4.8
4	Spain	4.7
5	Hungary	4.7
6	Iceland	4.5
7	Denmark	4.5
8	Switzerland	4.3
9	Netherlands	4.3
10	Taiwan	4.3
11	Ireland	4.3
12	Australia	4.3
13	France	4.0
14	Israel	4.0
15	United Kingdom	4.0
16	Sweden	4.0
17	Jordan	3.8
	EUROPEAN UNION AVERAGE	3.8
18	South Africa	3.7
19	Vietnam	3.7
20	Germany	3.7
21	Turkey	3.7
22	Slovenia	3.7
23	New Zealand	3.7
24	Bulgaria	3.7
25	United States	3.7
26	Austria	3.5
27	China	3.3
28	Indonesia	3.3
29	El Salvador	3.3
30	Thailand	3.3
31	Trinidad and Tobago	3.3
32	Canada	3.3
33	Lithuania	3.3
34	Latvia	3.3
35	Chile	3.2
36	Belgium	3.2
37	Slovak Republic	3.2
38	Norway	3.2
	GROUP 1998 AVERAGE	3.1
	GROUP 2000 AVERAGE	3.0
39	Mauritius	3.0
40	Jamaica	3.0
41	Russia	3.0
42	Japan	3.0
43	Mexico	3.0
44	Egypt	3.0
45	Peru	3.0
46	Argentina	2.8
47	India	2.8
48	Philippines	2.8
49	Panama	2.7
50	Italy	2.7
51	Greece	2.7
52	Brazil	2.7
53	Nigeria	2.7
54	Poland	2.7
55	Estonia	2.7
56	Sri Lanka	2.7
57	Uruguay	2.7
58	Korea	2.7
59	Costa Rica	2.7
60	Colombia	2.5
61	Bolivia	2.3
62	Portugal	2.3
63	Dominican Republic	2.3
64	Malaysia	2.3
65	Czech Republic	2.0
66	Romania	1.7
67	Paraguay	1.7
68	Ukraine	1.7
69	Nicaragua	1.7
70	Venezuela	1.7
71	Ecuador	1.5
72	Bangladesh	1.3
73	Zimbabwe	1.0
74	Guatemala	1.0
75	Honduras	1.0

6. Capital Accumulation

RANK	COUNTRY	VALUE
1	Singapore	6.5
2	China	5.9
3	Korea	4.5
4	Mauritius	4.4
5	Malaysia	4.4
6	Slovak Republic	4.4
7	Hong Kong SAR	4.2
8	Honduras	4.1
9	Nigeria	4.1
10	Vietnam	4.1
11	Ireland	4.0
12	Japan	4.0
13	Trinidad and Tobago	4.0
14	Czech Republic	4.0
15	Slovenia	3.9
16	Hungary	3.8
17	Jamaica	3.7
18	Sri Lanka	3.7
19	Norway	3.7
20	Portugal	3.7
21	Switzerland	3.7
	GROUP 1998 AVERAGE	**3.7**
22	Spain	3.6
23	Latvia	3.5
24	Taiwan	3.5
25	Russia	3.5
26	Netherlands	3.5
27	Dominican Republic	3.4
28	Poland	3.4
29	Indonesia	3.4
30	Jordan	3.4
31	Panama	3.4
32	Greece	3.3
33	Belgium	3.3
34	Austria	3.3
35	Estonia	3.3
36	Denmark	3.3
37	Ukraine	3.2
	EUROPEAN UNION AVERAGE	**3.2**
38	Chile	3.2
39	Thailand	3.2
40	Finland	3.1
41	Egypt	3.1
42	India	3.1
43	Philippines	3.1
44	Australia	3.1
45	Germany	3.1
	GROUP 2000 AVERAGE	**3.0**
46	Turkey	2.9
47	Lithuania	2.9
48	Mexico	2.9
49	Paraguay	2.9
50	Iceland	2.9
51	France	2.9
52	Canada	2.8
53	Brazil	2.8
54	Italy	2.8
55	Ecuador	2.7
56	Peru	2.6
57	Sweden	2.5
58	New Zealand	2.5
59	Venezuela	2.5
60	Israel	2.4
61	Romania	2.4
62	United Kingdom	2.3
63	United States	2.2
64	Bolivia	2.2
65	South Africa	2.1
66	Bangladesh	2.0
67	Costa Rica	2.0
68	Argentina	2.0
69	El Salvador	1.9
70	Zimbabwe	1.9
71	Guatemala	1.8
72	Bulgaria	1.8
73	Uruguay	1.4
74	Colombia	1.4
75	Nicaragua	1.0

7. Low Taxes

RANK	COUNTRY	VALUE
1	Hong Kong SAR	6.1
2	Singapore	5.0
3	Estonia	5.0
4	Malaysia	4.5
5	Taiwan	4.4
6	Nigeria	4.3
7	Mauritius	4.3
8	Panama	4.0
9	Thailand	3.9
10	United States	3.9
11	Jordan	3.8
12	Ukraine	3.8
13	Costa Rica	3.7
14	Sri Lanka	3.7
15	Latvia	3.7
16	El Salvador	3.7
17	India	3.7
18	Ireland	3.6
19	Ecuador	3.6
20	Bolivia	3.6
21	Dominican Republic	3.6
22	Japan	3.5
23	Finland	3.5
24	United Kingdom	3.5
25	Guatemala	3.5
26	Indonesia	3.4
27	Hungary	3.4
	GROUP 1998 AVERAGE	**3.3**
28	Trinidad and Tobago	3.3
29	Philippines	3.3
30	Brazil	3.3
31	Australia	3.3
32	Korea	3.2
33	Egypt	3.2
34	Honduras	3.2
35	New Zealand	3.2
36	Spain	3.2
37	Bangladesh	3.2
38	Nicaragua	3.2
39	Lithuania	3.2
40	Jamaica	3.1
41	China	3.1
42	Iceland	3.1
43	South Africa	3.1
44	Chile	3.1
45	Slovenia	3.0
46	Peru	2.9
47	Venezuela	2.9
48	Canada	2.9
49	Mexico	2.8
50	Colombia	2.8
51	Turkey	2.8
52	Vietnam	2.7
53	Netherlands	2.7
	GROUP 2000 AVERAGE	**2.7**
54	Portugal	2.7
55	Poland	2.6
56	Czech Republic	2.6
	EUROPEAN UNION AVERAGE	**2.6**
57	Israel	2.6
58	Greece	2.5
59	Argentina	2.5
60	Austria	2.4
61	Slovak Republic	2.4
62	Norway	2.4
63	Russia	2.3
64	Bulgaria	2.2
65	Germany	2.2
66	Italy	2.2
67	France	2.1
68	Belgium	2.1
69	Romania	2.0
70	Sweden	1.9
71	Denmark	1.7
72	Zimbabwe	1.6
73	Uruguay	
74	Switzerland	
75	Paraguay	

8. Innovation

RANK	COUNTRY	VALUE
1	United States	5.9
2	Finland	5.9
3	Israel	5.7
4	France	5.7
5	Netherlands	5.6
6	Germany	5.6
7	Switzerland	5.6
8	Taiwan	5.5
9	Sweden	5.5
10	Japan	5.5
11	Singapore	5.3
12	United Kingdom	5.3
13	Austria	5.3
14	Denmark	5.2
15	Canada	5.2
16	Belgium	5.1
	EUROPEAN UNION AVERAGE	5.1
17	Ireland	5.1
18	Australia	5.0
19	Iceland	4.9
20	Italy	4.9
21	Norway	4.8
22	Spain	4.7
23	Korea	4.5
24	New Zealand	4.4
25	Hong Kong SAR	4.3
26	Hungary	4.2
27	South Africa	4.2
28	Slovenia	4.1
29	Sri Lanka	4.0
30	Estonia	4.0
	GROUP 1998 AVERAGE	4.0
31	Brazil	4.0
32	India	3.9
33	Portugal	3.9
34	China	3.9
35	Malaysia	3.9
36	Costa Rica	3.8
37	Poland	3.8
38	Trinidad and Tobago	3.8
39	Czech Republic	3.8
40	Slovak Republic	3.7
41	Chile	3.7
42	Russia	3.7
43	Jamaica	3.7
44	Latvia	3.6
45	Uruguay	3.6
46	Panama	3.6
47	Thailand	3.6
48	Greece	3.5
49	Ukraine	3.5
50	Lithuania	3.5
51	Jordan	3.5
52	Philippines	3.4
53	Mauritius	3.4
54	Indonesia	3.3
	GROUP 2000 AVERAGE	3.3
55	Argentina	3.3
56	Mexico	3.3
57	Colombia	3.3
58	Turkey	3.3
59	Vietnam	3.2
60	Egypt	3.2
61	Zimbabwe	3.1
62	Nigeria	3.1
63	Venezuela	3.1
64	Bulgaria	3.1
65	Paraguay	2.9
66	Peru	2.9
67	Guatemala	2.8
68	El Salvador	2.8
69	Nicaragua	2.7
70	Ecuador	2.6
71	Romania	2.6
72	Bangladesh	2.5
73	Honduras	2.4
74	Bolivia	2.3
75	Dominican Republic	

9. Technology Transfer

RANK	COUNTRY	VALUE
1	Singapore	6.1
2	Malaysia	6.0
3	Hungary	5.8
4	Romania	5.8
5	Hong Kong SAR	5.7
6	United Kingdom	5.7
7	Egypt	5.6
8	Netherlands	5.6
9	Poland	5.6
10	Brazil	5.6
11	Ireland	5.6
12	Australia	5.5
13	Chile	5.5
14	Taiwan	5.5
15	Belgium	5.5
16	Israel	5.5
17	India	5.5
18	Mexico	5.5
19	Thailand	5.4
20	Slovak Republic	5.4
21	Venezuela	5.4
22	Portugal	5.4
23	Italy	5.4
24	Canada	5.4
25	Czech Republic	5.3
26	Argentina	5.3
27	Spain	5.3
28	Austria	5.3
29	South Africa	5.3
	GROUP 1998 AVERAGE	5.3
30	Philippines	5.3
31	New Zealand	5.2
	EUROPEAN UNION AVERAGE	5.2
32	Estonia	5.2
33	Costa Rica	5.2
34	Turkey	5.1
35	Germany	5.1
36	Denmark	5.1
37	Sri Lanka	5.0
38	France	5.0
39	Korea	5.0
40	Nigeria	5.0
41	Iceland	4.9
42	Japan	4.9
43	Jordan	4.9
44	Trinidad and Tobago	4.9
45	Vietnam	4.9
46	Norway	4.9
47	Greece	4.9
48	Switzerland	4.9
49	Jamaica	4.9
	GROUP 2000 AVERAGE	4.8
50	Indonesia	4.8
51	Mauritius	4.8
52	Peru	4.8
53	Latvia	4.7
54	Colombia	4.7
55	Panama	4.7
56	United States	4.6
57	Honduras	4.6
58	El Salvador	4.6
59	Sweden	4.6
60	Finland	4.6
61	Slovenia	4.5
62	Lithuania	4.5
63	Zimbabwe	4.4
64	China	4.4
65	Uruguay	4.3
66	Ecuador	4.2
67	Guatemala	4.1
68	Bangladesh	4.1
69	Russia	3.8
70	Bulgaria	3.8
71	Nicaragua	3.8
72	Ukraine	3.8
73	Paraguay	3.7
74	Bolivia	3.5
75	Dominican Republic	

10. New Economy

RANK	COUNTRY	VALUE
1	Finland	6.6
2	Iceland	6.5
3	Sweden	6.4
4	Singapore	6.4
5	United States	6.3
6	Norway	6.3
7	Denmark	6.2
8	Canada	6.2
9	Netherlands	6.2
10	Hong Kong SAR	6.2
11	Australia	6.1
12	Switzerland	6.1
13	Austria	6.1
14	United Kingdom	6.1
15	Germany	6.0
16	Taiwan	6.0
17	New Zealand	6.0
18	Ireland	6.0
	EUROPEAN UNION AVERAGE	**5.9**
19	Belgium	5.9
20	Estonia	5.9
21	France	5.9
22	Korea	5.9
23	Israel	5.8
24	Japan	5.8
25	Portugal	5.7
26	Spain	5.6
27	Italy	5.5
28	Slovenia	5.5
29	Czech Republic	5.4
	GROUP 1998 AVERAGE	**5.4**
30	Hungary	5.3
31	Slovak Republic	5.2
32	Chile	5.2
33	Malaysia	5.2
34	Uruguay	5.1
35	Greece	5.1
36	Latvia	5.0
37	Poland	4.9
38	Brazil	4.8
39	Argentina	4.8
40	South Africa	4.8
41	Mauritius	4.8
42	Costa Rica	4.7
	GROUP 2000 AVERAGE	**4.7**
43	Lithuania	4.7
44	Trinidad and Tobago	4.6
45	Turkey	4.6
46	Mexico	4.6
47	Jamaica	4.6
48	Venezuela	4.5
49	Panama	4.5
50	Bulgaria	4.4
51	Colombia	4.4
52	Jordan	4.3
53	Thailand	4.2
54	Russia	4.2
55	Philippines	4.1
56	China	4.0
57	Dominican Republic	4.0
58	Peru	4.0
59	Romania	4.0
60	El Salvador	3.9
61	Egypt	3.8
62	Ukraine	3.8
63	Ecuador	3.6
64	Paraguay	3.6
65	Bolivia	3.5
66	Guatemala	3.5
67	Indonesia	3.4
68	India	3.4
69	Sri Lanka	3.4
70	Honduras	3.2
71	Nicaragua	3.2
72	Zimbabwe	3.1
73	Vietnam	2.8
74	Nigeria	2.2
75	Bangladesh	2.0

11. Education

RANK	COUNTRY	VALUE
1	United States	6.3
2	Finland	6.3
3	Denmark	6.1
4	Norway	6.1
5	Austria	6.0
6	Switzerland	6.0
7	Japan	6.0
8	Ireland	5.9
9	Netherlands	5.8
10	Sweden	5.8
11	Australia	5.8
12	Belgium	5.8
13	Canada	5.7
14	France	5.7
15	New Zealand	5.7
16	Korea	5.5
17	Singapore	5.5
18	Estonia	5.5
19	Iceland	5.5
20	Germany	5.4
	EUROPEAN UNION AVERAGE	**5.4**
21	Latvia	5.3
22	Taiwan	5.2
23	Israel	5.1
24	Czech Republic	5.1
	GROUP 1998 AVERAGE	**5.1**
25	Slovenia	5.1
26	Hungary	5.0
27	Hong Kong SAR	4.9
28	Spain	4.8
29	Slovak Republic	4.7
30	Malaysia	4.7
31	United Kingdom	4.7
32	Italy	4.7
33	Poland	4.7
34	Romania	4.4
35	Greece	4.4
36	Costa Rica	4.3
	GROUP 2000 AVERAGE	**4.3**
37	Jamaica	4.2
38	Ukraine	4.0
39	South Africa	4.0
40	Trinidad and Tobago	3.9
41	Chile	3.9
42	Portugal	3.8
43	Bulgaria	3.7
44	Uruguay	3.7
45	Mauritius	3.6
46	Philippines	3.6
47	Thailand	3.5
48	Lithuania	3.5
49	Vietnam	3.5
50	Argentina	3.4
51	Jordan	3.3
52	Sri Lanka	3.2
53	Panama	3.2
54	Indonesia	3.1
55	Russia	3.0
56	Brazil	3.0
57	Peru	3.0
58	Paraguay	3.0
59	Egypt	2.8
60	Colombia	2.8
61	Mexico	2.8
62	Turkey	2.7
63	China	2.7
64	Zimbabwe	2.6
65	Ecuador	2.4
66	El Salvador	2.3
67	India	2.2
68	Dominican Republic	2.1
69	Nigeria	2.0
70	Venezuela	1.9
71	Bolivia	1.8
72	Guatemala	1.7
73	Nicaragua	1.6
74	Bangladesh	1.3
75	Honduras	1.3

12. Infrastructure

RANK	COUNTRY	VALUE
1	Canada	6.8
2	Netherlands	6.8
3	Germany	6.7
4	Belgium	6.7
5	Switzerland	6.6
6	Sweden	6.5
7	Austria	6.5
8	United States	6.5
9	Finland	6.3
10	Czech Republic	6.3
11	France	6.3
12	Singapore	6.2
13	Iceland	6.2
14	Denmark	6.2
15	United Kingdom	6.1
	EUROPEAN UNION AVERAGE	**6.1**
16	Norway	6.1
17	Hong Kong SAR	6.1
18	Australia	6.1
19	Israel	6.0
20	New Zealand	6.0
21	Malaysia	6.0
22	Chile	6.0
23	Spain	5.9
24	Japan	5.8
25	Argentina	5.7
26	Estonia	5.7
27	Portugal	5.6
28	Korea	5.6
29	Thailand	5.5
	GROUP 1998 AVERAGE	**5.4**
30	Ireland	5.4
31	Hungary	5.4
32	Taiwan	5.3
33	Brazil	5.3
34	Italy	5.3
35	South Africa	5.3
36	Greece	5.2
37	Slovenia	5.2
38	Slovak Republic	5.1
39	Uruguay	5.1
40	Jordan	5.1
41	Egypt	5.1
42	Latvia	5.0
43	Dominican Republic	4.8
44	El Salvador	4.7
45	Turkey	4.6
46	Poland	4.6
47	Panama	4.6
48	Jamaica	4.5
49	Venezuela	4.5
50	Colombia	4.5
51	Indonesia	4.3
52	Peru	4.3
53	Lithuania	4.2
	GROUP 2000 AVERAGE	**4.2**
54	India	4.2
55	Russia	4.1
56	Zimbabwe	4.1
57	Mexico	4.0
58	China	4.0
59	Ukraine	4.0
60	Guatemala	3.9
61	Philippines	3.9
62	Trinidad and Tobago	3.8
63	Bulgaria	3.7
64	Sri Lanka	3.6
65	Bolivia	3.5
66	Paraguay	3.5
67	Costa Rica	3.3
68	Nigeria	3.2
69	Romania	3.1
70	Mauritius	3.0
71	Ecuador	3.0
72	Bangladesh	2.7
73	Honduras	2.6
74	Vietnam	2.5
75	Nicaragua	2.3

13. Rule of Law

RANK	COUNTRY	VALUE
1	United States	7.0
2	Hong Kong SAR	7.0
3	United Kingdom	6.8
4	Israel	6.8
5	Switzerland	6.8
6	Germany	6.8
7	Denmark	6.5
8	France	6.5
9	Ireland	6.5
10	Japan	6.5
11	Finland	6.5
12	Italy	6.4
13	Belgium	6.4
	EUROPEAN UNION AVERAGE	**6.3**
14	New Zealand	6.3
15	Canada	6.3
16	Australia	6.3
17	Austria	6.3
18	Netherlands	6.3
19	Singapore	6.1
20	South Africa	6.0
21	India	6.0
22	Portugal	5.9
23	Hungary	5.9
24	Iceland	5.8
25	Chile	5.8
26	Poland	5.8
27	Norway	5.8
28	Uruguay	5.8
29	Spain	5.8
30	Mauritius	5.8
31	Sweden	5.6
32	Greece	5.6
33	Jordan	5.6
34	Brazil	5.5
35	Jamaica	5.5
	GROUP 1998 AVERAGE	**5.3**
36	Sri Lanka	5.3
37	Estonia	5.3
38	Philippines	5.3
39	Thailand	5.0
40	Costa Rica	5.0
41	Slovenia	5.0
42	Turkey	4.9
43	Trinidad and Tobago	4.9
44	Argentina	4.6
45	Korea	4.5
46	Czech Republic	4.5
47	Slovak Republic	4.4
48	Egypt	4.4
49	Latvia	4.3
50	Mexico	4.3
51	Romania	4.3
52	Venezuela	4.0
53	Russia	4.0
54	Paraguay	3.8
55	Taiwan	3.8
56	Zimbabwe	3.8
57	China	3.8
	GROUP 2000 AVERAGE	**3.7**
58	Vietnam	3.6
59	Malaysia	3.5
60	Colombia	3.3
61	Bangladesh	3.3
62	Bulgaria	3.3
63	Indonesia	3.3
64	Nigeria	3.0
65	Panama	3.0
66	Peru	2.8
67	El Salvador	2.8
68	Nicaragua	2.5
69	Lithuania	2.5
70	Guatemala	2.5
71	Ukraine	2.5
72	Dominican Republic	2.5
73	Honduras	2.5
74	Bolivia	1.3
75	Ecuador	1.3

14. Red Tape

RANK	COUNTRY	VALUE
1	Trinidad and Tobago	7.0
2	Estonia	6.5
3	Switzerland	6.5
4	United Kingdom	6.5
5	Sri Lanka	6.5
6	Singapore	6.5
7	Finland	6.5
8	Iceland	6.5
9	Spain	6.5
10	Hong Kong SAR	6.5
11	Ireland	6.0
12	Netherlands	6.0
13	New Zealand	5.5
14	United States	5.5
15	Jamaica	5.5
	EUROPEAN UNION AVERAGE	**5.1**
16	Austria	5.0
17	Sweden	5.0
18	India	5.0
19	Canada	5.0
20	Malaysia	5.0
21	Slovenia	5.0
22	Chile	5.0
23	Australia	5.0
24	Germany	5.0
25	Colombia	5.0
26	Taiwan	5.0
27	Philippines	5.0
28	Denmark	4.8
	GROUP 1998 AVERAGE	**4.8**
29	Belgium	4.8
30	Mauritius	4.5
31	El Salvador	4.5
32	France	4.5
33	Japan	4.5
34	Guatemala	4.5
35	Argentina	4.5
36	Brazil	4.5
37	Ecuador	4.5
38	Mexico	4.5
39	Czech Republic	4.5
40	Nigeria	4.5
41	Indonesia	4.5
42	Bangladesh	4.5
43	Romania	4.5
44	Korea	4.5
45	Norway	4.5
46	Uruguay	4.5
47	Portugal	4.5
48	China	4.3
49	Venezuela	4.3
50	Lithuania	4.0
51	Ukraine	4.0
52	Zimbabwe	4.0
53	Honduras	4.0
54	Bulgaria	4.0
55	Latvia	4.0
56	Hungary	4.0
57	Nicaragua	4.0
	GROUP 2000 AVERAGE	**3.9**
58	Poland	3.8
59	Russia	3.5
60	Israel	3.5
61	South Africa	3.5
62	Panama	3.5
63	Costa Rica	3.5
64	Jordan	3.5
65	Peru	3.5
66	Italy	3.3
67	Paraguay	3.0
68	Greece	3.0
69	Slovak Republic	3.0
70	Thailand	3.0
71	Egypt	3.0
72	Turkey	3.0
73	Vietnam	3.0
74	Dominican Republic	2.5
75	Bolivia	1.5

15. Corruption

RANK	COUNTRY	VALUE
1	Iceland	7.0
2	Finland	6.8
3	Denmark	6.6
4	New Zealand	6.5
5	Singapore	6.5
6	Sweden	6.5
7	Canada	6.4
8	Australia	6.4
9	United Kingdom	6.4
10	Netherlands	6.3
11	United States	6.3
12	Hong Kong SAR	6.3
13	Norway	6.2
14	Chile	6.1
15	Japan	6.1
16	Israel	6.1
17	Lithuania	6.0
18	Belgium	6.0
19	Austria	6.0
20	Switzerland	5.9
21	Ireland	5.9
	EUROPEAN UNION AVERAGE	**5.9**
22	Taiwan	5.9
23	Germany	5.8
24	France	5.6
25	Spain	5.6
26	Italy	5.4
27	Hungary	5.4
28	Portugal	5.2
29	Estonia	5.1
30	Peru	5.1
31	South Africa	5.1
32	Trinidad and Tobago	5.0
33	Slovenia	4.9
34	Bulgaria	4.9
	GROUP 2000 AVERAGE	**4.9**
35	Slovak Republic	4.9
36	Jordan	4.8
37	Jamaica	4.8
	GROUP 1998 AVERAGE	**4.8**
38	Malaysia	4.7
39	Uruguay	4.7
40	Mauritius	4.6
41	Costa Rica	4.6
42	Colombia	4.5
43	Latvia	4.5
44	Egypt	4.5
45	Dominican Republic	4.4
46	Brazil	4.4
47	Mexico	4.4
48	Greece	4.4
49	Poland	4.4
50	El Salvador	4.3
51	Turkey	4.3
52	China	4.3
53	Korea	4.2
54	Russia	4.2
55	Thailand	4.2
56	Sri Lanka	4.2
57	Panama	4.2
58	Romania	4.1
59	Bolivia	4.1
60	Argentina	4.0
61	Venezuela	4.0
62	Guatemala	4.0
63	Czech Republic	4.0
64	Ecuador	3.9
65	India	3.7
66	Nicaragua	3.7
67	Honduras	3.7
68	Philippines	3.6
69	Vietnam	3.5
70	Zimbabwe	3.5
71	Indonesia	3.3
72	Ukraine	3.3
73	Paraguay	2.8
74	Nigeria	2.8
75	Bangladesh	2.1

16. Competition

RANK	COUNTRY	VALUE
1	United States	7.0
2	Netherlands	6.7
3	Germany	6.7
4	Switzerland	6.3
5	Finland	6.3
6	Vietnam	6.0
7	Denmark	6.0
8	France	6.0
9	United Kingdom	6.0
10	Austria	5.8
11	Canada	5.8
	EUROPEAN UNION AVERAGE	5.7
12	Trinidad and Tobago	5.7
13	Sweden	5.7
14	Singapore	5.7
15	Japan	5.7
16	Australia	5.7
17	Slovak Republic	5.7
18	Belgium	5.7
19	Taiwan	5.7
20	New Zealand	5.7
21	Poland	5.7
22	Spain	5.7
23	Nigeria	5.7
24	Hungary	5.7
25	Brazil	5.7
26	Ireland	5.5
	GROUP 1998 AVERAGE	5.4
27	Czech Republic	5.3
28	Hong Kong SAR	5.3
29	Estonia	5.3
30	Chile	5.3
31	India	5.3
32	China	5.3
33	Slovenia	5.2
34	Norway	5.0
35	Uruguay	5.0
36	Greece	5.0
37	Thailand	5.0
38	Israel	5.0
39	Panama	5.0
40	Lithuania	5.0
	GROUP 2000 AVERAGE	4.8
41	Jordan	4.7
42	Bulgaria	4.7
43	Philippines	4.7
44	Dominican Republic	4.7
45	Latvia	4.7
46	South Africa	4.7
47	Italy	4.7
48	Iceland	4.7
49	Colombia	4.7
50	Sri Lanka	4.7
51	Portugal	4.5
52	Russia	4.3
53	Argentina	4.3
54	Costa Rica	4.3
55	Malaysia	4.3
56	Peru	4.3
57	Jamaica	4.3
58	Mexico	4.3
59	Guatemala	4.3
60	Nicaragua	4.3
61	Korea	4.3
62	El Salvador	4.3
63	Indonesia	4.3
64	Bangladesh	4.3
65	Turkey	4.3
66	Ukraine	4.3
67	Egypt	4.0
68	Bolivia	4.0
69	Venezuela	4.0
70	Romania	4.0
71	Paraguay	3.7
72	Mauritius	3.7
73	Zimbabwe	3.3
74	Ecuador	3.3
75	Honduras	3.3

17. Local Supplier Depth

RANK	COUNTRY	VALUE
1	United States	6.3
2	Germany	6.1
3	Finland	6.0
4	Japan	6.0
5	Switzerland	5.7
6	Austria	5.7
7	United Kingdom	5.6
8	Australia	5.5
9	France	5.5
10	Netherlands	5.5
11	Taiwan	5.4
12	Canada	5.3
13	Denmark	5.3
14	Czech Republic	5.3
15	Italy	5.3
16	Spain	5.3
	EUROPEAN UNION AVERAGE	5.2
17	Brazil	5.1
18	Norway	5.0
19	New Zealand	5.0
20	India	5.0
21	Sweden	5.0
22	Slovak Republic	4.8
23	China	4.8
24	Belgium	4.8
25	South Africa	4.8
	GROUP 1998 AVERAGE	4.7
26	Ireland	4.7
27	Israel	4.7
28	Russia	4.7
29	Hungary	4.7
30	Poland	4.6
31	Korea	4.5
32	Estonia	4.5
33	Hong Kong SAR	4.5
34	Portugal	4.5
35	Singapore	4.4
36	Iceland	4.4
37	Uruguay	4.3
38	Slovenia	4.3
39	Lithuania	4.3
40	Mexico	4.3
41	Chile	4.3
	GROUP 2000 AVERAGE	4.3
42	Latvia	4.2
43	Turkey	4.2
44	Ukraine	4.2
45	Costa Rica	4.0
46	Thailand	4.0
47	Romania	4.0
48	Argentina	3.9
49	Bulgaria	3.9
50	Jordan	3.8
51	Peru	3.7
52	Jamaica	3.7
53	Panama	3.7
54	Greece	3.7
55	Colombia	3.5
56	Dominican Republic	3.5
57	Sri Lanka	3.5
58	Indonesia	3.5
59	Paraguay	3.5
60	Nigeria	3.5
61	Philippines	3.4
62	Venezuela	3.3
63	Guatemala	3.3
64	Trinidad and Tobago	3.3
65	El Salvador	3.3
66	Vietnam	3.3
67	Malaysia	3.3
68	Egypt	3.2
69	Mauritius	3.2
70	Zimbabwe	3.0
71	Ecuador	2.6
72	Honduras	2.2
73	Nicaragua	2.2
74	Bangladesh	2.2
75	Bolivia	2.2

18. Workplace Incentives

RANK	COUNTRY	VALUE	1 ———————— 7
1	United States	6.2	
2	Singapore	6.0	
3	Sweden	5.8	
4	Hong Kong SAR	5.8	
5	Canada	5.8	
6	Finland	5.7	
7	United Kingdom	5.6	
8	Denmark	5.6	
9	Australia	5.6	
10	Norway	5.6	
11	Estonia	5.6	
12	Germany	5.5	
13	Taiwan	5.4	
14	New Zealand	5.4	
15	Ireland	5.4	
16	Iceland	5.4	
17	Switzerland	5.3	
18	Belgium	5.3	
19	Malaysia	5.2	
20	Israel	5.2	
21	Hungary	5.2	
22	France	5.1	
	EUROPEAN UNION AVERAGE	**5.1**	
23	Costa Rica	5.0	
24	Ukraine	5.0	
25	Latvia	5.0	
	GROUP 1998 AVERAGE	**4.9**	
26	Spain	4.9	
27	Trinidad and Tobago	4.8	
28	China	4.8	
29	Philippines	4.8	
30	Netherlands	4.8	
31	El Salvador	4.8	
32	Czech Republic	4.8	
33	Austria	4.8	
34	Japan	4.7	
35	Vietnam	4.7	
36	Jamaica	4.7	
37	Slovenia	4.6	
38	Nigeria	4.6	
39	Romania	4.6	
40	Portugal	4.6	
41	Brazil	4.6	
42	Egypt	4.5	
43	Lithuania	4.5	
44	Thailand	4.4	
45	Poland	4.4	
46	South Africa	4.4	
	GROUP 2000 AVERAGE	**4.3**	
47	Korea	4.2	
48	Mexico	4.2	
49	Dominican Republic	4.2	
50	Slovak Republic	4.2	
51	Italy	4.0	
52	Russia	4.0	
53	Sri Lanka	4.0	
54	Indonesia	3.9	
55	Zimbabwe	3.7	
56	Argentina	3.7	
57	Jordan	3.7	
58	Greece	3.7	
59	Panama	3.7	
60	Turkey	3.7	
61	Venezuela	3.7	
62	Uruguay	3.6	
63	Chile	3.6	
64	Peru	3.6	
65	Mauritius	3.4	
66	Bulgaria	3.4	
67	Guatemala	3.2	
68	Colombia	3.2	
69	India	3.2	
70	Nicaragua	3.1	
71	Paraguay	3.0	
72	Bolivia	2.6	
73	Ecuador	2.5	
74	Bangladesh	2.2	
75	Honduras	1.8	

19. Labor Market Flexibility

RANK	COUNTRY	VALUE	1 ———————— 7
1	Romania	7.0	
2	Ukraine	7.0	
3	Singapore	6.3	
4	Peru	6.3	
5	Hong Kong SAR	6.3	
6	United Kingdom	6.0	
7	United States	6.0	
8	Nigeria	5.7	
9	China	5.5	
10	Czech Republic	5.5	
11	Iceland	5.3	
12	Switzerland	5.3	
13	Chile	5.0	
14	Trinidad and Tobago	5.0	
15	Turkey	5.0	
16	Bangladesh	5.0	
17	Korea	5.0	
18	Nicaragua	5.0	
19	Latvia	5.0	
20	Dominican Republic	5.0	
21	Denmark	5.0	
22	Canada	4.8	
23	Hungary	4.7	
24	Estonia	4.7	
25	Russia	4.7	
26	Bolivia	4.7	
27	Taiwan	4.7	
28	Israel	4.7	
29	Jordan	4.7	
30	Indonesia	4.7	
31	Malaysia	4.7	
	GROUP 2000 AVERAGE	**4.6**	
32	Thailand	4.5	
33	Brazil	4.3	
34	New Zealand	4.3	
35	El Salvador	4.3	
36	Egypt	4.2	
	GROUP 1998 AVERAGE	**4.1**	
37	Bulgaria	4.0	
38	Jamaica	4.0	
39	Guatemala	4.0	
40	Costa Rica	4.0	
41	Argentina	3.8	
42	Sri Lanka	3.7	
43	Venezuela	3.7	
44	Paraguay	3.7	
45	Slovak Republic	3.7	
46	Vietnam	3.5	
47	India	3.3	
48	Japan	3.3	
49	Netherlands	3.3	
50	Portugal	3.3	
51	Poland	3.3	
52	Lithuania	3.3	
53	Colombia	3.3	
54	Honduras	3.2	
55	Uruguay	3.2	
56	Mexico	3.0	
57	Philippines	3.0	
58	Panama	3.0	
59	Australia	3.0	
	EUROPEAN UNION AVERAGE	**2.9**	
60	Spain	2.7	
61	South Africa	2.7	
62	Austria	2.7	
63	Finland	2.7	
64	Ireland	2.3	
65	Norway	2.3	
66	Slovenia	2.3	
67	Greece	2.3	
68	France	2.3	
69	Germany	2.2	
70	Belgium	2.0	
71	Sweden	2.0	
72	Italy	1.8	
73	Ecuador	1.3	
74	Zimbabwe	1.2	
75	Mauritius	1.0	

20. Cluster Development

RANK	COUNTRY	VALUE	1 7
1	Italy	6.0	
2	United States	6.0	
3	Finland	5.5	
4	India	5.0	
5	Korea	5.0	
6	Portugal	5.0	
7	Trinidad and Tobago	5.0	
8	Germany	5.0	
9	Taiwan	5.0	
10	Japan	5.0	
11	Norway	5.0	
12	Mauritius	5.0	
13	Ireland	5.0	
14	United Kingdom	5.0	
15	Switzerland	5.0	
16	Israel	5.0	
17	Sweden	5.0	
18	Canada	5.0	
19	Belgium	4.5	
	EUROPEAN UNION AVERAGE	**4.1**	
20	France	4.0	
21	Romania	4.0	
22	Russia	4.0	
23	Turkey	4.0	
24	Ukraine	4.0	
25	Singapore	4.0	
26	Thailand	4.0	
27	Lithuania	3.0	
28	Indonesia	3.0	
29	Chile	3.0	
30	Hong Kong SAR	3.0	
31	Malaysia	3.0	
32	Mexico	3.0	
33	Austria	3.0	
34	Philippines	3.0	
35	New Zealand	3.0	
36	Brazil	3.0	
37	Spain	3.0	
38	South Africa	3.0	
39	Panama	3.0	
40	Poland	3.0	
41	Slovak Republic	3.0	
42	Peru	3.0	
	GROUP 2000 AVERAGE	**2.6**	
43	Uruguay	2.5	
44	Egypt	2.5	
45	Estonia	2.0	
46	Argentina	2.0	
47	Sri Lanka	2.0	
48	Greece	2.0	
	GROUP 1998 AVERAGE	**2.0**	
49	China	2.0	
50	Costa Rica	2.0	
51	Slovenia	2.0	
52	Jamaica	2.0	
53	Colombia	2.0	
54	El Salvador	2.0	
55	Bolivia	2.0	
56	Denmark	2.0	
57	Hungary	2.0	
58	Netherlands	2.0	
59	Ecuador	2.0	
60	Iceland	2.0	
61	Dominican Republic	2.0	
62	Latvia	2.0	
63	Bangladesh	2.0	
64	Vietnam	2.0	
65	Jordan	2.0	
66	Guatemala	2.0	
67	Australia	2.0	
68	Venezuela	2.0	
69	Zimbabwe	1.5	
70	Nicaragua	1.0	
71	Czech Republic	1.0	
72	Honduras	1.0	
73	Paraguay	1.0	
74	Bulgaria	1.0	
75	Nigeria	1.0	

References

de Melo, Martha, Cevdet Denizer, and Alan Gelb. 1997. "From Plan to Market: Patterns of Transition," in *Macroeconomic Stabilization in Transition Economies.* Mario I. Blejer and Marko Skreb, eds. (Cambridge; New York, and Melbourne: Cambridge University Press), pp. 17–72.

Havrylyshyn, Oleh, Ivailo Izvorski, and Ron van Rooden. 1998. Recovery and Growth in Transition Economies 1990–97: A Stylized Regression Analysis. International Monetary Fund Working Paper: WP/98/141, September.

World Economic Forum. 2001. *The Global Competitiveness Report 2001–2002* (Oxford: Oxford University Press).

New Data on Restructuring and Growth in Transition Regions and Countries

ANDREW M. WARNER, Center for International Development
at Harvard University

The most fundamental economic objective of transition has always been to achieve sustainable growth by shifting economic resources to new sectors and new industries. The reason for this was not complicated. Demand for the output of older sectors that existed to produce goods for the Soviet economic network was never likely to grow. Therefore, growth must come from newer sectors in transition economies. This means that the ability to grow in a fast and sustainable fashion depends on achieving effective structural change.

The purpose of this paper is to present new data on structural change in selected regions of transition countries by combining data from standard sources as well as a survey of enterprises conducted for this *Report*. The results from this new survey are presented for the first time in this *Report*. The data are based on small (100- to 200-firm) surveys of enterprises in 16 regions in central Europe, southeastern Europe, and the former Soviet Union. In Russia, the data cover three cities: Ekaterinburg, Tomsk, and Voronezh. These are combined with similar data from 13 other transition regions or countries: Armenia, Belarus, Bulgaria, Croatia, Estonia, Kazakhstan, Kyrgyzstan, Lithuania, Montenegro, Romania, Serbia, Ukraine, and Uzbekistan. Through this survey we have collected economic data separately for four main types of firms: state firms, privatized firms, spin-offs of former state firms, and completely new private firms. A *spin-off* is defined as an enterprise that was once part of a state firm but has been reestablished as a separate legal entity. For example, if a hotel of a state firm were reestablished as a privately owned hotel, the hotel would be a spin-off.

The data were collected along these lines because such data are vital to understanding the success of current reform efforts and future growth prospects. Macroeconomic data in transition countries are usually not presented separately according to these categories. There are exceptions, of course, but not for a broad sample of countries. Also, structural change in general means that resources are being shifted between sectors. To measure structural change accurately, therefore, one needs to split up the economy along the lines across which the structural change is happening. In transition counties, the important fault lines are not the traditional sectors such as agriculture, manufacturing, construction, or mining, for example. The fault line that matters is the public versus private divide, or, more simply: new sectors versus old sectors. This kind of data does not exist in the official publications for a large sample of countries and must be constructed from scratch.

Interpreting structural change

Structural change is by definition a fluid situation because some sectors are growing while others are declining. This fact means that the interpretation of what lies behind any aggregate growth rates is not straightforward. Specifically, there are pitfalls in using past growth rates as indicators of the success of structural change or of reform efforts. There are also pitfalls in using current growth rates as indicators of where the economy is headed in the future.

We take up this last point with an example. Economies in the midst of rapid structural change can easily have negative growth rates but good future prospects. Consider a simple example of an economy with 40 percent of total GDP in the private sector and 60 percent in the state sector. Further assume that the private sector is growing at 10 percent and state sector is declining at 10 percent. Such an economy would record an aggregate growth rate of −2 percent (40 percent of +10 plus 60 percent of −10). One might be tempted to say that this economy would be stagnating. But in 10 years, such an economy would be growing at 6 percent and in 20 years at 9 percent, *even though none of the underlying private sector or state sector growth rates would have changed*, because the weight of the declining sector will fall to 0. In contrast, a single-track economy where every sector is declining at −2 percent would never achieve positive growth. Both economies would look the same at the start of the process, but in fact would have very different futures.

What is driving the result in this example is that, if the declining sector keeps declining, its weight in the economy will decline as well, so that far in the future all that will really matter is the growth rate of the growing sector. The example serves to make the general point that aggregate growth can be a misleading indicator in circumstance where there is a lot of shifting between sectors. However, the implicit assumption in this example—that private sector growth would continue forever—is very unlikely to happen.

What we really should be focusing on in these circumstances is the rate of growth of the growing sector and whether that rate of growth specifically is sustainable. In transition countries, this means focusing on the growth rate of new sectors, which are basically the newly emerging private sectors. It should be mentioned, however, that this does not mean that all former state companies and industries will not grow, but it seems clear that the bulk of the growth in transition countries is likely to come from new sectors.

Once we focus on growth in newer sectors, there is an interesting twist. Such growth will generally be a product of two developments. One is normal growth in the productivity of the firms and industries in these newer sectors. But the other is that growth will be temporarily boosted as productive resources are being transferred from the state sectors to the new private sectors. Therefore private sector growth is likely to undergo a boom period for several years in transition countries before tapering off to more normal rates of increase. The key question is, once the structural change runs its course, to what growth rate will these sectors settle down? In particular, will it be fast enough to ensure fast catch-up to European levels of GDP?

We now turn to graphs that present simple estimates of the contribution of the private sector to growth in transition countries. The way to keep track of the private sector's contribution to overall growth is to look at its growth rate times its share in the economy. A fast-growing private sector will have little impact is if is just a tiny share in the economy. Similarly, even a moderate growth in the private sector can make an important contribution if the private sector represents a big share in the overall economy.

In Figure 1 we plot the contribution to growth of the new private sector in all of the European transition countries and the countries of the former Soviet Union for which data are available. Each small circle in the figure represents the growth rate for a particular country for a particular year. There is also a horizontal line that connects the median growth for each year. One can see from this line that there is a pattern whereby the private sectors' contribution to growth has gone through a boom period several years after transition started. On average in transition countries, this boom period started in 1993 and reached its apex in 1997. It is likely that this is the period where the resource transfers between the state sectors and the private sectors were taking place especially rapidly.

In Figure 2, we show the same information plotted against transition time rather than calendar time. *Transition time* is simply the number of years since transition started. Because transition started in different years in different countries, this yields a different picture than that of Figure 1 of when the structural changes were taking place. In terms of transition time, structural changes on average started in the second year of transition and reached their apex in the fifth year of transition.

The delay in shifting resources to the private sector in former Soviet countries can be seen by comparing Figures 3 and 4, which separate former Soviet countries from other countries. Structural changes occurred most strongly between 1991 and 1994 in the central European transition countries, and between 1994 and 1997 in the former Soviet countries. In the central European countries, private sector growth has settled down to an average annual rate of growth between 5 and 7 percent since 1995. In contrast, private sector growth in the Soviet counties peaked in 1997, dropped sharply in 1998 and 1999, and recovered slightly in 2000.

Figure 1: This graph plots the contribution to growth of the private sector in transition countries from 1991 through 2000. The private sector boomed between 1993 and 1997, as resources were shifted rapidly from the state to the private sector. But the growth tapered off between 1997 and 1999. In 2000, the median growth of the private sector rose to 6 percent. It is unclear whether this is a temporary recovery or a new trend.

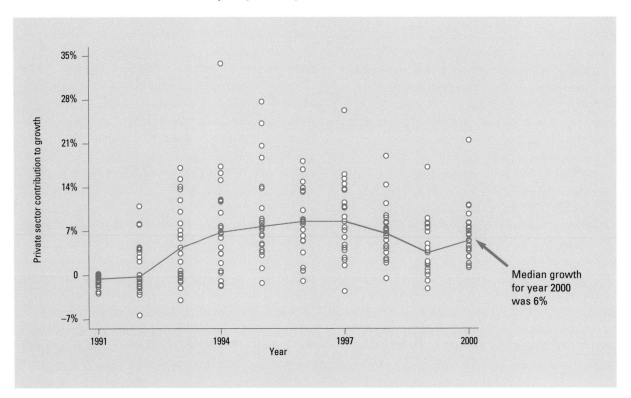

Figure 2: This graph is similar to Figure 1, but it plots growth of the private sector against transition time rather than calendar year. This graph shows that the private sector boom was between the second and the seventh year of transition, on average. Once again we can detect a recovery phase, in this case lasting from the eight to the tenth year of transition, although there are only four countries in their tenth year of transition.

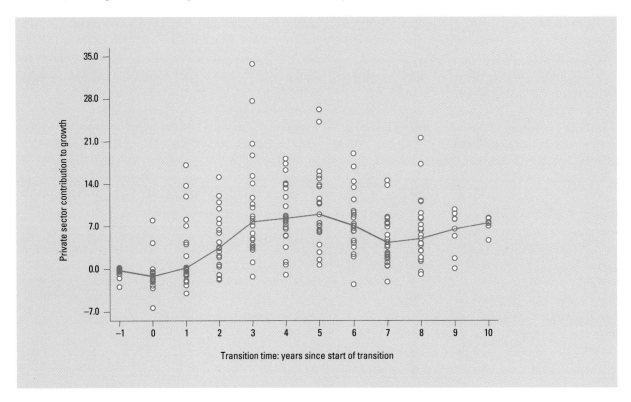

Figure 3: Same as Figure 1 but only for non–former Soviet transition countries. One can see that the private sector boom associated with fast structural change was earlier for these countries than for the former Soviet countries (shown in Figure 4).

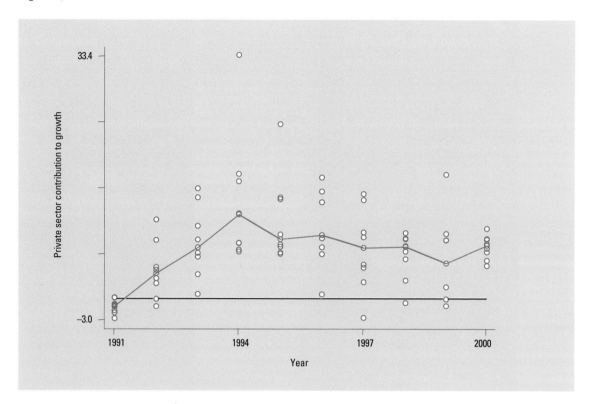

Figure 4: Same as Figure 1 but only for former Soviet transition countries. The private sector boom period started late for these countries and reached its apex in 1997, before being interrupted by the Russian crisis of 1998. There were signs of a recovery in the private sector starting in 2000.

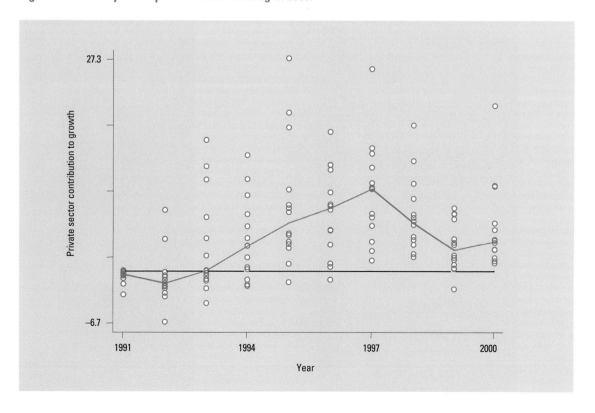

New data on the extent of structural change in transition regions

In the four figures above, one can see when the shift from the state sector to the private sector took place in the transition countries and how the timing of this resource shift was different in different regions. What we will show now are the results of a survey in a number of regions that tries to measure specific dimensions of this structural change. Although the figures above are designed to provide an overall picture of the shift to private industries, the survey data measure specifically the movements of capital and labor, and what types of capital and labor have moved.

This information is useful because it helps us know the nature of the structural changes and whether or not structural changes have been completed in specific economies. This information in turn gives us a better foundation from which to assess future growth prospects. For example, if we see fast private sector growth today in a country that has not yet shifted a lot of resources to the private sector (Belarus or Uzbekistan, for example), it could be that this growth is only a temporary boom that will end when the resource shift has ended. In contrast, if we see fast private sector growth in a country that has completed its structural change, this growth is more likely to be sustainable.

The shift of resources from the state to the private sector has two obvious dimensions: the decline of state industries and the rise of private industries. First we look at measures of the decline of state industries. This is followed by data on the shift of different types of capital to new industries and the shift of different types of labor. Finally we look at the extent to which the sectors have different rates of employment growth.

We start with a simple description of the sample and the number of firms surveyed in each region. Table 1 shows that there were a total of 2,114 firms interviewed. Of these, 471 are state firms, 567 are privatized firms, 284 were spin-offs of state firms, and 792 were newly created private firms. The composition of the sample of firms was chosen to be roughly proportional to employment across different types of firms and industries. However, state firms are typically larger than new private firms, so the sample covers a larger fraction of state employment than it does of private sector employment.

One of the few measures of restructuring available for transition countries are the estimates of the share of the economy in the private sector by the European Bank for Reconstruction and Development (EBRD). The latest estimates from the EBRD are shown in Table 2. We regard these estimates as complementary to our survey. They provide general impressions while the data here give more detail and measure additional aspects of restructuring.

Note that, of the regions in our data, the EBRD estimates that three have less than 50 percent of the economy in the private sector: Belarus with 20 percent, Serbia with 40 percent, and Uzbekistan with 45 percent. According to the EBRD estimates, these are the economies with the greatest amount of remaining restructuring. The rest of the regions in our sample have achieved private sector shares of approximately 70 percent. This is close to the maximum one would expect once restructuring is complete.

We show an additional measure of remaining restructuring in Table 3. The first column shows estimates from managers of state enterprises about the fraction of the labor force that should be in the private sector in their country. Since these estimates are from managers of state enterprises, we would expect their estimates of the private sector share to be on the low side. Nevertheless, if one looks at the first column, the averages for most countries give percentages that are higher than the EBRD estimates (shown again in column 2). In other words, even managers of state enterprises suggest that private sector employment in transition countries should eventually be on the order of 80 percent or higher. If we take this 80 percent figure as the long-run target, it implies that a fair amount of restructuring remains to be accomplished in the transition regions in our sample. These estimates are shown in the fourth column of Table 3.

When we look at specific countries, we see more support for a larger state role in Belarus and Ukraine than in the other countries, according to managers of state enterprises at least. But even according to these biased estimates, the optimal share of the private sector would be 57 percent and 67 percent on average. We can see from the third column of Table 3 that if we take these numbers as a guide, there is still a lot of restructuring left to accomplish in Armenia, Belarus, Croatia, Romania, Serbia, and Uzbekistan. If we instead use 80 percent as the target figure for the long-run share of the private sector, we see in column 4 that Belarus, Serbia, and Uzbekistan, in that order, have the most restructuring left to accomplish. What this means is that private sector growth in the short run could be high in each country if and when this restructuring gets under way. If these countries have achieved their required decline in state industries without any accompanying rise in private industries, they could experience temporary very fast growth as the idle resources are taken up by new private industries. It is in this sense that short run increases in growth can be misleading indicators.

Table 1. Number of firms surveyed

Country	State firm	Privatized former state firm	Private spin-off of a state firm	New private firm	Total firms
Armenia	16	1	27	56	100
Belarus	59	51	25	65	200
Bulgaria	36	61	24	122	243
Croatia	17	24	7	51	99
Estonia	4	15	6	73	98
Kazakhstan	4	31	14	51	100
Kyrgyzstan	63	85	38	40	226
Lithuania	16	33	7	52	108
Montenegro	58	9	12	21	100
Poland	44	57	19	31	151
Romania	33	24	13	29	99
Russia (Ekaterinburg)	17	22	24	37	100
Russia (Tomsk)	7	23	6	60	96
Russia (Voronezh)	9	39	10	43	101
Serbia	55	15	4	21	95
Ukraine	14	47	25	12	98
Uzbekistan	19	30	23	28	100
Average	**471**	**567**	**284**	**792**	**2,114**

Table 2: Estimates of the share of the private sector from the EBRD

Country	EBRD estimate of private sector share (mid 1991)
Armenia	60%
Belarus	20
Bulgaria	70
Croatia	60
Estonia	75
Kazakhstan	60
Kyrgyzstan	60
Lithuania	70
Montenegro	n/a
Poland	75
Romania	65
Russia (Ekaterinburg)	70*
Russia (Tomsk)	70*
Russia (Voronezh)	70*
Serbia	40
Ukraine	60
Uzbekistan	45

Source: *Transition Report 2001*, EBRD. Table 2.1.
* Estimates for Russia

Table 3: Estimates of structural changes yet to be accomplished

COUNTRY	Percent of labor force that should be in the private sector in the future[1]	Percent of output in the private sector today (EBRD estimate)[2]	Difference (column 3 = column 1 minus column 2)	80 minus EBRD estimate (column 4 = 80 minus column 2)
	1	2	3	4
Poland	82	75	7	5
Armenia	88	60	28	20
Belarus	57	20	37	60
Bulgaria	77	70	7	10
Croatia	83	60	23	20
Estonia	89	75	14	5
Kazakhstan[3]	—	60	—	20
Kyrgyzstan	75	60	15	20
Lithuania	84	70	14	10
Montenegro	82	n/a	—	n/a
Romania	90	65	25	15
Russia (Ekaterinburg)	65	70	–5	10
Russia (Tomsk)	79	70	9	10
Russia (Voronezh)	76	70	6	10
Serbia	82	40	42	40
Ukraine	67	60	7	20
Uzbekistan	68	45	23	35

[1] Mean response from survey of managers of state enterprises when asked "What percent of your country's labor force should be working in state industries in the future?"

[2] EBRD estimate of percent of output in the private sector, mid 2001.

[3] Insufficient number of respondents.

Note: Numbers are left blank when five or fewer firms responded; n/a = not available in the EBRD *Transition Report*.

Table 4: Estimates of employment cuts necessary in state firms and privatized firms

Country	STATE FIRMS				PRIVATIZED FIRMS			
	Employment today	Optimal employment in 10 years	Remaining employment cuts	In percent	Employment today	Optimal employment in 10 years	Remaining employment cuts	In percent
Poland	69,140	48,500	20,640	30	78,386	57,530	20,856	27
Armenia	2,766	5,555	−2,789	−101	1,334	1,358	−24	−2
Belarus	10,429	10,315	114	1	26,110	18,480	7,630	29
Bulgaria	8,444	5,752	2,692	32	6,866	8,978	−2,112	−31
Croatia	6,781	6,737	44	1	27,726	18,475	9,251	33
Estonia	4,612	3,785	827	18				
Kazakhstan	2,000	2,200	−200	−10				
Kyrgyzstan	6,636	9,506	−2,870	−43	3,148	3,355	−207	−7
Lithuania	1,581	575	1,006	64	2,847	820	2,027	71
Montenegro	197	130	67	34	25,920	22,248	3,672	14
Romania					233,484	138,200	95,284	40
Russia (Ekaterinburg)	5,637	5,950	−313	−6	3,645	5,430	−1,785	−49
Russia (Tomsk)					17,380	4,820	12,560	72
Russia (Voronezh)					7,320	9,050	−1,730	−24
Serbia	4,772	4,661	111	2	10,926	7,679	3,247	30
Ukraine	17,580	21,970	−4,390	−25	2,426	4,800	−2,374	−98
Uzbekistan	3,295	3,852	−557	−17	1,674	1,495	179	11

Notes: The first column is the sum over all firms of current employment. The second column is the sum of the estimates by each manager of what optimal employment would be in his/her enterprise in 10 years. The third column is the difference between these two: a positive number indicating that employment should decline; a negative number indicating that employment should rise. Numbers are left blank when less than five firms responded.

Table 5: Employment reductions in the state sector

Country	Employment in 2000 as a percent of employment at the start of transition (countries with largest reductions listed first)		
	State firm	Privatized former state firm	Private spin-off of a state firm
Estonia	20	52	60
Armenia	49		36
Kyrgyzstan	52	37	27
Uzbekistan	59	44	34
Montenegro	60	66	80
Ukraine	60	56	59
Poland	65	59	46
Russia (Voronezh)	69	50	75
Kazakhstan	72	34	27
Croatia	73	65	100
Bulgaria	76	61	42
Russia (Ekaterinburg)	84	73	83
Lithuania	85	42	19
Russia (Tomsk)	92	46	116
Belarus	93	88	144
Serbia	93	95	120
Romania	96	97	93
Average	**70**	**60**	**68**

Note: Numbers are left blank when five or fewer firms responded

We asked the same managers of state enterprises to estimate optimal employment not for their country but rather for their firm specifically. These figures are shown in Table 4. We would expect each manager to be somewhat more optimistic about the employment prospects in his or her own firm that for the state sector in the country at large. But even here, the table shows that some of the state managers anticipate additional large cuts in employment in their firms. For state firms in Poland, for example, managers estimate that employment still needs to be cut 30 percent from current levels. In Lithuania the figure is 64 percent. Among privatized firms, one can see that managers are more likely to anticipate employment increases in their firms. This is to be expected in part because the firms that are more economically viable were more likely to be privatized. It is worth bearing in mind that the estimates in Table 4 contain a double bias: first because managers are asked about their own firms specifically; second because they are managers in state enterprises or privatized enterprises. Yet, despite this double bias, a substantial number of managers anticipate that state employment needs to be cut further.

It is useful to combine these data on estimates for the future with data on the amount of labor that has already left the state sector. In Table 5 we show employment levels in the year 2000 compared with employment at the start of transition. For each country shown, these figures measure the ratio of employment in 2000 as a percentage of employment at the start of transition. We show these figures for three kinds of firms: state firms, privatized state firms, and spin-offs of former state firms.

The table shows that employment in these firms' ranges between an average of about 60 to 70 percent of employment at the start of transition. This tells us that the state firms in our sample that have survived the transition process through early 2001 have cut their workforce on average of 30 to 40 percent. The full decline in employment of the state sector would be larger than this because there are some state firms in each country that have closed down entirely. These will not appear in any survey because they are not around to be interviewed anymore.

What is significant is the small amount of labor force cuts among the surviving state firms in countries such as Romania, Serbia, Belarus, Tomsk and Ekaterinburg in Russia, and even Lithuania. It is also interesting that in three of these countries, the spin-offs have actually added employment on average. This is consistent with the view that spin-offs are often the most economically viable parts former state firms. State managers have been accused of asset stripping where the most valuable parts of the state firm is set up as a state entity, and then the managers of the state firm switch to become managers of the profitable spin-off and leave the rest of the state firm in the hands of the state as an implicit liability of the taxpayers or the workers left behind. These data indicate that the countries that have been most aggressive in cutting employment in former state firms are Estonia, Armenia, Kyrgyzstan, and Uzbekistan.

Shifts of capital

A second measure of restructuring is the shift of real capital from state industries to other industries. This is not typically measured in other data. To measure this we ask directly: "how much of your current real capital was once owned by a state entity or the government?" Purchases by a new private firm of land or office space or industrial equipment from a state firm or from the government would count as transfer of capital from the state to the private sector. On the other hand, purchases of new computers or the construction of new buildings would not be a transfer but simply be new investments. Our expectation was that most of the transfers of capital to the private sector would be land or building purchases rather than purchases of equipment or other productive assets. We further thought that it was possible that this number was very small. A small percentage would indicate that private sector growth relied more extensively on new capital accumulation rather than transfers from the state sector.

Knowing the extent to which new private firms relied on capital from the state sector would help to understand the relative importance of policy measures that were designed to promote an orderly decline of state industries. At one extreme, one can imagine an economy where all private industries grew by employing young workers who just entered the labor market and by acquiring new capital. In this extreme case, one could argue that the shutdown of state industries would have little importance for private sector growth. On the other hand, an economy where private industries need state assets in order to expand would be more constrained if such a transfer were delayed.

Even in transition regions, such as the former Soviet Union, in which the shutdown of state industries was delayed, labor was relatively free to leave state firms. Therefore, transfers of labor to the private sector were never really constrained. What was constrained was the transfer of land and structures. The act of not closing a state firm implicitly delays that transfer of resources because the land and buildings are not for sale. In addition to this, lack of efficient bankruptcy rules can delay shutdown and thus act as a barrier to the transfer of resources. Further, lack of clearly defined property rights over land and structures can delay restructuring because this introduces more uncertainty for new firms thinking about acquiring former state properties. In this circumstance, even if the state firms are shut down, the properties can remain idle rather than being used in the private industries.

Table 6: When you were established, what percent of your fixed assets (land, buildings, equipment) in terms of market value were previously owned by a state-owned firm or the government?

Country	Private spin-off of a state firm	New private firm
Armenia	93	5
Belarus	43	7
Bulgaria	88	21
Croatia	36	5
Estonia	50	15
Kazakhstan	48	3
Kyrgyzstan	64	8
Lithuania	79	34
Montenegro	88	79
Poland	86	10
Romania	100	
Russia (Ekaterinburg)	36	8
Russia (Tomsk)		7
Russia (Voronezh)	91	3
Serbia		36
Ukraine	93	27
Uzbekistan	58	20
Average	**70**	**18**

Note: Numbers are left blank when five or fewer firms responded.

Table 7. What percent of your fixed assets (land, buildings, equipment) today, in terms of market value, was previously owned by a state-owned firm or the government?

Country	Private spin-off of a state firm	New private firm
Armenia	14	0
Belarus	36	6
Bulgaria	43	12
Croatia	12	0
Estonia	17	0
Kazakhstan	36	11
Kyrgyzstan	38	1
Lithuania		17
Montenegro	33	13
Poland	54	6
Romania	58	4
Russia (Ekaterinburg)	26	10
Russia (Tomsk)		9
Russia (Voronezh)	93	16
Serbia		12
Ukraine	43	18
Uzbekistan	32	8
Average	**38**	**8**

Note: Numbers are left blank when five or fewer firms responded.

When we observe in Tables 6 and 7 that a relatively low proportion of the assets of new private firms were once owned by state entities, we cannot be sure of the extent to which this is because the assets were not released or because the assets were not wanted/needed. However, if constraints on releasing state assets were driving the results, we would expect to see that private firms in slow-reform regions such as Serbia, Belarus, and Ukraine would have a smaller share of former state assets that private firms in regions where these assets were release more easily. In fact, however, we see the opposite. Private firms in the slow reform regions tend to have a larger, not smaller, share of former-state assets on their books.

Tables 6 and 7 differ in that Table 6 asks for an assessment at the time of establishment and Table 7 asks for an assessment now (end of 2000). By comparing these tables, we can obtain some idea of the rate at which the former economy is receding into the background. The average percent of state assets was 64 percent for spin-offs at the time of establishment and only 34 percent at the end of 2000. For new private firms, the average percent of state assets was 18 percent at the time of establishment and only 8 percent at the end of 2000.

From both tables, one can see that the legacy of the older state economy in terms of capital was quite small for the new private sector by the end of the first decade of transition. Put simply, new firms in transition regions are not using much of the old state capital. The picture that emerges is that of a new private sector that has accumulated most of its productive assets anew, and whose growth has not employed many of the assets of the former state sector. In this sense, the private and the state sectors have dynamics that are not highly interconnected.

Shifts of labor skills

The legacy of the old state sector is seen most clearly in the shifts of labor between the sectors. In Table 8 we show results from the question: "What percent of your work force were previously employed more than 5 years in the state sector?" The average response across all countries for the state firms was 78 percent. This ranged from 93 and 97 percent in the Russian cities of Voronez and Tomsk to 44 percent in Croatia. When we look across firms within regions, we see that the number of former state workers drops off, but only slightly. The average is 71 percent in privatized firms and 67 percent in private spin-offs. Therefore, if we measure "old" labor as workers who acquired more than 5 years of experience in state industries, then the majority of workers in all four kinds of firms are old workers. Because of demographics and the fact that the normal aging process proceeds at a gradual

Table 8: What percent of your work force were previously employed more than 5 years in the state sector?

Country	State firm	Privatized former state firm	Private spin-off of a state firm	New private firm
Armenia	76	.	75	52
Belarus	80	78	78	69
Bulgaria	87	78	67	46
Croatia	44	56	66	38
Estonia		79	83	54
Kazakhstan		67	65	38
Kyrgyzstan	63	63	50	44
Lithuania	86	64	72	42
Montenegro	63	79	56	37
Poland	71	69	70	64
Romania	82	75	67	49
Russia (Ekaterinburg)	80	64	60	33
Russia (Tomsk)	93	70		20
Russia (Voronezh)	97	66	51	44
Serbia	72	77		47
Ukraine	87	78	81	55
Uzbekistan	88	72	68	59
Average	**78**	**71**	**67**	**47**

Note: Numbers are left blank when five or fewer firms responded.

Table 9: What percent of your managers have some foreign experience?

Country	State firm	Privatized former state firm	Private spin-off of a state firm	New private firm
Armenia	8	.	5	9
Belarus	2	5	5	8
Bulgaria	8	7	9	14
Croatia	10	5	3	3
Estonia		9	6	16
Kazakhstan		5	8	7
Kyrgyzstan	2	2	3	0
Lithuania	9	9	1	11
Montenegro	1	0	1	1
Poland	6	4	3	4
Romania	3	6	25	46
Russia (Ekaterinburg)	0	2	8	9
Russia (Tomsk)	5	2	2	7
Russia (Voronezh)	1	1	1	3
Serbia	3	1		5
Ukraine	4	2	5	13
Uzbekistan	1	7	2	8
Average	**4**	**4**	**5**	**10**

Note: Numbers are left blank when five or fewer firms responded.

rate, we know that old labor will be around for several decades. What these tables show is that there has not been an extreme partition of the labor force whereby only the new workers of the younger generation become employed in the new private sector and the older workers stay in the state sector. Even in fast-reforming Poland, firms in the new private sector report that 64 percent of their work force acquired more than 5 years of their work experience in the state sector.

This characterization of such workers as "old" workers is surely unfair in the implication that they necessarily have old skills. Obviously, many of the labor skills are easily transferable with no depreciation in value, and furthermore there is always scope for additional learning. However, the numbers in Table 8 do highlight the fact that sheer demographics place a limit on how fast the private sector can acquire new labor.

In Table 9 we continue with measures of labor skills. Table 9 shows average results from the question asking for the percentage of managers that have some foreign experience. This percentage is very small on average. The Romania figures seem unusually high and should probably be discounted. For the other countries, the share of managers with foreign experience is usually lower than 10 percent. This number is only very slightly higher in new private firms, but only by a very small margin. In Table 10 we ask the same question of production workers rather than managers. Again the percentages are extremely small.

Table 10. What percent of your production workers have some foreign experience?

Country	State firm	Privatized former state firm	Private spin-off of a state firm	New private firm
Armenia	5		1	6
Belarus	0	1	1	5
Bulgaria	7	2	7	8
Croatia	4	3	2	3
Estonia		2		8
Kazakhstan		4	1	2
Kyrgyzstan	2	2	5	1
Lithuania	2	4		7
Montenegro	3	0	0	1
Poland	2	3	2	0
Romania	0	2	5	8
Russia (Ekaterinburg)	0	3	2	5
Russia (Tomsk)	1	0	1	2
Russia (Voronezh)	1	0	0	0
Serbia	9	1		11
Ukraine	3	1	2	13
Uzbekistan	1	6	2	3
Average	**3**	**2**	**2**	**5**

Note: Numbers are left blank when five or fewer firms responded.

45

Table 11: What percent of your workers are comfortable with a computer?

Country	State firm	Privatized former state firm	Private spin-off of a state firm	New private firm
Armenia	35		18	53
Belarus	14	20	19	42
Bulgaria	29	13	19	44
Croatia	45	30	51	48
Estonia		14	15	48
Kazakhstan		21	38	44
Kyrgyzstan	4	2	2	4
Lithuania	24	20	7	34
Montenegro	10	10	31	34
Poland	42	40	39	23
Romania	23	28	37	50
Russia (Ekaterinburg)	25	16	55	52
Russia (Tomsk)	26	16	56	49
Russia (Voronezh)	26	15	36	33
Serbia	18	10		22
Ukraine	15	11	13	67
Uzbekistan	9	12	14	20
Average	**23**	**17**	**28**	**39**

Note: Numbers are left blank when five or fewer firms responded.

Table 12: Current growth rates of employment, by sector (weighted averages)

Country	State firm	Privatized former state firm	Private spin-off of a state firm	New private firm
Armenia	3	10	4	48
Belarus	77	48	59	50
Bulgaria	13	41	39	25
Croatia	11	16	23	25
Estonia	8	16	10	41
Kazakhstan	2	18	24	18
Kyrgyzstan	4	3	8	7
Lithuania	28	26	21	70
Montenegro	8	10	22	31
Poland	−10	−10	−7	0
Romania	24	−7	−2	55
Russia (Ekaterinburg)	11	35	69	62
Russia (Tomsk)	1	6	21	197
Russia (Voronezh)	14	23	55	45
Serbia	24	11	43	23
Ukraine	−3	−10	89	74
Uzbekistan	9	11	136	100
Average	**13**	**15**	**36**	**51**

Note: Numbers are left blank when five or fewer firms responded.

In Table 11 we show results from the survey question on the fraction of the labor force that are comfortable with a computer. The first thing that stands out in this table are Kyrgystan's low numbers. Other countries with low shares are Uzbekistan and Montenegro (especially for state firms or privatized firms).

In summary, what we see here is a picture of substantial movements of labor from the state sector to the private sector. Private firms on average do have a lower fraction of former state workers than the state sectors, but the numbers are not greatly lower. In addition, workers in most sectors have very little foreign experience, and about 25 to 30 percent of workers are comfortable with computers. There is not a huge difference in computer literacy between former state industries and private industries.

Further growth

We have seen earlier that not even managers of state enterprises or privatized firms think that there is a lot of scope for expansion of the state sector. If this is correct, it means that if there is growth in transition countries, most growth will come from the private sector. In this connection it is interesting to compare current rates of growth by type of firm. Is it the case that growth is coming from new private firms and not from the former state sector?

In Table 12 we show mean responses to the question on the rate of growth of employment over the last 2 years. Recall that we are asking questions of firms that still exist, so we will miss any drops in employment from firms that have shut down in the past 2 years. For this reason, we should expect these numbers to be higher than actual employment growth by each type of firm. The numbers show clearly that employment growth has been faster in spin-offs and new private firms than in state firms or privatized firms. This confirms what we would expect: that growth is predominately private sector growth. Note that in Ukraine and Uzbekistan, the growth rates of the private sector firms are much greater than state firms and privatized firms. This is consistent with the view that structural change in such countries has been accelerating in recent years. In a more mature country such as Poland, we see less of a difference in growth rates across sectors.

Conclusions

This paper has attempted to document a number of facts. First, not even managers of state enterprises in transition countries say that the state sector in transition countries should be any more than 20 or 30 percent of the labor force. If, as seems reasonable, the state sector is not likely to expand, this means that to understand growth prospects one needs to look specifically at private sector growth. During structural change episodes, such growth will be influenced both by normal productivity growth and also by the rate of transfer of resources from the state sector to the private sector. As these transfers are taking place, we should see that private sector growth is temporarily high, but of course it cannot be sustained at that level once the transfers are accomplished. Data from transition countries suggest that former Soviet economies have experienced such transfers relatively recently, and several still have the bulk of the transfers in front of them. The data also show that central European transition countries achieved the bulk of such transfers during the first 4 years of transition.

Information from surveys of enterprises in transition regions indicates that relatively little state capital has been transferred to new private firms. Most of the accumulation of new firms has apparently been new investments rather than acquisitions of older capital from the state sectors. The main resource that has been transferred from the state to the private sector has been labor. Even in new private firms, the average percentage of workers who received more than 5 years of work experience in state firms was 47 percent. The transfers have been predominantly transfers of labor rather than transfers of capital.

The paper also shows estimates of how much faster employment has recently been growing in private firms than in state firms. The differences in growth rates are quite high for some countries that have delayed reforms for several years. Two examples of this are Ukraine and Uzbekistan, perhaps indicating that structural changes are starting to accelerate in such countries.

The most recent data on growth of the private sector from the year 2000 indicate that growth rates did increase across the region after the slump associated with the Russia crisis. For example, in non–former Soviet countries, the median private sector growth was about 6 percent per year. In former Soviet countries, the median was slightly lower than this, although there was more cross-country dispersion. It is still too early to tell if these growth rates are a temporary boom or a long-term trend. They are higher than anticipated, however, and if sustained would suggest faster convergence to European income levels than previously thought.

References

European Bank for Reconstruction and Development. 2001. *Transition Report* (London: EBRD).

Entrepreneurship and Growth: Evidence from Russia

DANIEL BERKOWITZ and **DAVID N. DEJONG**,[i]

Department of Economics, University of Pittsburgh

Introduction

A broad range of national-level evidence indicates that entrepreneurial activity has been a critical source of growth in post-socialist economies. For example, synthesizing a large body of work focusing on the experiences of Poland, China, and Russia, McMillan and Woodruff (2001) conclude that the robust economic growth enjoyed by Poland and China is attributable in large part to the substantial entrepreneurial development they have experienced, while the relative economic stagnation Russia has endured during its transition has as a root source its record of relatively sluggish entrepreneurial development. The purpose of this paper is to report on complementary research we have conducted. This research has indicated the existence of strong links observed at the regional level within Russia between entrepreneurial activity established in the early stages of Russia's economic transition and subsequent economic growth (Berkowitz and DeJong 2001; forthcoming [2002a,b]).

Despite the relatively modest development of entrepreneurial activity experienced in Russia and the economic stagnation it has endured at the aggregate level during its transition, Russia provides an excellent laboratory for econometric analysis because it contains a large number of regions that exhibited striking variation in initial conditions, in the adoption of policy reforms, and in entrepreneurial activity in the early stages of its transition. It has also experienced striking regional variation in subsequent growth.

The data we have analyzed cover 70 of Russia's 89 regions. As examples of the regional variation noted above, consider the variables that have been the primary focus of our analyses: entrepreneurial activity and economic growth. Entrepreneurial activity is quantified as the number of legally registered small private enterprises in place in each region by the end of December 1995; they are concentrated primarily in construction, trade, commerce, and small-scale industry. These enterprises consist of small-scale startup firms and private spin-offs from previously state-owned enterprises. Measured as the number of enterprises per thousand inhabitants, this variable ranges from a low of 1.71 in the Kursk Oblast to 16.61 in Moscow; its average is 4.19, and its standard deviation is 2.29. Economic growth is measured as the average annual growth rate of real per capita income. Measured between 1993:IV and 1997:IV,[ii] regional growth averaged 1.46 percent within Russia, with a standard deviation of 4.75 percentage points; the maximum growth rate observed over this period is an astounding 22 percent

(Moscow), and the minimum is an equally astounding −8.18 percent (Sakhalin Oblast). Measured between 1993:IV and 2000:IV, average growth falls to −7.31 percent, with a standard deviation of 3.25 percentage points; one reason for this striking drop is the financial crisis Russia suffered in August of 1998.

In evaluating the relationship between early patterns of entrepreneurial activity and subsequent growth, we have sought to account for factors that may have had a joint impact on entrepreneurial activity and growth. We have also attempted to control for potential problems arising from the possibility that our measure of entrepreneurial activity in part reflects optimism regarding prospects for subsequent growth. Thus, our analyses have incorporated a broad range of measures intended to quantify regional patterns of initial conditions and also of policy reform measures that predate our measures of entrepreneurial activity and growth. The goal has been to provide a conditional characterization, which is free from potential simultaneity bias, of the relationship between entrepreneurial activity and subsequent growth.

Our main focus here will be on the results of our most recent analysis (Berkowitz and DeJong 2001), which is based on the broadest set of regions we have considered and the most recent measures of economic growth.[iii] There, using a two-stage least-squares estimation procedure, we found that regional entrepreneurial activity has had a strong and enduring relationship with growth. Specifically, our estimates indicate that a one-standard-deviation increase in regional entrepreneurial activity is associated with an increase in real economic growth of 1.52 annual percentage points over the period 1993:IV through 1997:IV, and 1.07 percentage points over the period 1993:IV through 2000:IV.

Among the variables we used as instruments for entrepreneurial activity in our analysis, educational attainment had the strongest explanatory power. Perhaps surprisingly, the policy reform measures we considered (which quantified the regional implementation of privatization reforms) exhibited quantitatively and statistically insignificant links between regional patterns of initial policy reform implementation and growth. Indeed, to the extent that we observed links between policy reform measures and growth, they were indirect, with entrepreneurial activity serving as a critical conduit.

Data description

Besides real income growth and entrepreneurial activity, the data set we analyzed contains regional measures of initial conditions and initial policy reform measures. By *initial*, we mean measurements taken as close to the beginning of Russia's transition period as possible. Most variables are measured as of 1993; none are measured later than 1994. Our purpose in compiling initial measurements was to use them either as instruments for our measure of entrepreneurial activity, or as conditioning variables in growth regressions—thus the importance of obtaining measurements early in the transition process.

As noted, the data set covers 70 of Russia's 89 regions. Most of the excluded regions are now-autonomous Oblasts, Okrugs, and Krais that were part of then-conglomerate regions early in Russia's transition process, and thus for whom separate measurements of "initial" variables are unavailable. The war-torn Chechen Republic is also excluded for lack of data. The 70 regions covered in our data set represent all 11 of Russia's geographic territories.

We quantified initial conditions using six variables that summarize regional population, industrial, and locational characteristics. The variables are as follows: educational attainment (EDU—the share of the population 15 years old and older as of 1994 that completed high school and received at least some post-secondary training); the initial reformist orientation of the population (REF—the share of the population that voted for pro-reformist candidates in the December 1993 parliamentary elections); initial living standards (INITIAL—the average ratio of money income per capita to the cost of a uniform basket of 25 food goods during 1993:IV); initial production potential (IO—a measure of the international competitiveness of the industrial structure of each region as of 1985); the importance of the defense industry (DEFENSE—the number of workers employed in the defense industry per thousand employed workers, as of 1985); and logged distance from Moscow (LNDIST).

We used two variables to quantify regional variations in the implementation of policy reforms early in Russia's economic transition: the extent of small- and large-scale privatization. These are measured as the number of enterprises privatized by local (SPRIV) and federal (LPRIV) governments in 1993 per thousand inhabitants in each region. In Berkowitz and DeJong (2002a,b), we also evaluated regional measures of price-liberalization reforms, and found that these measures had minimal explanatory power.

49

Table 1: Summary statistics

Variable	Timing	Average	Median	Standard Deviation	Minimum	Maximum
Growth	1993:IV–1997:IV	1.46%	1.54%	4.75%	–8.18%	22.06%
Growth	1993:IV–2000:IV	–7.31%	–7.70%	3.25%	–14.63%	3.49%
Small Private Enterprises	Dec. 31, 1995	4.19	3.87	2.29	1.71	16.61
Education	1994	13.73%	12.70%	3.69%	9.20%	33.40%
Initial Income	1993:IV	8.80	8.11	2.64	3.29	19.57
Reformist Voting	Dec. 1993	33.30%	32.40%	10.16%	13.00%	61.00%
IO	1985	5.11	7.19	14.45	–771.74	42.30
Defense	1985	0.23	0.22	0.13	0.00	0.57
Distance from Moscow (ln)		7.04	7.07	1.37	0.00	9.37
Large-Scale Privatization	1993	0.05	0.05	0.04	0.00	0.16
Small-Scale Privatization	1993	0.20	0.20	0.12	0.00	0.78

Table 2: Two-stage least-squares estimates, growth measured through 1997

Small Private-Enterprise (ENT) Regression

Explanatory Variable	Coefficient Estimate	Standard Error	t statistic	p value	Standard Deviation of Variable	Quantitative Significance
Constant	–1.515	1.269	–1.195	0.232	0.000	0.000
Education	0.458	0.063	7.299	0.000	3.695	1.693
Distance (ln)	–0.127	0.161	–0.786	0.432	1.375	–0.174
Large-Scale Privatization	4.873	7.373	0.661	0.509	0.036	0.175
Small-Scale Privatization	0.337	1.981	0.170	0.865	0.118	0.040
R²: 0.589						

Growth Regression, 1993–1997

Explanatory Variable	Coefficient Estimate	Standard Error	t statistic	p value	Standard Deviation of Variable	Quantitative Significance
Constant	–11.778	1.937	–6.081	0.000	0.000	0.000
Initial Income	0.349	0.112	3.112	0.002	2.643	0.924
IO	0.063	0.029	2.175	0.030	14.446	0.907
Defense	0.064	0.031	2.030	0.042	12.930	0.824
Reformist Voting	0.143	0.045	3.176	0.001	10.163	1.453
Small Private Enterprises (fitted)	0.866	0.376	2.303	0.021	1.758	1.522
R²: 0.448						

Note: Standard errors are heteroskedasticity consistent (White 1980). *Quantitative Significance* indicates the estimated impact of a one-standard-deviation increase in the indicated independent variable on the dependent variable.

Summary statistics for the variables we analyzed are provided in Table 1. We noted in the introduction that Russia has experienced striking regional variation in entrepreneurial activity and subsequent growth; similar variation is observed in most of the additional variables as well. For example, the voting shares quantified under REF range from 13 percent (Dagestan) to 61 percent (St. Petersburg), with a mean of 33.3 percent and standard deviation of 10.16 percent. As an exception, EDU is relatively tightly dispersed, with a mean of 13.73 percent and a standard deviation of only 3.69 percent.

Findings

Our analyses have focused on two measures of growth: that observed between 1993:IV and 1997:IV (Berkowitz and DeJong 2001; 2002a,b); and between 1993:IV and 200:IV (Berkowitz and DeJong 2001). In part, we considered the former measure in our most recent work (Berkowitz and DeJong 2001) to illustrate how our 70-region analysis compared with our previous analyses. Also, we were interested in learning whether the relationship between small private enterprise formation and growth has changed appreciably over time.

Table 3: Two-stage least-squares estimates, growth measured through 2000

Explanatory Variable	Coefficient Estimate	Standard Error	t statistic	p value	Standard Deviation of Variable	Quantitative Significance
Constant	−12.915	1.531	−8.435	0.000	0.000	0.000
Initial Income	0.032	0.127	0.253	0.800	2.643	0.085
IO	0.059	0.018	3.283	0.001	14.446	0.851
Defense	0.013	0.027	0.476	0.634	12.930	0.164
Reformist Voting	0.068	0.038	1.803	0.071	10.163	0.695
Small Private Enterprises (fitted)	0.586	0.221	2.657	0.008	1.758	1.030
R^2: 0.279						

Note: The regression model used to obtain fitted values of small private enterprise formation is that reported in Table 2.

We guarded against problems arising from potential simultaneity by conducting a two-stage least-squares (2SLS) estimation procedure in which we used, as instruments for entrepreneurial activity, a subset of the variables introduced above that quantify regional differences in initial conditions and reform policies. Although each variable qualifies as a valid instrument *a priori*, we used only a subset of the variables as instruments in our analysis to guard against the possibility of over-fitting small private enterprise formation in our first-stage regression. The instruments we used were selected by regressing growth measured through 1997:IV on each of the additional variables included in our data set; variables whose coefficients were statistically insignificant at the 20 percent level in this regression were selected as instruments in our two-stage procedure. Four variables were thus selected: EDU, LNDIST, LPRIV, and SPRIV.

The application of our 2SLS analysis to growth measured through 1997:IV is presented in Table 2. The first-stage regression of entrepreneurial activity (ENT) on (EDU, LNDIST, LPRIV, and SPRIV) produced an R^2 statistic of 0.589, despite the fact that only EDU was statistically significant. Second-stage estimates were obtained by regressing GROWTH on the fitted version of ENT and the variables that were not used as instruments in the first-stage regression (INITIAL, IO, DEFENSE, and REF). Note that the variables used as first-stage instruments were excluded from the second-stage growth regression: these exclusion restrictions served to identify the model. To evaluate the validity of these restrictions, we added each instrumental variable to the list of explanatory variables in the second-stage regression, one at a time, and re-estimated the model. In no case did the included instrument turn out to be statistically significant at the 20 percent level in the re-estimated growth regression, thus the exclusion restrictions seem valid empirically.

As Table 2 indicates, each variable included in the second-stage growth regression is statistically significant at the 5 percent level, and is quantitatively significant as well. To characterize quantitative significance, we report in the seventh column of the table the impact on annual growth of a one-standard-deviation increase in each of the independent variables. Notably, a one-standard-deviation increase in small private enterprise formation corresponds with a 1.52 percentage point increase in annual growth. The quantitative significance of the remaining variables ranges from 0.824 (DEFENSE) to 1.453 (REF).

Next, we applied our 2SLS analysis to growth measured through 2000:IV; these results are reported in Table 3. (The first-stage regression is precisely that reported in Table 2, and is not replicated in Table 3.) Comparison of the estimates obtained in this case with their counterparts reported in Table 2 yields the following observations. First, the statistical and quantitative significance of INITIAL is no longer evident measuring growth through 2001:IV: the regional divergence in income observed through 1997 seems to have been subsequently reversed. A similar reversal is found for DEFENSE. Second, the significance of IO is virtually unchanged across time periods (its measure of quantitative significance drops only slightly, from 0.907 to 0.851). Finally, REF and ENT remain statistically significant, although their quantitative significance is lower over the longer time horizon (REF's measure falls from 1.453 to 0.695; ENT's falls from 1.522 to 1.03).

These results indicate that the regional pattern of entrepreneurial activity that had been established in Russia by the mid-1990s has had a substantial and enduring relationship with subsequent economic growth. It is therefore of considerable interest to understand how regional variations in the adoption of policy reforms may have influenced small private enterprise formation. Since the measures of policy reforms we analyzed were compiled very early in Russia's transition, we were able to offer only a limited characterization of this influence in that work. We conclude here by summarizing this characterization, and by outlining our plans for extending this line of inquiry.

As noted, the preceding 2SLS analysis was conducted using a limited subset of instruments; this was done in order to avoid over-fitting entrepreneurial activity in the first-stage regression. Running an ordinary least squares regression of entrepreneurial activity on the entire set of initial and policy variables considered in Berkowitz and DeJong (2001), we obtain one notable change: REF turns out to be quantitatively and statistically significant in this case. Specifically, a one-standard-deviation increase in REF corresponds with an additional 0.596 new enterprises per thousand inhabitants; moreover, REF is statistically significant at the 1 percent level. The quantitative significance of LPRIV and SPRIV remains modest, and each variable remains statistically insignificant. Finally, the strong link between EDU and ENT established in the original regression remains evident, as illustrated by the quantitative significance measure of 1.229 we obtain in this case.

In sum, it appears that regions with relatively well-educated citizens sympathetic to the adoption of economic reforms have enjoyed relatively high levels of small private enterprise formation, which has exhibited a strong and lasting relationship with economic growth. In contrast, there is little direct evidence that privatization activity has had substantive economic effects, but since our measures of these activities were compiled in an early stage of the transition process, caution should be taken in basing general conclusions on this finding.

We are currently seeking to overcome this caveat by conducting a dynamic analysis of the empirical relationship observed between the regional implementation of economic reforms, the development of entrepreneurial activity, and economic growth. Considerable attention has been given in the theoretical literature on transition to issues regarding the timing of the implementation of privatization and price reforms (for a thorough discussion of alternative viewpoints, see Roland 2000, Chapter 6, and references therein). Proponents of a "big-bang" strategy have supported rapid implementation, arguing that this would eliminate inefficiencies associated with state control and ownership of enterprises, and would also eliminate market distortions that result in queuing, rent seeking, and input diversion. Gradualists have emphasized economic and political benefits that can result from a steady sequencing of reforms that enable agents to learn and experiment with private ownership and flexible pricing. As it turns out, not only has there been substantial regional variation within Russia in the extent of privatization and price reforms, but there has also been substantial variation in the *timing* of the implementation of these reforms. Our intention is to exploit this variation in assessing whether regional variations in timing exhibit discernable links with regional variations in the evolution of entrepreneurial activity and economic growth.

Conclusion

Exploiting the rich regional variation in entrepreneurial activity and initial conditions that existed within Russia early in its transition, in addition to the regional variation in subsequent growth it has realized, we have found a strong and enduring relationship between entrepreneurial activity and growth. This intra-national evidence thus complements evidence of the importance of entrepreneurial activity for growth that has emerged from international comparisons of transitional economies. The fact that we observe such a strong statistical relationship in this case is particularly noteworthy given Russia's relatively poor showing in these international comparisons.

References

Berkowitz, Daniel and David N. DeJong. "Entrepreneurship and Post-Soviet Growth." Manuscript, University of Pittsburgh, 2001.

Berkowitz, Daniel and David N. DeJong. "Accounting for Growth in Post-Soviet Russia." *Regional Science and Urban Economics*, forthcoming (2002a).

Berkowitz, Daniel and David N. DeJong. "Policy Reform and Growth in Post-Soviet Russia." *European Economic Review*, forthcoming (2002b).

McMillan, John and Christopher Woodruff. "Entrepreneurs in Economic Reform." Manuscript, Stanford University Business School, 2001.

Roland, Gerard. *Transition and Economics: Politics, Markets, and Firms.* Cambridge: MIT Press, 2000.

White, Halbert. "A Heteroskedasticity-Consistent Covariance Matrix Estimator and Direct Test for Heteroskedasticity," *Econometrica* (48) (1980): 817–838.

Notes

[i] Prepared for the World Economic Forum, Andrew Warner, Editor. This paper summarizes the findings presented in Berkowitz and DeJong (2001; 2002a,b), which benefited from financial support provided by the National Council for Soviet and East European Studies (under contracts #807-09 and #811-12); the National Science Foundation (under grant SBR-9730499); and the Center for Russian and East European Studies at the University of Pittsburgh.

[ii] IV indicates the fourth quarter of the year in question.

[iii] Due to data limitations, our earlier analyses (Berkowitz and DeJong, forthcoming [2002a,b]) were based on measures of growth observed for 48 regions over the period 1993:IV through 1997:IV. The results of all three analyses are qualitatively quite similar.

Trade Integration with the European Union: Where Do the Transition Economies Stand?

PETER K. CORNELIUS, World Economic Forum
FRIEDRICH VON KIRCHBACH, International Trade Centre
YONG ZHANG, World Economic Forum

Economists are not good at predicting the impact of drastic policy changes even in the short run. Predicting trade flows two or three decades after a radical transformation of the CEEC [central and eastern European countries] economies takes us well into the "twilight zone" of economic understanding. The best way to proceed in such circumstances is to admit that any answers will be little more than a rough guess, and then to base that guess on simple and transparent assumptions. (Baldwin 1994, pp. 81–82).

Ten years into the transformation process, we are still in the twilight zone. In several countries, economic reforms, especially structural ones, are far from being complete. The industrial structure in central and eastern Europe (CEE) and the member countries of the Commonwealth of Independent States (CIS) remains subject to deep changes,[i] the institutional framework continues to be under construction, and the direction and composition of foreign trade is considerably influenced by the ongoing evolution of trade arrangements, which in many cases has followed a piecemeal approach driven not least by short-term political considerations. Probably the single most important factor of uncertainty, however, consists of the expected accession of several transition economies to the European Union (EU).

Nevertheless, after a decade of economic transformation, it seems worthwhile to look at where the CEE and CIS countries stand at this point in time in terms of redirecting trade and becoming more integrated into the EU. How successful have these countries been in penetrating new markets? To what extent have firms been able to develop and export new products to the West, as opposed to shifting sales from eastern to western markets? What are the products for which CEE and the CIS seem to possess a comparative advantage? Are recent developments consistent with earlier predictions, and, 10 years into the transition, can we say anything more about the long-term trade pattern?

The major aim of this paper is therefore to provide a detailed empirical analysis of the present foreign trade structure of CEE and the CIS, both with regard to its geographical distribution and its product composition. In doing so, we examine specifically the extent to which the transition economies have been successful in gaining increasing shares in markets that enjoy particularly strong growth as opposed to those markets whose overall size is stagnating or even shrinking. These findings are juxtaposed both with the original trade structures in individual countries of CEE and the CIS and with earlier predictions that have been developed as benchmarks for predicting the long-term evolution of foreign trade in these countries. It is beyond the scope of the paper, however, to explain the evolutionary process of foreign trade in these countries that has led to the current geographical distribution and product composition. This process has remained extremely complex, with trade flows affected, inter alia, by trade policy (and other structural) reforms, exchange-rate policies, bilateral and multilateral trade agreements, and various supply and demand shocks that have taken place over the last decade. Rather, we are concerned with an empirical snapshot of the trade structure of the CEE countries on their way to a long-term equilibrium.

The pre-reform structure of foreign trade

Although rigid quantitative controls on prices and production in the pre-reform CEE countries discouraged foreign trade with the West, central planning did aim at establishing a socialist division of labor among the member countries of the Council of Mutual Economic Assistance (CMEA). This was most pronounced within the former Soviet Union (FSU), where each republic was fully integrated into the planning process.

As Table 1 shows, intra-CMEA trade indeed accounted for the bulk of total trade of most pre-reform transition economies.[ii] In the case of Bulgaria, for example, exports to non-CMEA countries represented only about 10 percent of total trade in 1985. In the case of the former Czechoslovakia, the share was around 21 percent, while in Hungary and Poland the respective shares amounted to 42 and 45 percent. On the import side, the picture was not materially different. In the case of Bulgaria, almost 80 percent of imports came from other former centrally planned economies, while the shares of Hungary and Poland were around 40 percent and 47 percent, respectively.

At the same time, misguided domestic pricing and exchange-rate policies led to serious distortions regarding the product composition of foreign trade (shown in Table 2 for 1988). Although intra-CMEA trade was probably most affected, it can be doubted that trade with the West was in accordance with the underlying pattern of comparative advantage (Collins and Rodrik 1991, p. 51). Thus, it was generally expected that trade flows with the West were not a good guide to predict the future trade pattern.

As far as eastern Europe is concerned, manufactures accounted for the bulk of foreign trade with the West in 1988, both on the export and import sides. Although eastern Europe overall appears to have had a revealed comparative disadvantage in this product category, this disadvantage was relatively small. However, a considerable comparative disadvantage seems to have existed in machinery, as indicated by a substantial deficit in net exports. On the other hand, comparative advantages appear to have existed in basic and miscellaneous manufactures.

By contrast, the FSU had comparative advantages only in crude materials and fuels. For most other product categories, substantial disadvantages seem to have existed in the pre-reform period, most importantly in machinery and miscellaneous manufactures, but also food.

Table 3 permits us to look more closely at the composition of trade flows between the three Visegrad countries (the former Czechoslovakia, Hungary, and Poland) and the EU. In 1988, these countries exported mainly agricultural, forestry, fishery products, ferrous and non-ferrous ores and metals, chemical products, and textiles and clothing. Some variations among the three countries are worth noting. The former Czechoslovakia, for instance, exported relatively few agricultural, forestry, and fishery products. By contrast, Hungary exported relatively more meat and meat products to the EU than the other two countries did.

The Visegrad countries' imports from the EU were dominated by chemical products, agricultural machinery, electronic goods, textiles, and clothing. In Hungary and Poland, imports of motor vehicles had also a sizeable share. By contrast, imports of mineral products, ferrous and non-ferrous ores and metals, and meat and meat products played only a minor role.

Table 1: CEE countries' direction of foreign trade, 1985, US$ (million)

EXPORTS FROM:	TO:		
	EU	**EFTA**	**CMEA countries**
Bulgaria	402	61	9,855
Czechoslovakia	1,532	596	12,541
Hungary	1,326	749	4,464
Poland	2,502	688	5,998
Romania	2,595	302	4,018

IMPORTS BY:	FROM:		
	EU	**EFTA**	**CMEA countries**
Bulgaria	1,338	383	10,071
Czechoslovakia	1,642	522	13,360
Hungary	1,756	840	4,034
Poland	2,074	562	6,372
Romania	835	168	3,706

Source: Winters and Wang (1994), p. 22.

Trade Integration with the European Union: Where Do the Transition Economies Stand?

55

Table 2: Eastern Europe and the Former Soviet Union: Product composition of trade with the West and revealed comparative advantage, 1988 (US$ billion, except where indicated)

PRODUCT CATEGORY	EXPORTS TO WEST		IMPORTS FROM WEST		ADVANTAGE INDEX[1]	
	Eastern Europe	Soviet Union	Eastern Europe	Soviet Union	Eastern Europe	Soviet Union
Primary products	5.7	4.0	3.7	5.1	0.17	−0.09
food	3.2	0.5	1.9	4.2	0.21	−0.77
crude materials	2.2	3.5	1.5	0.7	0.14	0.68
Fuels	3.4	14.6	0.5	0.2	0.72	0.97
Manufactures	17.6	6.1	20.0	20.8	−0.11	−0.52
chemicals	3.2	1.5	4.4	3.1	−0.20	−0.32
basic manufactures	6.6	3.3	4.9	6.6	0.10	−0.31
machinery	3.4	1.1	8.6	9.0	−0.46	−0.77
miscellaneous manufactures	4.3	0.2	2.0	2.1	0.32	−0.82
Total	**26.8**	**24.8**	**24.3**	**26.3**		

[1] The index of revealed comparative advantage is calculated as $(X - aM)/(X + aM)$ for each category, where a is an adjustment coefficient for unbalanced trade (a = 1.10 and 0.94 for eastern Europe and the former Soviet Union, respectively).

Source: Rodrick (1994), Table 2.8.

Table 3: Visegrad countries' trade structure with the European Union (1988, in percent)

	CZECHOSLOVAKIA	HUNGARY	POLAND
Agricultural, forestry and fishery products			
Exports	3.8	14	11.1
Imports	3.2	1.3	4
Ferrous and non-ferrous ores and metals			
Exports	13	9	14.7
Imports	3.4	5.3	5.7
Non-metallic mineral products			
Exports	8	2.5	3.2
Imports	1.6	1.8	1.8
Chemical products			
Exports	14.2	10.9	6.1
Imports	23.8	26.2	26
Agricultural and industrial machinery			
Exports	7.5	5.1	3.5
Imports	31.4	20.7	23.4
Electrical goods			
Exports	3.3	6.5	3.4
Imports	8.5	9.4	5.6
Motor vehicles			
Exports	3.3	0.9	4.4
Imports	1.9	3.6	4
Meat, meat preparations and preserves			
Exports	3	12.9	3.8
Imports	2.7	1.2	1.9
Textiles and clothing			
Exports	10.1	14.1	9.4
Imports	10.7	13.9	12.3

Source: Halpern (1994), Table 3.2.

Potential trade flows: Early estimates

Against this background, one of the key questions at the onset of the economic transformation (ie, at the end of the 1980s) was: What would pan-European trade look like, if the transition economies in CEE and the members of the CIS were as integrated with the West and themselves as western Europe is today?

Early predictions of changes in CEE and CIS trade flows were typically based on two assumptions (eg, Collins and Rodrik 1991, p. 28). First, once central planning was eliminated, the transition countries would be likely to trade less with each other and more with the rest of the world, and especially with western Europe. This was generally referred to as the "direction-of-trade effect." Second, to the extent that central planning had repressed trade, liberalization would lead to an overall expansion of these countries' trade, with the "volume-of-trade effect" coming about through an increase in openness and/or expansion of output.

In order to get at least a vague idea about potential trade flows, most researchers employed so-called gravity models whose roots date back to the mid-1960s (Linnemann 1966). Aiming to provide a long-term equilibrium view of the volume of trade and aggregate trade patterns, gravity models generally describe the trade flows from a particular origin to a particular destination in terms of supply factors in the origin, demand factors in the destination, and various stimulating or restraining factors relating to the specific flow.[iii] By contrast, gravity models are silent with regard to the composition of trade and thus avoid entirely the issues of what the transition economies will trade and how what they will trade will progress from any particular point in time.[iv]

Table 4 summarizes the findings of two different gravity models that are frequently cited in the literature (Baldwin 1994; and Winters and Wang 1994). These models differ in a number of important respects, such as their country coverage and the base year. Nevertheless, their results are largely consistent. Although different in terms of magnitude, both models forecast a strong re-orientation of CEE and exports to western Europe (EU and EFTA). For example, for the three Visegrad countries, Winters and Wang (1994) predict a 5- to 10-fold increase in exports to the EU; Baldwin's (1994) estimates are somewhat lower, with the ratios between potential and actual exports ranging from around 2 to 5. However, both models generally agree that exports to other CEE countries will be considerably lower once a long-term equilibrium is reached. In the case of Poland, however, their estimates do differ considerably, which might be due to different reference years.

As far as imports from western Europe are concerned, a similar picture emerges. Both models predict a strong re-orientation of trade toward the EU and EFTA, away from other former centrally planned economies. For the CEE countries as a whole, Winters and Wang (1994) predict increases in imports from western Europe of around 350 to 500 percent, with a particularly strong redirection of trade forecast for the former Czechoslovakia. By comparison, Baldwin's (1994) estimated increases are lower, ranging from 100 to 150 percent.

The results reported here are broadly similar to estimates by Collins and Rodrik (1991). Although they apply a substantially different methodology,[v] these authors also find that in the long-term equilibrium trade between the CEE countries and western Europe will be considerably larger, with predictions for the three Visegrad countries of the former Czechoslovakia, Hungary, and Poland ranging from around 300 percent to 750 percent.

Table 4: Gravity model estimates of potential trade (as ratio to actual trade)

EXPORTER IMPORTER								
	EU-12[3]	EFTA[4]	CEEC[5]	Bulgaria	Czechoslovakia	Hungary	Poland	Romania
Bulgaria								
Winters/Wang[1]	31.1	9.9	0.3					
Baldwin[2]	5.2	7.3						
Czechoslovakia								
Winters/Wang[1]	9.9	3.7	0.6					
Baldwin[2]	4.8	5.5	1.0					
Hungary								
Winters/Wang[1]	4.9	1.2	0.9					
Baldwin[2]	1.7	1.7	0.8					
Poland								
Winters/Wang[1]	5.1	3.8	1.5					
Baldwin[2]	2.1	2.0	0.8					
Romania								
Winters/Wang[1]	2.0	4.3	1.0					
Baldwin[2]	1.2	3.2	0.4					
EU-12[3]								
Winters/Wang[1]			5.8	2.0	9.5	3.9	6.7	7.0
Baldwin[2]			2.0					
EFTA[4]								
Winters/Wang[1]			4.4	1.8	4.6	1.3	5.5	9.1
Baldwin[2]			2.5					
CEEC[5]								
Winters/Wang[1]	5.0	3.8	0.6	0.3	0.5	1.0	1.5	1.2
Baldwin[2]								

[1] Winters and Wang's (1994) gravity model is based on 76 non-CEE countries averaged over the 1984–1986 period. Dummy variables are included for adjacency and mutual membership in preferential trade areas. Actual trade flows refer to 1985.

[2] Baldwin's (1994) gravity model includes 17 exporting countries and 20 partner countries. Trade flows between Iceland and Turkey are excluded, resulting in 339 bilateral flows. Data are obtained for the period 1979–1988. GDP numbers are corrected for price differences and are expressed in 1985 international dollars. Actual trade flows refer to 1989.

[3] EU-12 refers to the member countries of the European Union at the time prior to the reform process in eastern Europe, ie, Belgium, Denmark, Germany, Greece, France, Ireland, Italy, Luxembourg, the Netherlands, Portugal, Spain, and the United Kingdom.

[4] EFTA refers to Austria, Finland, Iceland, Norway, Sweden, and Switzerland.

[5] Winters and Wang (1994) include Bulgaria, the former Czechoslovakia, East Germany, Hungary, Poland, and Romania. In addition, Baldwin (1994) includes Albania, Croatia, Slovenia, Estonia, Latvia, and Lithuania, but excludes East Germany.

In sum, although these estimates differ in terms of the exact magnitude of the potential re-orientation of trade, the studies do agree that this potential is huge. In the following section we examine the extent to which the expected re-orientation has already taken place. We also evaluate how the transition economies' trade structure has evolved and look into trade flows in parts and components in search of evidence for the degree of integration of production processes between eastern and western Europe.

How much trade re-orientation has taken place?

As a matter of fact, trade integration between the CEE countries and the EU has deepened remarkably over the last decade or so. By 2000, the EU accounted for around two-thirds of the exports and imports of CEE-12 (Tables 5 and 6), up from 55 percent in 1993, the first year for which we have data for all 12 countries.[vi] This increase reflects a 2.5-fold rise of CEE-12 exports to the EU in dollar terms during this period, compared with an increase of total exports of about 110 percent from around US$ 59 billion to around US$ 125 billion.[vii]

The geographical re-orientation of CEE's exports toward the EU could already be observed in the preceding years, from 1989 to 1992, for which we have data for individual transition countries. In Hungary, for example, the EU's share rose from 33 percent to around 62 percent during these years; since then it has increased further, to 73 percent in 2000. Similarly, Poland's exports to the EU as a percentage of the country's total exports grew from around 40 percent in 1989 to 62 percent in 1992 and further to 68 percent until the end of the decade. In Bulgaria, finally, where total exports actually fell in value terms in 1989 to 1992, exports to the EU nearly doubled, resulting in a substantial increase in the EU's relative importance as the country's trading partner. Thus, it appears that, in some countries, the bulk of the re-orientation process took place in the early years of the transformation process.

On the import side, a similar pattern can be observed, with the share of the EU in CEE-12 imports rising from around 52 percent to more than 62 percent in 1993 to 2000. However, in dollar terms, import growth has clearly outperformed export growth. In 2000, imports from the EU alone amounted to more than US$ 110 billion, compared with only around US$ 40 billion in 1993. Although imports from the EU alone have risen particularly fast, imports from other countries have also shown high growth rates. To a considerable extent, central and eastern Europe's huge import demand has mirrored the countries' need for investment goods—and the technologies embodied therein—in order to rebuild a competitive capital stock which had virtually been depleted under central planning.

Thanks to the substantial increase in both exports and imports, the EU has become CEE's major trading partner. This is particularly true for the three Visegrad countries Poland, Hungary, and the Czech Republic, with their exports to and imports from the EU having increased by about 300 percent in 1993 to 2000. In 2000, these three countries accounted for about two-thirds of the CEE-12's total exports to and imports from the EU. If one includes the early years of economic transformation from 1989 to 1992, trade with the West has actually risen even more. For the entire period, Poland and Hungary have registered a ninefold increase regarding both exports to and imports from the EU.

While in the last few years the trajectory of trade integration has flattened somewhat, earlier predictions based on gravity models already seem to be proving to be too conservative. Joining the EU will no doubt provide additional momentum for further trade integration, as evidenced by the experience of some latecomers such as Spain and Portugal. Being a member of the EU does not necessarily mean joining the European Monetary Union (EMU). Denmark, Sweden, and the United Kingdom have until now decided to pursue their own monetary and exchange rate policies. Eventually, however, the EU accession countries might decide to participate in EMU, which could provide another stimulus for their external trade with other western European countries. Rose and Wincoop (2001), for example, estimate that joining the EMU could raise bilateral trade between current members (including Greece) and new members by 40 to 60 percent. Should the three outsiders (Denmark, Sweden, and the United Kingdom) join the EMU, the total effect would be somewhat smaller, but still significant. Eliminating national monetary barriers between the EU and the CEE may thus be expected to result in a sizeable increase in trade integration, going beyond the effects stemming from the reduction of direct trade barriers.

Although both CEE-12's exports to and imports from the EU have grown substantially faster than predicted at the onset of the economic transformation, over the past decade or so their aggregate trade deficit vis-à-vis the EU has widened considerably. In 2000, the gap reached more than US$ 30 billion, up from around US$ 8 billion in 1993 when the transition started in earnest. This may not seem surprising, taking into account central and eastern Europe's comparative advantages and disadvantages in the pre-reform period (see Table 2) and the economies' need to rebuild their capital stocks almost entirely new. Ten years into the transition, it seems necessary to examine the extent to which their export and import structures have changed in the wake of the structural reform process.

Table 5a: CEE countries' exports to the European Union, FOB, US$ (million)

COUNTRY	1989	1990	1991	1992	1993	1994	1995	1996	1997	1998	1999	2000
Albania	117	107	79	68	89	109	160	181	124	191	258	239
Bosnia and Herzegovina	—	—	—	—	34	14	29	80	168	253	367	450
Bulgaria	598	782	919	1,144	1,090	1,564	2,012	1,913	1,942	2,137	2,035	2,463
Croatia	—	—	—	—	2,214	2,531	2,672	2,302	2,220	2,172	2,088	2,234
Czech Republic	—	—	—	—	6,354	7,480	9,273	12,760	13,557	16,976	18,575	17,978
Hungary	3,247	4,350	5,972	6,644	4,982	6,818	8,077	8,234	13,603	16,782	18,927	19,681
Macedonia, Former Yug. Rep.	—	—	—	—	364	361	409	491	456	578	533	669
Poland	5,358	7,467	9,578	8,221	9,794	11,929	16,039	16,248	16,533	19,285	19,338	19,737
Romania	3,451	1,961	1,576	1,536	2,026	2,970	4,388	4,271	4,752	5,522	5,723	6,630
Slovak Republic	—	—	—	—	1,618	2,340	3,208	3,645	4,540	5,970	6,066	5,832
Slovenia	—	—	—	—	3,847	4,539	5,648	5,369	5,321	5,917	5,625	5,577
Yugoslavia Fed. Rep. of (Serbia/Motenegro)	—	—	—	—	3	5	38	516	1,055	1,026	564	673
Total	**12,771**	**14,667**	**18,124**	**17,613**	**32,415**	**40,660**	**51,953**	**56,010**	**64,271**	**76,809**	**80,099**	**82,163**

Table 5b: CEE countries' exports to the world, FOB, US$ (million)

COUNTRY	1989	1990	1991	1992	1993	1994	1995	1996	1997	1998	1999	2000
Albania	305	224	171	114	122	141	202	211	141	206	275	281
Bosnia and Herzegovina					85	36	52	181	381	511	611	689
Bulgaria	2,787	2,032	2,051	2,444	2,319	3,382	5,220	4,781	4,314	4,150	3,755	4,760
Croatia	—	—	—	—	3,904	4,260	4,632	4,512	4,332	4,557	4,226	4,071
Czech Republic	—	—	—	—	11,774	14,281	17,178	22,132	22,504	26,420	26,831	27,602
Hungary	9,682	9,593	9,972	10,728	8,598	10,588	12,861	13,145	19,100	23,005	24,849	27,454
Macedonia, Former Yug. Rep.	—	—	—	—	1,055	1,086	1,203	1,148	1,237	1,311	1,192	1,369
Poland	13,533	13,627	14,913	13,187	14,143	17,240	22,895	24,440	25,751	28,228	27,407	27,894
Romania	11,090	5,871	4,318	4,367	4,892	6,160	8,061	7,644	8,387	8,467	8,660	10,367
Slovak Republic	—	—	—	—	5,460	6,691	8,579	8,831	9,639	10,720	10,197	10,670
Slovenia	—	—	—	—	6,241	7,232	8,389	8,312	8,372	9,034	8,505	8,728
Yugoslavia Fed. Rep. of (Serbia/Motenegro)	—	—	—	—	4	57	66	678	1,267	1,414	817	995
Total	**37,397**	**31,347**	**31,425**	**30,840**	**58,597**	**71,154**	**89,338**	**96,015**	**105,425**	**118,023**	**117,325**	**124,880**

Table 5c: Proportion of CEE countries' exports to the European Union to its exports to the world

COUNTRY	1989	1990	1991	1992	1993	1994	1995	1996	1997	1998	1999	2000
Albania	0.38	0.48	0.46	0.60	0.73	0.77	0.79	0.86	0.88	0.93	0.94	0.85
Bosnia and Herzegovina	—	—	—	—	0.40	0.39	0.56	0.44	0.44	0.50	0.60	0.65
Bulgaria	0.21	0.38	0.45	0.47	0.47	0.46	0.39	0.40	0.45	0.51	0.54	0.52
Croatia	—	—	—	—	0.57	0.59	0.58	0.51	0.51	0.48	0.49	0.55
Czech Republic	—	—	—	—	0.54	0.52	0.54	0.58	0.60	0.64	0.69	0.65
Hungary	0.34	0.45	0.60	0.62	0.58	0.64	0.63	0.63	0.71	0.73	0.76	0.72
Macedonia, Former Yug. Rep.	—	—	—	—	0.35	0.33	0.34	0.43	0.37	0.44	0.45	0.49
Poland	0.40	0.55	0.64	0.62	0.69	0.69	0.70	0.66	0.64	0.68	0.71	0.71
Romania	0.31	0.33	0.36	0.35	0.41	0.48	0.54	0.56	0.57	0.65	0.66	0.64
Slovak Republic	—	—	—	—	0.30	0.35	0.37	0.41	0.47	0.56	0.59	0.55
Slovenia	—	—	—	—	0.62	0.63	0.67	0.65	0.64	0.65	0.66	0.64
Yugoslavia Fed. Rep. of (Serbia/Motenegro)	—	—	—	—	0.75	0.09	0.58	0.76	0.83	0.73	0.69	0.68
Total	**0.34**	**0.47**	**0.58**	**0.57**	**0.55**	**0.57**	**0.58**	**0.58**	**0.61**	**0.65**	**0.68**	**0.66**

Source: IMF Direction of Trade database, August 2001. Proportions are computed by the authors.
Note: "—" means data are unavailable.

Table 6a: CEE countries' imports from the European Union, CIF, US$ (million)

COUNTRY	1989	1990	1991	1992	1993	1994	1995	1996	1997	1998	1999	2000
Albania	157	196	239	432	300	124	500	694	519	658	721	817
Bosnia and Herzegovina	—	—	—	—	120	141	226	715	946	1,048	1,132	1,166
Bulgaria	2,081	1,790	1,504	1,609	1,908	2,379	2,098	1,780	1,628	2,325	2,611	2,858
Croatia	—	—	—	—	2,585	3,096	4,664	4,625	5,403	4,942	4,376	4,304
Czech Republic	—	—	—	—	7,058	8,813	12,847	17,834	15,423	20,197	20,262	24,191
Hungary	3,472	4,217	5,894	6,307	6,764	8,891	9,515	9,685	13,240	16,486	17,984	20,853
Macedonia, Former Yug. Rep.	—	—	—	—	402	551	688	630	650	695	721	1,024
Poland	4,796	4,615	10,083	9,048	12,204	14,087	18,782	23,739	27,000	31,030	29,829	34,790
Romania	646	2,215	1,802	2,564	2,955	3,429	5,292	5,205	5,848	7,055	6,597	7,400
Slovak Republic	—	—	—	—	1,946	2,432	3,354	4,434	5,646	7,210	6,428	6,756
Slovenia	—	—	—	—	4,266	5,140	6,685	6,368	6,308	6,991	6,805	6,842
Yugoslavia Fed. Rep. of (Serbia/Motenegro)	—	—	—	—	79	156	277	1,595	2,156	2,038	1,433	1,821
Total	**11,152**	**13,033**	**19,522**	**19,960**	**40,587**	**49,239**	**64,928**	**77,304**	**84,767**	**100,675**	**98,899**	**112,822**

Table 6b: CEE countries' imports from the world, CIF, US$ (million)

COUNTRY	1989	1990	1991	1992	1993	1994	1995	1996	1997	1998	1999	2000
Albania	387	423	496	574	421	161	651	909	620	795	899	1,063
Bosnia and Herzegovina	—	—	—	—	424	775	950	1,941	2,400	2,549	2,627	2,677
Bulgaria	5,145	3,462	2,715	4,345	4,481	4,685	5,469	4,891	3,880	5,044	5,220	6,362
Croatia	—	—	—	—	4,666	5,229	7,510	7,787	9,100	8,327	7,724	7,688
Czech Republic	—	—	—	—	13,805	16,325	22,973	30,685	29,687	31,777	31,660	35,414
Hungary	8,885	8,621	11,082	11,110	12,387	14,449	15,483	16,209	21,234	25,727	27,894	33,035
Macedonia, Former Yug. Rep.	—	—	—	—	1,199	1,484	1,712	1,627	1,773	1,915	1,796	2,157
Poland	11,357	8,976	17,084	15,204	18,834	21,569	29,050	37,137	42,307	47,053	45,911	52,326
Romania	9,951	10,293	5,957	6,140	6,522	7,113	10,388	9,964	11,142	12,107	10,786	13,054
Slovak Republic	—	—	—	—	6,968	7,272	9,648	12,030	12,892	14,380	12,431	13,747
Slovenia	—	—	—	—	6,866	8,026	9,645	9,429	9,357	10,068	9,889	10,089
Yugoslavia Fed. Rep. of (Serbia/Motenegro)	—	—	—	—	91	223	383	2,397	2,854	3,126	2,366	3,208
Total	**35,725**	**31,775**	**37,334**	**37,373**	**76,664**	**87,311**	**113,862**	**135,006**	**147,246**	**162,868**	**159,203**	**180,820**

Table 6c: Proportion of CEE countries' imports to the European Union to its imports from the world

COUNTRY	1989	1990	1991	1992	1993	1994	1995	1996	1997	1998	1999	2000
Albania	0.41	0.46	0.48	0.75	0.71	0.77	0.77	0.76	0.84	0.83	0.80	0.77
Bosnia and Herzegovina	—	—	—	—	0.28	0.18	0.24	0.37	0.39	0.41	0.43	0.44
Bulgaria	0.40	0.52	0.55	0.37	0.43	0.51	0.38	0.36	0.42	0.46	0.50	0.45
Croatia	—	—	—	—	0.55	0.59	0.62	0.59	0.59	0.59	0.57	0.56
Czech Republic	—	—	—	—	0.51	0.54	0.56	0.58	0.52	0.64	0.64	0.68
Hungary	0.39	0.49	0.53	0.57	0.55	0.62	0.61	0.60	0.62	0.64	0.64	0.63
Macedonia, Former Yug. Rep.	—	—	—	—	0.34	0.37	0.40	0.39	0.37	0.36	0.40	0.47
Poland	0.42	0.51	0.59	0.60	0.65	0.65	0.65	0.64	0.64	0.66	0.65	0.66
Romania	0.06	0.22	0.30	0.42	0.45	0.48	0.51	0.52	0.52	0.58	0.61	0.57
Slovak Republic	—	—	—	—	0.28	0.33	0.35	0.37	0.44	0.50	0.52	0.49
Slovenia	—	—	—	—	0.62	0.64	0.69	0.68	0.67	0.69	0.69	0.68
Yugoslavia Fed. Rep. of (Serbia/Motenegro)	—	—	—	—	0.87	0.70	0.72	0.67	0.76	0.65	0.61	0.57
Total	**0.31**	**0.41**	**0.52**	**0.53**	**0.53**	**0.56**	**0.57**	**0.57**	**0.58**	**0.62**	**0.62**	**0.62**

Source: IMF Direction of Trade database, August 2001. Proportions are computed by the authors.
Note: "—" means data are unavailable.

Trade flows between CEE countries and the EU have been driven primarily by exports and imports of manufactured goods (SITC-6), machines and transport equipment (SITC-7), and miscellaneous products (SITC-8). Tables 7 and 8 report the composition of SITC one-digit-level product groups based on the UN COMTRADE database. As far as EU's exports to the CEE are concerned, these goods represented around 80 percent of EU's total exports to the region in 2000. Although exports of chemicals and chemical products account for another 12 percent, the remaining SITC groups are of limited importance.

It is important to note that CEE's imports of machines and transport equipment have proved to be particularly dynamic. With the import value of SITC-7 products having increased more than tenfold from 1989 to 2000, the percentage of these goods in terms of the region's total imports from the EU rose from less than one-third to more than 46 percent during this period, helping replenish the transition economies' capital stock. By contrast, SITC-6 and SITC-8 products more or less stagnated in terms of their relative importance. The share of imports of chemical products actually declined, reflecting a below-average increase in imports in value terms.

As far as the EU's imports are concerned, manufacturing goods have also dominated the region's foreign trade with CEE countries. By 2000, SITC-6 to SITC-8 product groups have accounted for 85 percent of EU's total imports from the CEE, 32 percent higher than that in 1989. In value terms, CEE exports of machines and transport equipment (SITC-7) to the EU increased on average by around 140 percent per year in 1989 to 2000, reaching more than US$ 36 billion. As a percentage of EU's total imports from the region, SITC-7 products thus accounted for almost 43 percent in 2000, up from less than 15 percent at the onset of the transition. Miscellaneous manufactured products also gained in importance relative to other SITC groups, while EU's imports of manufactured goods from CEE basically increased in line with total imports from the region. By contrast, the increase in the value of CEE's exports of food and live animals to the EU remained very limited—partly thanks to the EU's Common Agricultural Policy (CAP)—failing to prevent the SITC group's percentage to fall substantially in 1989 to 2000.

Trade Integration with the European Union: Where Do the Transition Economies Stand?

61

Table 7a: The European Union's exports to CEE countries and Russia, US$ (million), 1989–2000

PRODUCT	1989	1990	1991	1992	1993	1994	1995	1996	1997	1998	1999	2000
Food and live animals	797	1,298	2,292	2,782	3,321	3,673	4,308	4,684	4,469	4,388	3,757	3,149
Beverages and tobacco	154	290	591	568	544	569	654	736	651	660	716	529
Crude materials, inedible	871	904	1,074	1,110	1,029	1,283	1,765	1,845	1,790	1,806	1,769	1,645
Fuels, lubricants, etc.	174	306	919	1,269	1,193	1,279	1,518	1,947	2,143	1,710	1,778	1,932
Animal, veg. oils, etc.	89	95	120	187	183	205	256	262	292	338	251	199
Chemicals, related prod. nes	2,362	2,542	4,372	5,078	5,315	6,666	8,897	10,221	10,957	11,571	11,690	11,598
Manufactured goods	2,865	3,415	7,121	8,574	9,360	11,876	16,426	18,551	19,737	22,226	21,269	21,554
Machines, transport equip	4,223	6,174	13,981	15,807	16,516	20,392	27,923	34,547	38,255	42,552	41,764	46,049
Misc. manufactured articles	1,234	2,112	4,124	4,968	5,543	7,020	9,026	10,398	11,079	11,943	11,660	11,148
Goods not classified by kind	169	223	451	499	522	549	1,164	689	1,720	3,735	3,104	1,224
CEE total	**12,938**	**17,360**	**35,045**	**40,841**	**43,528**	**53,511**	**71,936**	**83,880**	**91,092**	**100,928**	**97,759**	**99,028**
Russia	—	—	—	16,721	15,628	16,918	20,835	23,802	28,532	22,795	15,082	16356.83
World	896,723	1,078,670	1,486,916	1,579,501	1,443,254	1,649,067	2,016,764	2,077,536	2,091,244	2,148,088	2,139,434	1,996,338
CEE's proportion	**1.44**	**1.61**	**2.36**	**2.59**	**3.02**	**3.24**	**3.57**	**4.04**	**4.36**	**4.70**	**4.57**	**4.96**

Table 7b: Composition of the European Union's exports to CEE countries, percentage, 1989–2000

PRODUCT	1989	1990	1991	1992	1993	1994	1995	1996	1997	1998	1999	2000
Food and live animals	6.16	7.48	6.54	6.81	7.63	6.86	5.99	5.58	4.91	4.35	3.84	3.18
Beverages and tobacco	1.19	1.67	1.69	1.39	1.25	1.06	0.91	0.88	0.71	0.65	0.73	0.53
Crude materials, inedible	6.73	5.21	3.06	2.72	2.36	2.40	2.45	2.20	1.97	1.79	1.81	1.66
Fuels, lubricants, etc.	1.35	1.76	2.62	3.11	2.74	2.39	2.11	2.32	2.35	1.69	1.82	1.95
Animal, veg. oils, etc.	0.69	0.55	0.34	0.46	0.42	0.38	0.36	0.31	0.32	0.34	0.26	0.20
Chemicals, related prod. nes	18.26	14.64	12.47	12.43	12.21	12.46	12.37	12.19	12.03	11.46	11.96	11.71
Manufactured goods	22.15	19.67	20.32	20.99	21.50	22.19	22.83	22.12	21.67	22.02	21.76	21.77
Machines, transport equip.	32.64	35.56	39.89	38.70	37.94	38.11	38.82	41.19	42.00	42.16	42.72	46.50
Misc. manufactured articles	9.54	12.17	11.77	12.16	12.74	13.12	12.55	12.40	12.16	11.83	11.93	11.26
Goods not classified by kind	1.31	1.29	1.29	1.22	1.20	1.03	1.62	0.82	1.89	3.70	3.18	1.24

Source: Compiled by the authors based on UN COMTRADE database.

Table 8a: The European Union's imports from CEE countries and Russia, US$ (million), 1989–2000

PRODUCT	1989	1990	1991	1992	1993	1994	1995	1996	1997	1998	1999	2000
Food and live animals	2,142	2,350	3,747	3,469	2,591	2,969	3,139	3,121	2,999	2,986	2,941	2,572
Beverages and tobacco	79	117	227	250	238	247	282	298	305	305	300	281
Crude materials, inedible	1,532	1,675	2,279	2,640	2,132	2,636	3,237	2,770	2,866	2,842	3,047	3,007
Fuels, lubricants, etc.	2,180	1,859	2,219	1,823	1,947	2,083	2,305	2,203	2,092	2,023	1,855	2,195
Animal, veg. oils, etc.	57	53	87	80	64	65	56	71	48	52	53	32
Chemicals, related prod. nes	1,443	1,811	2,755	2,697	2,207	2,889	4,208	3,860	3,902	3,774	3,503	3,958
Manufactured goods	3,647	4,503	7,759	9,146	7,875	11,377	15,956	14,590	15,321	16,927	16,285	17,175
Machines, transport equip.	2,225	2,701	5,649	6,695	6,549	9,162	13,872	16,759	20,646	29,062	33,465	35,720
Misc. manufactured articles	2,122	2,771	8,443	9,774	9,851	11,687	14,397	15,611	15,959	17,965	18,174	17,507
Goods not classified by kind	79	107	356	402	364	421	590	558	554	174	139	610
CEE total	**15,507**	**17,946**	**33,521**	**36,977**	**33,817**	**43,535**	**58,043**	**59,841**	**64,692**	**76,109**	**79,763**	**83,057**
Russia	0	0	0	22,362	20,882	24,995	28,389	30,165	28,916	22,306	22,615	33,302
World	1,009,949	1,200,927	1,575,966	1,652,214	1,402,086	1,591,156	1,921,447	1,971,218	1,973,427	2,068,197	2,105,704	1,989,547
CEE's proportion	**1.54**	**1.49**	**2.13**	**2.24**	**2.41**	**2.74**	**3.02**	**3.04**	**3.28**	**3.68**	**3.79**	**4.17**

Table 8b: Composition of the European Union's imports from CEE countries, percentage, 1989–2000

PRODUCT	1989	1990	1991	1992	1993	1994	1995	1996	1997	1998	1999	2000
Food and live animals	13.81	13.09	11.18	9.38	7.66	6.82	5.41	5.21	4.64	3.92	3.69	3.10
Beverages and tobacco	0.51	0.65	0.68	0.68	0.71	0.57	0.49	0.50	0.47	0.40	0.38	0.34
Crude materials, inedible	9.88	9.33	6.80	7.14	6.30	6.05	5.58	4.63	4.43	3.73	3.82	3.62
Fuels, lubricants, etc.	14.06	10.36	6.62	4.93	5.76	4.78	3.97	3.68	3.23	2.66	2.33	2.64
Animal, veg. oils, etc.	0.37	0.29	0.26	0.22	0.19	0.15	0.10	0.12	0.07	0.07	0.07	0.04
Chemicals, related prod. nes	9.30	10.09	8.22	7.29	6.53	6.63	7.25	6.45	6.03	4.96	4.39	4.77
Manufactured goods	23.52	25.09	23.15	24.73	23.29	26.13	27.49	24.38	23.68	22.24	20.42	20.68
Machines, transport equip.	14.35	15.05	16.85	18.11	19.36	21.04	23.90	28.01	31.91	38.18	41.96	43.01
Misc. manufactured articles	13.69	15.44	25.19	26.43	29.13	26.84	24.80	26.09	24.67	23.60	22.79	21.08
Goods not classified by kind	0.51	0.60	1.06	1.09	1.08	0.97	1.02	0.93	0.86	0.23	0.17	0.73

Source: Compiled by the authors based on UN COMTRADE database.

As a result of these trends, the EU's trade surplus for manufactured goods increased from US$ 328 million in 1989 to US$ 8.8 billion in 2000. This tremendous increase implies a massive competitive advantage, which had already been detected in the pre-reform trade statistics (Table 2).

As manufacturers have constituted the driving force of the trade expansion of the CEE members, it is striking to notice the dramatic differences in the export structure among the CEE and CIS countries. Tables 9 through 11 take a more disaggregated look at exports (SITC 3-digit level) of the CEE, non-Russia CIS and Russia in 1995 to 1999. These growth rates are put into perspective by comparing them with world trade growth in these categories. In principle, four different scenarios are conceivable. First, a country or a group of countries outperforms in markets that show strong growth ("champions"). Second, a country or a group of countries may outperform in terms of gaining shares in markets that are shrinking ("achievers in adversity"). Third, a country or a group of countries may underperform in world markets that expand rapidly ("underachievers"). And, finally, a country or a group of countries may underperform in a shrinking world market ("losers in declining markets").

Table 9 shows the fast-growing main export products of CEE countries. In terms of export values, most of the top-ten products in CEE belong to SITC-7 (machinery and transportation equipment) and SITC-8 (miscellaneous manufactured articles). Interestingly, in all these categories CEE as a group has outperformed world market growth. In most of these cases, world markets have actually expanded at a rapid pace, classifying the CEE as champions. This applies, for instance, to passenger motor vehicles, internal combustion engines, and automatic data processing equipments, whose world demand increased by around 7 to 8 percent annually in 1995 through 1999. However, with the CEE enjoying triple- and even quadruple-digit growth rates per annum in these markets, their world market shares have risen appreciably. In the case of internal combustion engines, for example, CEE accounted for more than 5 percent of world trade by 1999.

Table 9. Main products of CEE exports, by SITC-3 digit code

Label	Exports 1999 (US$ million)	Share of CEE in world market (%)	CEE export growth, % per annum	World trade growth, % per annum	CEE export performance	LEADING EXPORTERS AMONG CEE COUNTRIES					
713 Internal Combus. Pstn. Engine	3,284	5.1	1,088.3	7.2	Champions	HUN	2,689	POL	257.3	CZE	196
752 Automatic Data Proc. Equip.	2,522	1.3	480.2	7.8	Champions	HUN	2,213	CZE	136.1	SVK	98
961 Coin Nongold Noncurrent	10	17.5	442.9	−13.9	Achievers in adv.	HUN	10		—		—
763 Sound Recorder, Phonograph	876	3.7	297.7	2.2	Champions	HUN	868	BGR	8.0		—
532 Dyeing, Tanning Materials	6	0.7	239.0	0.5	Champions	SVN	6		—		—
672 Ingots Etc., Iron or Steel	244	2.9	219.3	−5.5	Achievers in adv.	POL	127	ROM	41.3	CZE	41
781 Pass. Motor Vehcls., Ex.Bus	6,876	2.4	174.3	6.7	Champions	CZE	2,135	SVK	1,411.9	HUN	1,342
611 Leather	181	1.5	173.6	−2.9	Achievers in adv.	HUN	47	POL	38.1	SVN	32
762 Radio-Broadcast Receiver	269	1.4	154.0	−2.4	Achievers in adv.	HUN	266	BGR	3.3		—
882 Photo. Cinematograph Suppl	10	0.1	144.4	−2.0	Achievers in adv.	BGR	6	SVN	3.0	LTU	0
072 Cocoa	79	1.4	142.6	1.7	Champions	EST	79		—		—
759 Parts for Office Machines	1,411	1.1	140.4	8.5	Champions	HUN	1,094	CZE	133.1	ROM	100
231 Natural Rubber, Etc.	2	0.0	113.9	−16.8	Achievers in adv.	BGR	2		—		—
898 Musical Instruments, Etc.	215	0.7	110.2	1.6	Champions	HUN	81	CZE	62.8	POL	38
871 Optical Instruments, Nes	28	0.3	92.7	15.2	Champions	CZE	26	LTU	2.4		—
061 Sugars, Molasses, Honey	166	2.0	91.4	−7.3	Achievers in adv.	POL	110	HUN	27.2	SVK	9
761 Television Receivers Etc.	1,086	5.2	88.4	3.7	Champions	POL	543	HUN	378.1	CZE	70
848 Clothing, Nontextile; Headgear	127	1.0	85.3	−0.3	Achievers in adv.	HUN	46	POL	24.3	ROM	17
751 Office Machines	10	0.1	82.1	−4.9	Achievers in adv.	SVK	4	BGR	2.4	EST	2
246 Wood in Chips, Particles	27	1.1	80.1	−4.1	Achievers in adv.	EST	18	LVA	9.6		—
764 Telecomm. Equip. Parts Nes	1,414	0.9	78.8	9.8	Champions	HUN	458	EST	380.5	POL	218
621 Materials of Rubber	269	4.0	69.3	4.1	Champions	CZE	103	HUN	53.6	SVK	36
659 Floor Coverings, Etc.	36	0.5	68.3	−1.6	Achievers in adv.	CZE	11	POL	10.1	ROM	8
333 Petroleum Oils, Crude	41	0.0	66.7	−1.9	Achievers in adv.	LTU	28	CZE	13.6		—
678 Wire of Iron or Steel	180	5.1	66.4	−1.6	Achievers in adv.	CZE	115	ROM	20.1	SVK	13
211 Hides, Skins (Ex.Furs), Raw	117	3.2	64.4	−11.9	Achievers in adv.	POL	32	SVN	20.4	CZE	19
812 Plumbing, Sanitary Equipt., Etc	295	5.5	56.4	3.2	Champions	CZE	95	HUN	65.6	POL	43
971 Gold, Nonmonetary Excl Ores	27	0.1	56.0	−2.8	Achievers in adv.	CZE	14	HUN	9.6	BGR	3
896 Works of Art, Antiques, Etc.	117	1.2	54.6	12.0	Champions	CZE	110	BGR	7.5		—
884 Optical Goods Nes	87	0.6	53.7	8.8	Champions	CZE	30	HUN	27.4	SVN	24
675 Flat-Rolled, Alloy Steel	173	1.1	53.1	−3.0	Achievers in adv.	SVN	82	ROM	49.8	SVK	29
071 Coffee, Coffee Substitute	175	1.4	53.1	−4.2	Achievers in adv.	POL	89	CZE	35.8	HUN	21
895 Office, Stationery Supplies	69	0.9	51.4	4.6	Champions	CZE	38	SVN	17.2	HUN	10
653 Fabrics, Man-Made Fibers	180	0.8	50.6	−4.5	Achievers in adv.	CZE	45	LTU	40.7	HUN	31
696 Cutlery	36	0.7	50.4	4.0	Champions	POL	23	CZE	12.3	BGR	1

Source: International Trade Centre calculation based on UN COMTRADE statistics.

Note: Eastern Europe includes Bulgaria (BGR), the Czech Republic (CZE), Estonia (EST), Hungary (HUN), Latvia (LVA), Lithuania (LTU), Poland (POL), Romania (ROM), the Slovak Republic (SVK), and Slovenia (SVN).

63

Table 9 also provides a more detailed picture in terms of individual countries. Hungary and the Czech Republic seem to have been particularly successful in penetrating dynamic markets. However, in some individual areas, other countries have also shown considerable growth rates. For example, this applies to Poland (with television receivers), the Slovak Republic (with passenger vehicles), and Estonia (with telecommunications equipment).

By contrast, the non-Russia CIS countries, but also Russia itself, appear to have been less successful in transforming their export structure. As Tables 10 and 11 show, their exports continue to be dominated by mineral fuels, lubricants and related materials (SITC-3), non-fuel crude material (SITC-2), and manufactured goods chiefly classi- fied by materials (SITC-6). As far as non-Russia CIS is concerned, there exist only a limited number of SITC 3-digit product categories where the region is classified as a champion. Apart from several raw materials (zinc, pearls, precious stones, and un-manufactured tobacco), non-electric motor engines (SITC-714) represent the only product category where non-Russia CIS exports have grown faster than world trade in 1995 through 1999. Despite this outperformance, however, the region's market share has remained minuscule, amounting to only 0.2 percent in 1999. A closer look at the geographical distribution of leading exporters reveals that the Ukraine accounts for almost the entire share of non-Russia CIS.

In some categories, non-Russia CIS exports have actually fallen in markets where world demand has risen, resulting in an accelerated loss in market shares. On the other hand, in many product categories that account for the bulk of export revenues of non-Russia CIS countries, exporters are characterized as "achievers in adversity," implying that they have performed well in markets where world demand (in value terms) has been shrinking in the second half of the 1990s. As a result, their market shares have risen considerably, which may be taken as an additional sign that structural change has been slow—an

observation that is consistent with the analysis in other chapters of this *Report*.

As far as Russia is concerned, exports have remained dominated by natural resources, especially petroleum, petroleum products, and natural gas. World trade in these categories has more or less stagnated in value terms in 1995 through 1999, thanks to suppressed world market prices. With Russia's exports having actually fallen, the country's world market share has shrunk. However, in the case of natural gas, more than one-third of world trade still stems from Russia. A somewhat smaller but still substantial

Table 10: Main products of CIS exports (excluding Russia), by SITC 3-digit code

Label	Exports 1999 (US$ million)	Share of CIS in world market, 1999 (%)	CIS export growth, 1995–1999, % per annum	World trade growth, 1995–1999, % per annum	CIS export performance	LEADING EXPORTERS AMONG CIS COUNTRIES					
333 Petroleum Oils, Crude	2,139	1.1	—	-1.9		KAZ	1,568	AZE	390	TKM	106
673 Flat-Rolled Iron Etc.	1,202	5.1	26.5	-5.8	Achievers in adv.	UKR	773	KAZ	420	KGZ	3
263 Cotton	1,164	22.4	-12.5	-13.2	Achievers in adv.	UZB	814	TKM	139	KAZ	81
672 Ingots Etc., Iron or Steel	817	9.7	30.8	-5.5	Achievers in adv.	UKR	743	BLR	39	KAZ	22
671 Pig Iron, Spiegeleisn, Etc.	749	8.7	5.3	-6.8	Achievers in adv.	UKR	415	KAZ	302	GEO	26
676 Iron, Stl. Bar, Shapes, Etc.	626	3.2	12.5	-4.0	Achievers in adv.	UKR	482	MDA	95	BLR	37
334 Petroleum Products	621	1.0	25.0	-2.0	Achievers in adv.	UKR	192	TKM	111	BLR	101
041 Wheat, Meslin, Unmilled	481	4.8	21.9	-7.4	Achievers in adv.	UKR	267	KAZ	199	MDA	10
682 Copper	469	1.9	12.6	-5.5	Achievers in adv.	KAZ	369	UKR	51	UZB	30
282 Ferrous Waste and Scrap	463	7.6	63.0	-7.7	Achievers in adv.	UKR	345	KAZ	83	GEO	26
684 Aluminum	399	1.0	30.3	-1.2	Achievers in adv.	UKR	211	TJK	124	KAZ	44
562 Fertilizer, Except Grp272	390	2.8	—	-5.1		BLR	182	UKR	181	GEO	16
285 Aluminum Ore, Conctr., Etc.	374	8.0	-11.6	-0.8	Losers in decl. mkt	KAZ	230	UKR	141	AZE	3
522 Inorganic Chemical Elements	355	2.5	-2.8	-2.0	Losers in decl. mkt	UKR	271	KAZ	67	BLR	9
281 Iron Ore, Concentrates	328	3.3	4.2	-2.2	Achievers in adv.	UKR	252	KAZ	76		—
842 Women's, Girls' Clothing, X-Knit	320	0.8	—	2.1		UKR	196	BLR	77	MDA	31
288 Non-Ferrous Waste, Scrap	318	3.8	34.8	-5.2	Achievers in adv.	UKR	126	KAZ	116	KGZ	21
971 Gold, Nonmonetary Excl Ores	309	1.6	—	-2.8		KGZ	126	UZB	116	KAZ	49
679 Tubes, Pipes, Etc. Iron, Stl	281	1.6	-8.8	-1.2	Declining sectors	UKR	267	GEO	5	BLR	3
686 Zinc	219	4.8	43.2	4.9	Champions	KAZ	202	UZB	17	MDA	0
651 Textile Yarn	214	0.7	—	-1.5		UZB	86	BLR	41	TKM	38
792 Aircraft, Associated Equipment	196	0.2	—	14.5		KAZ	147	UKR	44	BLR	3
112 Alcoholic Beverages	195	0.7	-4.1	4.9	Underachievers	MDA	126	GEO	22	UKR	16
287 Ore, Concentrated Base Metals	194	3.7	21.2	-4.2	Achievers in adv.	KAZ	123	UKR	65	ARM	5
011 Bovine Meat	186	1.5	—	-2.3		UKR	157	MDA	13	KAZ	11
343 Natural Gas	182	0.6	22.8	1.6	Achievers in adv.	UKR	121	KAZ	61	TKM	0
841 Men's, Boys' Clothing, X-Knit	173	0.5	—	1.8		UKR	98	BLR	37	MDA	19
222 Oilseed (Sft. Fix Veg. Oil)	169	1.4	40.7	0.6	Achievers in adv.	UKR	147	MDA	10	GEO	7
121 Tobacco, Unmanufactured	168	2.7	36.4	2.8	Champions	KGZ	52	MDA	35	UZB	29
278 Other Crude Minerals	167	2.2	63.5	-1.7	Achievers in adv.	UKR	138	KAZ	16	BLR	9
674 Flat-Rolled Plated Iron	157	1.0	181.4	0.7	Achievers in adv.	KAZ	112	UKR	44	AZE	0
667 Pearls, Precious Stones	155	0.3	17.0	2.5	Champions	ARM	78	UKR	65	BLR	12
248 Wood, Simply Worked	137	0.5	60.5	-0.4	Achievers in adv.	BLR	67	UKR	61	GEO	7
321 Coal, Not Agglomerated	132	0.8	-7.2	-3.0	Losers in decl. mkt	KAZ	82	UKR	50	GEO	0
351 Electric Current	119	2.0	—	3.5		UKR	87	BLR	17	GEO	12
057 Fruit, Nuts Excl.Oil Nuts	119	0.4	33.6	0.7	Champions	KAZ	22	UZB	21	GEO	18
421 Fixed Veg. Fat, Oils, Soft	116	1.5	1.3	-2.5	Achievers in adv.	UKR	110	MDA	3	UZB	1
054 Vegetables	114	0.6	-0.1	-0.6	Achievers in adv.	KAZ	38	UZB	27	UKR	15
845 Other Textile Apparel, Nes	110	0.2	—	6.7		BLR	47	UKR	39	MDA	15
625 Rubber Tires, Tubes, Etc.	109	0.5	-8.8	3.2	Underachievers	UKR	97	BLR	12	ARM	0
525 Radioactive Materials	106	1.7	—	2.3		KAZ	57	UKR	35	GEO	12
714 Engines, Motors Non-Elect	102	0.2	22.4	16.2	Champions	UKR	99	UZB	1	TJK	1
652 Cotton Fabrics, Woven	101	0.6	—	-1.4		UZB	39	TKM	22	TJK	19

Source: International Trade Centre calculation based on UN COMTRADE statistics.
Note: "—" means data are unavailable.

percentage concerns nickel, one of the ten most important export products in terms of foreign exchange earnings. Aluminum, finally, has remained the fourth largest foreign exchange earner. With world trade in this highly energy-intensive good having stagnated in value terms in the second half of the 1990s, Russia has been able to increase its world market share to more than 10 percent.

There are also a number of areas where Russia has been able to raise its shares in dynamic markets of manufactured products, however. This applies, for instance, to telecommunications equipment and non-electronic motor engines, product categories for which world trade expanded by almost 10 percent and more than 16 percent, respectively, per annum in 1995 through 1999. Russian exporters have also been "champions" in exporting power-generating machinery and tools and certain electrical machinery. However, in most of these markets, Russia's importance remained relatively small, and export revenues accounted for only a rather small percentage.

Table 11: Main products of Russia's exports, 1995–1999, by SITC 3-digit code

Label	Exports 1999 (US$ million)	Share of Russia in world market (%)	Russia export growth, % per annum	World trade growth, % per annum	Russia export performance
333 Petroleum Oils, Crude	13,467	6.7	−7.5	−1.9	Losers in decl. mkt
343 Natural Gas	11,446	34.7	−7.4	1.6	Underachievers
334 Petroleum Products	5,359	7.0	—	−2.0	
684 Aluminum	4,121	10.2	3.9	−1.2	Achievers in adv.
673 Flat-Rolled Iron, Etc.	1,563	6.6	−6.3	−5.8	Losers in decl. mkt
672 Ingots Etc., Iron or Steel	1,524	18.1	−8.7	−5.5	Losers in decl. mkt
562 Fertilizer, Except Grp272	1,436	10.4	4.5	−5.1	Achievers in adv.
247 Wood Rough, Rough Squared	1,196	13.4	6.8	−7.9	Achievers in adv.
683 Nickel	1,126	22.7	−5.0	−3.8	Losers in decl. mkt
682 Copper	965	3.9	−4.4	−5.5	Achievers in adv.
793 Ship, Boat, Floating Structures	743	5.3	550.6	1.3	Champions
641 Paper and Paperboard	660	1.0	7.0	−1.4	Achievers in adv.
718 Other Power-Generating Machinery	658	11.3	81.5	4.2	Champions
248 Wood, Simply Worked	634	2.3	−0.6	−0.4	Losers in decl. mkt
695 Tools	627	3.5	584.7	2.5	Champions
282 Ferrous Waste and Scrap	614	10.1	26.4	−7.7	Achievers in adv.
891 Arms and Ammunition	597	15.2	1127.9	−2.0	Achievers in adv.
288 Non-Ferrous Waste, Scrap	490	5.9	36.2	−5.2	Achievers in adv.
676 Iron, Steel Bar, Shapes, Etc.	476	2.4	4.8	−4.0	Achievers in adv.
321 Coal, Not Agglomerated	436	2.6	−23.8	−3.0	Losers in decl. mkt
874 Measure, Control Instruments	424	0.7	133.9	4.1	Champions
671 Pig Iron, Spiegeleisn, Etc.	421	4.9	−1.8	−6.8	Achievers in adv.
699 Manufacts. Base Metal, Nes	415	0.9	43.5	6.7	Champions
714 Engines, Motors Non-Elect	381	0.9	17.7	16.2	Champions
522 Inorganic Chemical Elements	377	2.7	−5.4	−2.0	Losers in decl. mkt
251 Pulp and Waste Paper	367	2.1	−3.8	−8.8	Achievers in adv.
892 Printed Matter	306	1.2	4.2	1.7	Achievers in adv.
634 Veneers, Plywood, Etc.	275	1.7	16.8	0.6	Champions
232 Synthetic Rubber, Etc.	258	4.0	−15.9	−1.3	Losers in decl. mkt
689 Misc. Non-Ferrous Base Metal	250	6.9	−0.8	−0.5	Losers in decl. mkt
778 Electric Machine Appart. Nes	241	0.3	127.0	3.9	Champions
674 Flat-Rolled Plated Iron	207	1.3	4.8	0.7	Champions
781 Pass. Motor Vehicles. Ex. Bus	203	0.1	−30.1	6.7	Underachievers
764 Telecomm. Equip. Parts Nes	201	0.1	15.1	9.8	Champions
351 Electric Current	195	3.3	−23.6	3.5	Underachievers
511 Hydrocarbons, Nes, Derivatives	194	1.3	25.6	−4.6	Achievers in adv.
573 Polymers, Vinyl Chloride	192	2.7	31.4	−0.002	Achievers in adv.
034 Fish, Fresh, Chilled, Frozen	188	0.8	22.0	1.4	Champions
512 Alcohol, Phenol, Etc. Derivatives	175	1.5	−2.7	−4.6	Achievers in adv.
515 Organic-Inorganic Compounds	172	0.4	−2.9	12.5	Underachievers

Source: International Trade Centre calculation based on UN COMTRADE statistics.
Note: "—" means data are unavailable.

Finally, Tables 12 and 13 show the bilateral trade flows of parts and components between individual CEE countries and the EU.[viii] While the value of EU's exports of intermediate goods to these countries almost tripled between 1993 and 2000, the value of EU imports of such goods from the East has more than quadrupled.

A considerable percentage of foreign trade in parts and components between the EU and CEE represents intra-industry trade. In the late 1990s, the main intermediate goods exported by the EU comprised inputs for the production of motor vehicles, office equipment, telecommunications equipment, electricity equipment, and special industry machinery. Essentially, these products represent the most important items imported from the CEE. Although there is little information in the available statistics, there is reason to assume that a significant share of

imports and exports actually represents intra-firm trade. Indeed, a number of CEE countries have been important recipients of foreign direct investment (FDI) flows from EU members. This applies especially to the Czech Republic, Hungary, Poland, and Slovenia, which accounted for more than two-thirds of the CEE's imports from and exports to the EU in parts and components trade. The aggregated FDI inflows to these four countries rose from US$ 296 million in 1990 to almost US$ 15 billion in 1999 (World Bank 2001). According to UNCTAD's (2000) *World Investment Report*, the stock of inward FDI in the first three countries totaled around US$ 65 billion at end-1999, representing around two-thirds of the total stock in the CEE countries including the FSU.

Table 12. The European Union's exports of parts and components to CEE countries, US$ (million), 1993–2000

PARTNER	1993	1994	1995	1996	1997	1998	1999	2000
Bulgaria	93	121	166	145	135	180	207	155
Croatia	175	254	339	344	387	333	282	252
Czech Rep	870	1218	1786	2267	2521	2786	2907	3427
Hungary	766	1078	1666	2032	3132	3324	3732	3951
Poland	901	1123	2048	2691	3232	3222	3279	3364
Romania	165	197	304	356	397	414	478	568
Slovakia	219	341	668	762	894	1354	1268	1358
Slovenia	454	606	595	625	652	765	734	797
CEE countries, 8 total	**3,644**	**4,939**	**7,572**	**9,222**	**11,350**	**12,377**	**12,887**	**13,872**
World	141,256	160,073	196,488	208,393	206,517	218,789	224,193	215,652
Proportion	2.58	3.09	3.85	4.43	5.50	5.66	5.75	6.43

Source: Compiled by the authors based on UN COMTRADE database.

Table 13. The European Union's imports of parts and components from CEE countries, US$ (million), 1993–2000

PARTNER	1993	1994	1995	1996	1997	1998	1999	2000
Bulgaria	20	33	41	42	44	49	56	50
Croatia	49	61	73	64	58	85.12	93.82	92.81
Czech Rep	447	658	1,162	1,438	1,670	2,279	2,695	3,006
Hungary	503	722	1,030	1,250	1,541	2,152	2,561	2,698
Poland	291	419	695	790	993	1,189	1,420	1,625
Romania	23	39	90	147	166	221	319	394
Slovakia	61	153	337	413	493	672	737	706
Slovenia	265	345	454	444	458	568	562	597
CEE countries, 8 total	**1,658**	**2,430**	**3,881**	**4,589**	**5,423**	**7,216**	**8,445**	**9,169**
World	123,062	143,740	177,915	189,343	191,209	209,815	223,597	200,669
Proportion	1.35	1.69	2.18	2.42	2.84	3.44	3.78	4.57

Source: Compiled by the authors based on UN COMTRADE database.

Conclusions

In this paper, we have examined the extent to which central and eastern Europe has become more integrated with the EU through foreign trade. Starting from the pre-reform trade structure of the CEE and CIS, and early predictions of the re-direction of trade in the wake of their transition to market economies, we have analyzed the actual geographical distribution and the product composition of CEE's and CIS's foreign trade that have emerged over the past decade or so. The main findings are as follows:

- First, trade between CEE and the EU has intensified to an even larger extent than forecast by various gravity models at the beginning of the transition. As a matter of fact, the bilateral trade flows between CEE countries and the EU now account for around two-thirds of CEE's total trade. While the CIS countries, including Russia, have also become more integrated with the EU, the degree of integration has remained significantly smaller for these countries.

- Second, the re-direction of trade toward the EU has been accompanied by fundamental shifts in the composition of exports and imports. Manufactured goods, machinery and transportation equipment, along with miscellaneous manufactured articles, have become the driving forces of the trade integration, indicating the emergence of important competitive advantages in a number of the CEE countries.

- Third, Russia and, especially, the other members of the CIS, have made comparatively less progress in transforming their trade structures. The majority of their exports still consist of primary goods, whose importance in global trade has continued to decline.

- Fourth, trade integration between EU and CEE has been underpinned by growing production integration between these two economic areas. This is evidenced by continuously increasing bilateral trade flows in parts and components consistent with rising FDI flows.

With several countries in central and eastern Europe at the threshold to EU membership, there remains little doubt that trade integration will continue to intensify, resulting in a further re-direction of trade and changes in the product composition of exports and imports. Joining the European Monetary Union could result in a further boost, although this step does not seem imminent at this stage. To the extent that CIS countries speed up their economic transformation and open up their economies, they are also likely to become more integrated into the global economy and, more specifically, the EU. As the experience in other transition countries has shown, trade integration can be expected to be accompanied by increased FDI flows and production integration, fostering competitiveness and economic growth.

Trade Integration with the European Union: Where Do the Transition Economies Stand?

67

References

Baldwin, Richard E. 1994. *Towards an Integrated Europe* London: Centre for Economic Policy Research.

Belkindas, Misha V. and Matthew J. Sagers. 1990. "A Preliminary Analysis of Economic Relations among Union Republics of the USSR: 1970–1988," *Soviet Geography* 31 (November 1990)" 629–655.

Bergstrand, J. 1989. "The Generalized Gravity Equation, Monopolistic Competition and the Factors-Proportions Theory in International Trade," *The Review of Economics and Statistics* 71 (1989); 143–153.

Cicinskas, Jonas, Peter K. Cornelius, and Dalia Treigiene. 1996. "Trade Policies and Lithuania's Reintegration into the Global Economy," Working Paper No. 111. Stockholm: Stockholm Institute of East European Economies.

Collins, Susan M. and Dani Rodrik. 1991. *Eastern Europe and the Soviet Union in the World Economy.* Washington, DC: Institute for International Economics.

Halpern, Laszlo. 1994. "Comparative Advantage and Likely Trade Pattern of the CEECs," in *European Union Trade with Eastern Europe: Adjustment and Opportunities*, ed. by Riccardo Faini and Richard Portes. London: Centre for Economic Policy Research, pp. 61–85.

Helpman, Ehenan and Paul Krugman. 1985. *Market Structure and Foreign Trade.* Cambridge, Massachusetts and London: MIT Press.

IMF Direction of Trade database.

International Monetary Fund. 2001. Direction of Trade Statistics (Washington DC: International Monetary Fund, August.

Linnemann, H. 1966. *An Economic Study of International Trade Flows.* Amsterdam: North-Holland.

Nordhaus, William D., Merton J. Peck, and Thomas J. Richardson. 1991. "Do Borders Matter? Soviet Economic Reform after the Coup," *Brookings Papers on Economic Activity* 2 (1991): 321–340.

Rodrik, Dani. 1994. "Foreign Trade in Eastern Europe's Transition: Early Results," in *The Transition in Eastern Europe. Volume 2: Restructuring*, ed. by Olivier J. Blanchard, Kenneth A. Froot, and Jeffrey D. Sachs. Chicago and London: University of Chicago Press, pp. 319–352.

Rose, Andrew K. and Eric van Wincoop. 2001. "National Money as a Barrier to International Trade: The Real Case for Currency Union," *The American Economic Review* 91(2): 387–390.

United Nations Conference on Trade and Development. 2000. *World Investment Report.* New York and Geneva: United Nations.

UN COMTRADE database.

Winters, L. Alan and Zhen Kun Wang. 1994. *Eastern Europe's International Trade.* Manchester and New York: Manchester University Press.

The World Bank. 2001. *World Development Indicators.* Washington, DC: The World Bank.

World Economic Forum, *The Global Competitiveness Report 2001–2002.* 2001. Oxford: Oxford University Press.

Notes

[i] Unless otherwise specified, we use the acronym *CEE* for all transition economies in central and eastern Europe covered in this *Report*. The CIS members encompass the countries of the former Soviet Union (FSU) minus the three Baltic economies of Estonia, Latvia, and Lithuania, which are included in the CEE countries.

[ii] The data reported in Table 1 are taken from Winters and Wang (1994, p. 22). Although the authors have made important efforts to cross-check the data, they do emphasize that the figures are subject to severe reservations. Specifically, they point out (p. 21) that the data come from two different sources. For Hungary, Poland, and Romania, trade data are based on the IMF's Direction of Foreign Trade (DOT), which also provides the source for market economies' foreign trade. For other CEE countries, however, data were taken from various issues of *PlanEcon* for mutual trade. While the *PlanEcon* data for these countries' trade with market economies and for Hungary, Poland and Romania's total trade appear to match the DIT data reasonably well, this depends on two potentially highly distorted exchange rates. Intra-CMEA trade used to be reported in terms of so-called transferable rubles, requiring the authors to convert these first into local currency and then into dollars according to conversion factors provided by *PlanEcon*. According to Winters and Wang (1994, p. 21), there are two particular features that make the conversion factors, and hence the trade data, suspicious. First, the implied exchange rates between the transferable ruble and the dollar vary strongly by country and, second, the value of dollar trade suggested by the conversation factors appears huge for at least Bulgaria, the former Czechoslovakia, and former East Germany. Nevertheless, lacking more reliable sources, these data have generally been used by other researchers as well.

[iii] It has often been argued that the gravity model suffers from the absence of a cogent derivation based on economic theory. Although the gravity model may tell us something about what happens in international trade, it does not tell us why. For a discussion, see, for example, Winters and Wang (1994, pp. 13–15) and especially Baldwin (1994, pp. 82–87), who argues that the approach does have theoretical foundations related, inter alia, to the work of Helpman and Krugman (1985) and Bergstrand (1989).

[iv] Consisting of a single equation, bilateral trade flows are generally assumed to depend on five factors: the GDPs of the two countries, their populations, and the distance between them, with all variables in logs and X_{xi} representing exports for the exporter (country x) to the importer (country i), GDP and POP representing total GDP and populations of the relevant countries, and DISTxi being the distance between the two countries:

$$X_{xi} = \text{\ss}_0 + \text{\ss}_1(GDP_i/POP_i) + \text{\ss}_2 GDP_i +$$
$$\text{\ss}_3(GDP_x/POP_x) + \text{\ss}_4 GDP_x + \text{\ss}_5 DIST_{xi} + \text{dummies.}$$

Although this equation appears fairly straightforward, the model's empirical implementation faces a number of important challenges. First, appropriate level of product aggregation and country coverage need to be determined. As regards the latter, one particular problem may arise from the fact that for a few bilateral trade relations there is no reported trade. However, since the model is estimated in logs, solving this problem requires dropping such flows from the sample, substitute small values for the zeros, or using Tobit model estimation techniques, for example. Moreover, there are usually considerable discrepancies between import values reported by the importing country and export values reported by the exporting country. See, for example, Rodrik 1994. Second, obtaining trade flow data in volume terms is often difficult. Many researchers therefore run their regressions on value data. This is a valid procedure as long as single years are considered. However, using panel data for several years, which is clearly preferable to a single-year approach, requires volume data. Third, the measurement of distance is a difficult issue, and approaches to overcome this problem have differed considerably. For example, while some studies have tried to measure transport distance, others have relied on straight-line distances between capitals.

[v] In a first step, Collins and Rodrik (1991) fit an openness relationship across 91 countries, regressing the exports-to-GNP ratio on GNP, log GNP, log population, and a series of dummies, and then apply this to the estimates of GNP from *PlanEcon*. Regarding the geographical distribution of trade, they then estimate Western partners' shares in each CEE country's total exports and imports by updating a 1928 trade matrix. In a third step, they run a regression model on trade shares from six comparator countries (Austria, Finland, Germany, Italy, Spain, and Portugal), regressing partners shares in these countries' totals in 1989 on a constant, the corresponding shares in 1928 and a series of dummies for each partner. Finally, they apply this estimated relationship to East European trade shares in 1928 to predict their patterns in 1989.

[vi] CEE-12 comprises Albania, Bosnia Herzegovina, Bulgaria, Croatia, Czech Republic, Hungary, Macedonia, Poland, Romania, Slovak Republic, Slovenia, and Yugoslavia.

[vii] All the trade flows data are compiled in current dollar terms; this may generate bias when we compare trade flows over time. However, as the inflation rates in the United States in 1989–2000 are rather low and stable, the bias is not significant and does not affect the overall conclusions.

[viii] Tables 12 and 13 show the data for only eight CEE countries: Bulgaria, Croatia, Czech Republic, Hungary, Poland, Romania, Slovakia, and Slovenia. These eight countries represent the majority of the trade in parts and components with EU.

The Cost of Capital and the Need to be CLEAR

PETER CORNELIUS, World Economic Forum

THOMAS HALL, University of Alabama in Huntsville

JOEL A. KURTZMAN, PricewaterhouseCoopers

FIONA PAUA, World Economic Forum

Introduction

The access of central and eastern European countries to international debt capital markets remains limited. As indicated by their small shares in the various benchmark emerging market bond indexes (eg, JP Morgan's Emerging Markets Bond Index (EMBI) + and the Euro EMBI Global Index), relatively few countries in transition have been able to issue international bonds. Although the sovereign debt of some countries has been assigned investment grade, in many cases bonds are considered to be highly speculative. To compensate for the substantial perceived risk of these instruments, investors are demanding higher interest rates. Thus, while yield spreads vis-à-vis mature markets, such as US Treasuries or Bunds (10-year German government bonds), have declined appreciably since the Russian crisis in mid-1998, they have remained sizeable. Consequently, foreign borrowing remains a costly source of balance-of-payments and budgetary financing.

The interest premium demanded by international investors reflects their evaluation of the risk that the issuer may be unable or unwilling to repay and service the debt. This risk is typically higher in the case of bonds issued in foreign (hard) currency as opposed to debt instruments in local currency. In order to be able to repay foreign currency bonds, countries must "earn" foreign exchange reserves through current or capital account transactions. By contrast, taxes are usually paid in domestic currency, making it comparatively easier for governments to service local debt. Even if investing in local-currency bonds creates exchange-rate risk for foreigners, the ratings agencies have, in most cases, attached relatively lower grades to foreign currency bonds.

The perceived risk of debt default generally varies inversely with investors' views of a country's ability to achieve sustained economic growth. It follows, then, that macroeconomic management plays an important role in this regard. However, other factors are equally, if not more, critical, as observers increasingly recognize. Many transition economies continue to suffer from serious institutional weaknesses. In several of these economies, the regulatory burden appears excessively cumbersome, corruption is common, and the rule of law is widely perceived to be insufficient. Further, in some countries the administrative capacity of the authorities has remained weak, and government operations are often inefficient. By raising the perceived risk of debt default, all these factors affect the cost at which governments can borrow from abroad.

Other factors, of course, affect the price tag at which countries—and firms located within those countries—are able to borrow. One such factor is investor confidence that government policies are understandable, consistent, reliable, and predictable. In a word, investors will demand a greater premium on loaned funds if government policies are not transparent. Where opacity dominates the investment environment, bondholders will demand a higher premium.

How big is this opacity premium? And by how much could the cost of capital facing the sovereign borrowing programs of national governments be reduced by becoming CLEAR? This acronym, derived from the PricewaterhouseCoopers Opacity Index, indicates five aspects of opacity: (1) Corruption; (2) Legal opacity; (3) opacity in government Economic policies; (4) opacity in Accounting standards and information release by corporations, banks, and governments; and (5) Regulatory opacity. These two related questions are the focus of the present chapter, which is based on an ongoing project of the PricewaterhouseCoopers Endowment for the Study of Transparency and Sustainability.

In the balance of this paper, we discuss the progress of central and eastern Europe (CEE), including the Baltic states and member countries of the Commonwealth of Independent States (CIS), in terms of upgrading their governance structures and reducing opacity as they make the transition to market economies. We then assess the access of these countries to international debt capital markets and the importance of sovereign bond issuance to the region's balance-of-payments needs. Thereafter, we describe in greater detail the CLEAR factors as variables affecting the cost of capital, and we outline our approach to estimating their effects. Building on our quantitative estimates, we conclude with a discussion of policies necessary to reduce opacity and, in turn, lower the high-risk premium paid by many CEE countries.

Economic transformation and opacity

As discussed in other chapters of this *Report*, most EU accession countries started to introduce comprehensive reform programs at the beginning of the 1990s, led by Poland (January 1990) and Hungary (March 1990). After the collapse of the former Soviet Union (FSU), the Baltic countries (Estonia, Latvia, and Lithuania) followed suit in mid-1992. By contrast, reform efforts in many other FSU republics began in earnest only with considerable delay, and in some, notably Turkmenistan, economic transformation has been extremely limited (Fischer and Sahay 2000).

Initially, many countries perceived macroeconomic stabilization as the most urgent reform task; it was considered a prerequisite to arresting and reversing the sharp fall in output characterizing the period immediately after the beginning of the "transition" phase of political and economic reform away from state socialism. Soon, however, a general consensus emerged on the desirability of introducing a comprehensive approach encompassing liberalization, structural transformation, and institutional change. Virtually all of the reform programs have received substantial external assistance from various sources, including the International Monetary Fund (IMF), the World Bank, and the European Bank for Reconstruction and Development (EBRD).

Although at the beginning of the present decade, some of the early reformers were able to reach their pre-reform level of output or even exceed it (notably Poland), others, where progress has remained less advanced, have yet fully to recover from the decline in economic activity at the onset of the transition. This applies especially to many FSU countries, but also to some other countries such as Bulgaria and Romania.

To be sure, all transition countries, including those relatively advanced in the transformation process, continue to face important challenges in structural reform and institution building. Although most countries have achieved significant progress in privatizing small enterprises and reforming their trade and foreign exchange regimes, it has proved much more difficult to develop well-functioning securities markets and non-bank financial institutions and to implement an efficient competition policy. In several countries, however, the most daunting task continues to lie in creating market-supporting institutions, improving governance, and accelerating enterprise reform (EBRD 2000).

Institutional performance in the CEE countries, the Baltics, and the CIS continues to vary widely. According to a study by Weder (2000), only Hungary and Slovenia currently possess an institutional framework the quality of which approaches that of the European Union and other industrialized countries. While Poland, the Czech Republic, the Slovak Republic, and the Baltics also enjoy relatively well-functioning market-supporting institutions, most CIS countries lag substantially behind (see Table 1). This assessment is based on five indicators: (1) voice and accountability, (2) government effectiveness, (3) regulatory burden, (4) rule of law, and (5) graft, with the overall index calculated as a simple average ranging from −25 to +25. Taking into account that data uncertainty and differing degrees of coverage and data availability for different countries make precise rankings difficult, the individual countries are then grouped into five quintiles.

71

Table 1. Institutional quality: Quintiles, 1997–1998

HIGHEST QUINTILE	
Hungary	(8.0)
Slovenia	(8.0)
SECOND QUINTILE	
Poland	(6.7)
Czech Rep.	(6.6)
Estonia	(5.8)
Lithuania	(2.4)
Latvia	(2.2)
Slovak Rep.	(2.1)
THIRD QUINTILE	
Croatia	(–0.5)
Bulgaria	(–0.8)
Moldova	(–2.0)
FOURTH QUINTILE	
Macedonia	(–3.2)
Armenia	(–4.3)
Russia	(–5.1)
Kyrgyz Rep.	(–5.6)
Georgia	(–5.8)
Ukraine	(–6.4)
Kazakhstan	(–6.8)
LOWEST QUINTILE	
Albania	(–6.5)
Belarus	(–8.3)
Azerbaijan	(–8.6)
Bosnia Herzegovina	(–9.6)
Uzbekistan	(–11.8)
Turkmenistan	(–13.8)
Tajikistan	(–14.3)

Source: Weder (2000).

72

Table 2. Public institutions index

PUBLIC INSTITUTIONS		CONTRACTS AND LAW		CORRUPTION	
Country	**Index**	**Country**	**Index**	**Country**	**Index**
Hungary	5.20	Hungary	4.70	Lithuania	6.07
Estonia	4.99	Estonia	4.55	Hungary	5.69
Slovenia	4.90	Slovenia	4.50	Estonia	5.42
Lithuania	4.70	Poland	4.32	Slovenia	5.29
Slovak Rep.	4.54	Romania	4.30	Slovak Rep.	5.13
Poland	4.40	Slovak Rep.	3.95	Bulgaria	5.12
Latvia	4.18	Czech Rep.	3.85	Latvia	4.73
Bulgaria	4.07	Latvia	3.62	Poland	4.48
Romania	4.06	Lithuania	3.34	Russia	4.38
Czech Rep.	4.04	Bulgaria	3.01	Czech Rep.	4.23
Russia	3.68	Russia	2.97	Romania	3.82
Ukraine	3.15	Ukraine	2.84	Ukraine	3.47

Source: *Global Competitiveness Report 2001–2002*

Weder's assessment is based on work performed at the World Bank (Kaufmann et al 1999), aimed at aggregating a large number of different governance indicators for around 150 countries. Specifically, more than 300 such indicators have been included from two types of sources: ratings produced by commercial risk ratings agencies and other institutions, reflecting expert opinions; and surveys of firms and households, compiled by international organizations and other institutions. These indicators are grouped into six categories, among which political instability and violence represent an additional indicator not considered by Weder (2000).

Unfortunately, there exist no time series data for the index of institutional quality employed by Weder, which is based solely on data collected for the period 1997 to 1998. One important source for calculating the index as a comparative snapshot of the situation at that time was the World Economic Forum's Executive Opinion Survey. What do this year's Survey results tell us about the further progress of individual countries in upgrading their institutional frameworks?

Table 2 presents a public institutions index for the transition economies included in the *Global Competitiveness Report 2001–2002*. The index is comprised of two subindexes of equal weight, a contracts and law index and a corruption index. The first consists of the average score of economies on questions concerning neutrality in government procurement, judicial independence, clear delineation and respect for property rights, and costs related to organized crime. The latter measures the pervasiveness of bribery in three key public service areas: imports and exports, connection to public utilities, and tax collection. The public institutions index and the two subindexes range from a score of 1 (poor institutional framework) to 7 (excellent institutional framework).

Overall, Table 2 suggests that there remain important differences among the countries in transition with respect to their institutional development. Hungary and Slovenia continue to be the most advanced economies in central and eastern Europe, but the Baltics seem to be catching up. Poland, a leader in Weder's quality index, seems to have been slipping relative to others. This does not necessarily mean that Poland's institutional framework has actually deteriorated; rather, others are perceived to have moved ahead faster. In this context, note that Poland scores relatively poorly in terms of the perceived degree of corruption, both in absolute terms and relative to the transition economies. Finally, Russia and the Ukraine remain at the bottom of the rankings, a finding consistent with Weder's quality index.

Although the public institutions index and the institutional quality index are not directly comparable, they both suggest that the lack of institutions and governance represent an important challenge in the further transition process. Although some countries are more advanced than others, it appears that even the top performers need to continue institutional reforms.

The channels through which such reforms affect economic growth are complex. In the following, we focus on the cost of capital in an attempt to attach a price tag to opacity.

Balance-of-payments needs and international bond financing

Transforming the former centrally planned economies into market-oriented economies requires substantial resources. Old plants and equipment, meant for production of low-quality communist-era goods, must be retooled. Competitive new industries must be financed, and old firms must be restructured. Most countries undergoing this transition have witnessed a substantial surge in imports of goods and capital. As a result, their aggregate current account deficit widened markedly from around US$5 billion in 1992 to almost US$30 billion in 1998. With international reserves initially low or nonexistent, the current account gap was largely determined by the availability of external financing from official creditors, including the IMF and the World Bank, and private sources. Foreign direct investment (FDI) inflows increased considerably during this period but remained concentrated on relatively few countries. Portfolio investment inflows also increased appreciably until 1998; however, they have fallen sharply in the aftermath of Russia's debt default.

Debt issuance from central and eastern Europe lags in comparison to debt issuance from peers. As of 2000, the external debt stock of Latin America and East Asia comprised 32 percent and 26 percent of total emerging market debt stock, respectively, while the external debt of transition economies accounts for only 15 percent of the total.

Nevertheless, external borrowing has increased dramatically over the last 10 years. Aggregate external debt rose from US$152 billion in 1990 to US$381 billion in 2000. Within the region, nearly all countries posted increases in external debt in the last decade. During this period, Russia borrowed a net US$113 billion. Other countries, such as Armenia, Georgia, Kyrgyz Republic, Moldova, and Tajikistan experienced high increases in percentage terms, as these countries had minimal external debt at the beginning of the transition.

Although the expansion of external debt stock in the region has been remarkable, it masks a lack of access to private financing in international debt markets. Indeed, a closer examination of the composition of debt reveals that for many transition countries, much of the debt stock consists of concessional credit from bilateral and multilateral sources rather than debt securities issued abroad to private bondholders. Armenia is a case in point, with 94 percent of its external debt consisting of multilateral claims and official bilateral loans. Other countries that have over 80 percent of external debt stock from bilateral and multilateral sources include Tajikistan, Albania, Kyrgyz Republic, Ukraine, and Georgia.

As of the year 2000, ten countries—Albania, Armenia, Azerbaijan, Belarus, Georgia, Kyrgyz Republic, Macedonia, Tajikistan, Turkmenistan, and Uzbekistan—have not issued debt securities abroad. Yugoslavia and Moldova have been able to issue debt securities, but in only minimal amounts, at US$10 million and US$75 million, respectively.

Countries that have been able to raise substantial amounts of capital from international debt markets were able to do so mostly within a limited time period—from 1995 to 1997—when overall flows to emerging markets were increasing. From barely US$4 billion in 1994, international bond placements in the region grew to US$16 billion in 1997, a fourfold increase. Even during this 3-year period, however, the region comprised, at most, 13 percent of international bond placements from developing countries.

Sovereign debt issuance gained momentum rapidly in the region in 1996, the year when 12 countries managed to raise capital in international debt markets. The Czech Republic, Russia, and Romania each raised over a billion dollars. In 1997, encouraged by the successful placements of the previous year, 13 countries from the region issued debt securities. Russia alone increased its issuance to nearly US$7 billion. Other notable borrowers in 1997 were Croatia and Ukraine, which issued international bonds amounting to US$530 million and US$450 million, respectively.

That the bulk of sovereign debt issuance occurred during the 1995 to 1997 period is not surprising, given the favorable environment for sovereign issuers at that time. During this period, average bond maturities lengthened as investor confidence was bolstered by the structural reforms that accompanied the improvement in economic fundamentals of various emerging markets. More important still, the cost of issuing sovereign debt fell dramatically as interest spreads contracted to reflect growing investor appetite for emerging market bonds. Secondary market yield spreads in the EMBI fell from 1,752 basis points in March 1995 to 537 basis points by the end of 1996. By 1997, Romania was able to sell a 5-year 600 million German mark bond yielding 7.75 percent, a mere 300 basis point premium over comparable German government debt—a remarkable feat, given that the country carried a noninvestment-grade credit rating.

Access to international credit markets started to deteriorate in late 1997 when investor appetite for emerging market securities waned as a result of the Asian financial crisis. Fears of contagion arose as the Czech Republic experienced its own financial crisis in the same year. Increased perception of risk was evident in the rise in yield spreads of the EMBI (excluding Russia) from about 450 basis points prior to the Asian crisis in April 1997 to above 600 basis points by November 1997.

But the event that most severely curtailed the region's ability to tap international debt markets occurred on August 17, 1998, when Russia stopped payment on US$40 billion worth of bonds and allowed its currency to devalue. When news of Russia's partial debt moratorium was released, yield spreads on the EMBI excluding Russia rose above 1,400 basis points from the 780 basis points that had prevailed several days earlier. Russia itself saw its secondary-market yield spreads hover near 7,000 basis points, up from 400 basis points a year earlier. Sovereign issuers most adversely affected were Ukraine, Romania, and Kazakhstan, which saw yield spreads increase to 9,000 basis points, 5,700 basis points, and 2,300 basis points respectively, between 1997 and 1998. Not surprisingly, the pipeline for new sovereign issues slowed to a trickle in the year following the Russian default. Yield spreads began to recover in 2000 and the first half of 2001, with the EMBI spreads (premium over industrialized country debt) hovering at about the 700-basis-point level (International Monetary Fund 2001).

Although the new issue pipeline and yield spreads have not recovered to pre-Russian crisis levels, one of the remarkable developments that has since emerged in the region is the issuance of bonds denominated in euro. Hungary was the first to issue bonds in euro in 1999, at favorable terms with a yield of only 70 basis points higher than comparable German Bunds and 30 basis points above Euribor. This year, Poland launched 10-year euro bonds at

a spread over German Bunds and Euribor of 80 basis points and 35 basis points respectively. More recently, in the aftermath of the Turkey crisis, Croatia launched its first benchmark 10-year euro bond and was able to garner a spread of 215 basis points over comparable German Bunds. The favorable reception to the euro bond placements of these sovereign issuers—Hungary, Poland, and Croatia—can be attributed to the limited supply of investment-grade European Union accession/convergence plays. This means that, even at this stage, investors anticipate capital gains from the decline in interest rate differentials that is expected to occur as the accession candidates implement institutional and other reforms in their bid to join the European Union.

Estimates of the cost of opacity in transition economies

Although some of the incremental cost of government borrowings can be realistically attributed to crises and their aftermath, some countries in the region face higher costs than others even when no crisis threatens. As the previous section has shown, investors demand a lower premium on Hungarian debt than, for example, on debt issued by Croatia. One reason for this difference is that Hungary has a thriving industrial sector exporting products to the European Union and abroad (a success purchased at the cost of a relatively deep restructuring, including a large infusion of foreign direct investment accompanied by skilled managers trained abroad). As long as such markets continue to purchase Hungarian goods, a stable flow of hard currency will result. Thus, the ability of Hungary to service hard-currency-denominated debt is fairly secure.

Another reason why borrowers may demand a higher premium in some countries than in others has to do with their assessment of the government issuing sovereign debt. Governments perceived to be riddled with corruption, inconsistent in applying regulations, lax in the administration of policies, rules, and procedures, and burdened with inadequate legal and accounting systems will pay more for their capital. These are kinds of opacity, and they return us to the PricewaterhouseCoopers Opacity Index, based on five CLEAR factors as discussed in the first section of this paper. The higher the level of opacity, the lower the degree of trust among informed investors, and the higher the premium the government must pay to access international capital markets.

Table 3. Opacity in central and eastern Europe

Country	O-Factor	Borrowing Premium	Tax-Equivalent	Deterred FDI	Deterred FDI (millions of USD)
Czech Republic	71	8.99%	33%	194%	5,964
Hungary	50	3.70%	17%	83%	1,738
Lithuania	58	5.84%	23%	128%	768
Poland	64	7.24%	28%	157%	9,874
Romania	71	9.15%	34%	197%	2,874
Russia	84	12.25%	43%	263%	9,802
FOR COMPARISON:					
United States	36	n/a	n/a	n/a	n/a
United Kingdom	38	n/a	n/a	n/a	n/a

The Opacity Index is based on a survey of knowledgeable individuals (bankers, corporate chief financial officers, equity analysts, and in-country PricewaterhouseCoopers personnel), from which statistically valid estimates are developed. As Table 3 illustrates, the O-factor—a measure of the degree of opacity in various countries around the world—varies somewhat among transitional economies. The table includes all countries in central and eastern Europe surveyed in the initial round of Index, published in January 2001. As in the other indicators thus far explored in this paper, Russia performs the worst while Hungary performs the best.

The various columns in the table demonstrate different ways of measuring the negative effects of opacity (the first few columns are based on Barth et al 2001). In the O-factor column, which indicates the overall opacity score derived from survey responses, a higher score indicates greater opacity. In the adjoining column, the borrowing premium reflects the addition to sovereign rates of borrowing estimated to result from opacity, assuming that a higher O-factor affects all countries in the same way. This number is based on statistical regression analysis, with the dependent variable being the premium or spread above the US sovereign bond yield (holding for accumulated foreign reserves). Essentially, the column indicates that countries with higher levels of opacity will have to pay more for the same debt. For example, Lithuania has to pay 5.84 percent more on sovereign debt than it would have to pay if it had the same level of opacity as, say, the United States or Great Britain.

The tax-equivalent column shows another way to measure the effects of opacity, which can be viewed as a hidden surtax on foreign direct investment and ongoing corporate operations in a host country. In Poland, for example, the Index in combination with other publicly available data estimates that opacity levies a hidden 28-percent tax on FDI, with a resulting decline in the amount of FDI that Poland is able to attract.

Another way to view the implications of opacity on foreign direct investment is indicated in the last two columns, based on statistical analysis of the effect of opacity on the quantity of FDI during the period 1997 to 1999 (Wei and Hall 2001). During this time, the effects of the Asian and Russian financial crises had a large impact on portfolio flows. However, FDI tends to be less sensitive than portfolio flows to year-on-year fluctuations. For this reason, these numbers probably reflect the long-term effects of opacity. The columns indicating deterred FDI indicate, for example, that if Russia were able to reduce its opacity to the level of the opacity of the United States or the United Kingdom, it would receive more than two-and-a-half times as much foreign direct investment—nearly US$10 billion more in FDI.[i] As noted earlier, only a few countries in the region account for most of the FDI directed there. It is probably no coincidence that the Czech Republic, Hungary, and Poland, with O-factors of less than 62, receive significantly more FDI than, say, Romania and Russia, with average O-factors of about 78.

Conclusion

The cost of capital in central and eastern Europe is determined by two major forces: factors that are little if at all under the control of governments (eg, the Asian and Russian financial crises of 1997 and 1998) and factors that can indeed be controlled (eg, the level of opacity/transparency across the CLEAR dimensions).

Overall, investors are skeptical of the willingness of governments in central and eastern Europe to honor debt obligations. Some countries, however, have been much better able to commit credibly to servicing international debt, and these countries enjoy the benefits of cheaper borrowing. Many former Soviet countries, such as Azerbaijan, Georgia, and the Central Asian states, have been unable to access private international debt markets during the decade following the break-up of the Soviet Union, even in favorable climates for emerging-market bond issuance. On the other hand, countries in east central Europe have been more successful: Hungary and Slovenia have been able to borrow abroad, sometimes in significant amounts and at a low premium over what is charged to EU countries such as Germany.

Patterns of foreign direct investment mirror the pattern of sovereign debt. The Czech Republic, Hungary, and Poland, for example, have been able to attract significant quantities of FDI, measured on a per capita basis. This reflects the willingness of national authorities to sell some former state-owned assets to foreigners, as well as the willingness of foreigners to trust those governments. At the same time, statistical analysis of the level of opacity shows that the amount of foreign direct investment could be increased by cultivating a more transparent environment.

Governments often cannot affect the international environment, where a crisis in one part of the world spills over in the form of higher borrowing costs elsewhere. However, the level of opacity can be altered over time, with due effort and consultation, by national authorities. Given the positive benefits of a lower cost of capital, and arguably other social benefits as well, the clear policy implication of this analysis is that governments can benefit in tangible ways by reducing corruption, increasing the efficiency and professionalism of their legal system, maintaining consistent and predictable rules for setting economic policy, enhancing accounting transparency, and enacting clear and consistently enforced regulations. [ii] These are the CLEAR dimensions of opacity, and they are, in our view, as much a part of the infrastructure of economic progress as good roads, good railways, and good telecommunications.

References

Barth, James R., Thomas W. Hall, Joel Kurtzman, Shang-Jin Wei, and Glenn Yago. . *The Opacity Index*. January, 2001. Available at www.opacityindex.com.

European Bank for Reconstruction and Development. 2000. *Transition Report 2000*. London: EBRD.

Fischer, Stanley and Ratna Sahay. 2000. "The Transition Economies After Ten Years," IMF Working Paper 00/30. Washington, DC: International Monetary Fund.

Hall, Thomas. *Opacity in Latin America: The Economic Costs of Opacity in Mercosur and Neighboring Countries*. May, 2001. Available at www.opacityindex.com.

International Monetary Fund. Emerging Market Financing: Quarterly Report on Developments and Prospects. August 8, 2001. Washington, DC: International Monetary Fund.

International Monetary Fund. *World Economic Outlook: Focus on Transition Economies*. October 2000. Washington, DC: International Monetary Fund.

International Monetary Fund. *International Capital Markets: Developments, Prospects, and Key Policy Issues*. September 1999. Washington, DC: International Monetary Fund.

International Monetary Fund. *International Capital Markets: Developments, Prospects, and Key Policy Issues*. November 1997. Washington, DC: International Monetary Fund.

Joint BIS-IMF-OECD-World Bank Statistics on External Debt. http://www.oecd.org/dac/debt/.

Kaufmann, Daniel, Aart Kraay, and Pablo Zoido-Lobatón. 1999. Governance Matters. World Bank PRD Working Paper No. 2196. Washington DC: The World Bank.

Weder, Beatrice. 2000. Institutional Reform in Transition Economies: How Far Have they Come? Unpublished; Washington, DC: International Monetary Fund.

Wei, Shang-Jin and Thomas Hall. *Investigating the Costs of Opacity: Deterred Foreign Direct Investment*. April, 2001. Available at www.opacityindex.com.

The World Bank. *Global Development Finance 1997*. Washington, DC: The World Bank.

World Economic Forum, *The Global Competitiveness Report 2001–2002*. 2001. Oxford: Oxford University Press.

Notes

i These calculations assume that the level of opacity elsewhere remained the same. For details on empirical specification, etc., please see the technical appendix in Wei and Hall (2001).

ii For example, in Latin America at least, opacity seems, on initial analysis, to be related to less deep capital markets and greater income inequality, as measured by the gini coefficient. See Hall (2001).

Part 2

European Enlargement:
The View from Important Regions

European Union Enlargement: Economic Consequences and Perspectives for the European Union

JAN FIDRMUC, SUSANNE MUNDSCHENK, IULIA TRAISTARU,
and **JÜRGEN VON HAGEN,** Center for European Integration
Studies, University of Bonn

Introduction

The European Union (EU) is preparing itself for the next round of enlargement, which could eventually bring the number of its members up to 27. Ten candidate countries aim to complete negotiations in 2002. As the European Council at Nice decided last year, they could then participate in the next European Parliament elections, implying that they would become regular members by June 2004. This puts a rather tight clock on the process of negotiations, as enlargement requires a full-fledged revision of the Treaty on European Union and, therefore, a full round of ratifications by the incumbent members. Currently, the issues that remain to be resolved in the ongoing negotiations are agriculture, regional policy, budget institutions, and "other." The first three issues, which have important financial implications for the EU, are to be negotiated between the EU and the candidates within the existing budgetary framework for the period 2000 to 2006, which was passed in 1999 to provide a basis sufficient for the accession of 10 Member States in 2004.

How will the next enlargement change the EU and its policies? This paper develops some perspectives on this question. We begin with a short description of the economic characteristics of the prospective new members. This serves to point out two important facts about the enlargement. The first is that, despite the large number of potential entrants, the enlargement is small in economic terms from the point of view of the current EU. Although accession is a big economic event for the new members, the overall economic consequences of the next enlargement on the incumbent EU economies will be small.[i] Available estimates of the costs and benefits of enlargement (Baldwin et al 1997; Breuss 2001) indicate that the overall balance will be positive for the new members and the incumbent EU states. Breuss (2001) estimates that most of the incumbent EU members will experience gains on the order of 0.5 percent of GDP in the first six years and 0.25 percent over the following 10 years after the enlargement. The small size of the expected overall benefits is reflected in the noticeable absence of interest in the issue among the incumbent EU population. Eurobarometer polls indicate that less than 30 percent of EU citizens regard enlargement as a political priority (Heinemann, 2000). This does not preclude the possibility that the enlargement will have large effects on individual sectors, regions, or specific policies in the incumbent EU. Regarding regional effects, Breuss (2001) estimates that the largest gains will accrue to the countries bordering East and Central Europe, Austria, Germany, and Italy, while Spain, Portugal, Sweden, and Denmark may incur modest losses. We think that enlargement will have important consequences in three areas: EU institutions, labor markets, and regional and structural policies.

The second point is that the enlargement will increase the heterogeneity among the EU Member States significantly. This implies that the current pattern of transfers among the EU members will change, with some current net recipients loosing out, and that the demand for income redistribution in the EU will increase. The reform of EU institutions is affected by this tendency, as the richer among the incumbent members will want to protect themselves against a future majority of poor states.

Basic economic characteristics

EU enlargement to include 12 candidate countries (AC-12: Bulgaria, Cyprus, the Czech Republic, Estonia, Hungary, Latvia, Lithuania, Malta, Poland, Romania, Slovakia, and Slovenia) will increase the EU population by 28 percent and its area by 34 percent, while its GDP (at current exchange rates) will grow by only 5 percent and the EU average GDP per capita will be reduced by 15 percent.[ii] Although the size of the forthcoming enlargement is comparable with the entry of Greece, Spain, and Portugal in the 1980s, which added 22 percent to the EU population, the income differential between the incumbent and the new members is much larger.

As indicated by Table 1, average per-capita GDP of AC-12 measured in purchasing power standards (PPS) was, in 1998, 38 percent of the EU-15. In comparison, in 1980, the per capita GDP of Greece, Spain, and Portugal was 66 percent of the then EC-9 average. The combined GDP of AC-12 represents only 5 percent of the EU-15 GDP at current exchange rates and 11 percent in PPS. In contrast, the combined GDP of Greece, Spain, and Portugal was 10 percent at current exchange rates and 14 percent in PPS.

As shown in Table 2, a number of structural differences between EU-15 and AC-12 are significant. Employment by sector in AC-12 indicates greater shares of agriculture, 21 percent, compared with 5 percent for the EU-15 and a lower share of services, 47 percent, compared with 66 percent for the EU-15. Although employment rates (percent of population aged 15–64) are similar, female employment is higher and male employment is lower in the AC-12 than in the EU-15. The productivity level in AC-12 is 40 percent of the EU-15. The population in AC-12 is relatively younger: the share of those under 15 years is 20 percent compared with 17 percent for the EU-15, while those over 65 years amount to 13 percent of the population compared to 16 percent in EU-15. Population density (pop/km^2) is slightly lower in AC-12 (97.6) compared with the EU average (117.3).

Table 1. Key indicators related to the EU enlargement to AC-12 and the southern enlargement of 1980s

	EU-15, 1998	AC-12, 1998	EC-9, 1980	Greece, Spain, Portugal, 1980
GDP per capita in PPS	100	38.1	100	65.9
Population	100	28.1	100	21.6
GDP	100	4.6	100	7.7
GDP in PPS		10.7	100	9.8

EC-9: European Community: Belgium, Denmark, Germany, France, Ireland, Italy, Luxemburg, The Netherlands, and the United Kingdom.

EU-15: EC-9 plus Greece, Spain, Portugal, Austria, Finland, and Sweden.

AC-12: Bulgaria, Cyprus, Czech Republic, Estonia, Hungary, Latvia, Lithuania, Malta, Poland, Romania, Slovakia, and Slovenia.

Source: European Commission, "The Economic Impact of Enlargement," Enlargement Papers No. 4, June 2001, p. 8.

Table 2. Main indicators for AC-12, EU-15, and EU-27

INDICATOR	AC-12	EU-15	EU-27
Inhabitants, 1997(thousands)	106,084	374,168	480,252
Area (km^2)	1,086,568	3,189,838	4,276,406
Density (pop/km^2)	97.6	117.3	112.3
GDP per capita, 1997 PPS, EU-15 = 100	38.1	100	86.3
GDP per capita, 1997 PPS, EU-27 = 100	44.1	115.8	100
GDP per capita, 1997 PPS, euro	7298	19163	16542
Productivity 1997 EU-15 = 100	38.8	100	86.4
Productivity 1997 EU-27 = 100	44.3	115.7	100
Employment rate (% of population aged 15–64), 1999:			
total	60.6	61.8	62.4
female	54.6	51.8	53.5
male	66.8	71.8	71.3
Employment by sector (% of total), 1999:			
agriculture	20.9	4.7	8.1
industry	32.0	29.6	30.0
services	47.1	65.5	61.6
Demography, % of the population:			
< 15	19.5	17.4	17.7
15–64	67.8	67.0	67.1
65+	12.7	15.6	15.1

Source: C. Weise et al (2001). Annex 3, 196–198

Table 3: Regional disparities in EU-15 and EU-27

REGIONS	EU-15		EU-27
	1988	1998	1998
10%+	155.3	160.9	176.9
10%–	55.1	61.0	31.1
ratio	2.8	2.6	5.7
25%+	134.1	137.1	152.0
25%–	66.6	68.3	44.3
ratio	2.0	2.0	3.4

10%+ and 25%+: the regions with the highest GDP per head (PPS), accounting for 10% and 25%, respectively, of total population in the Union.

10%– and 25%–: the regions with the lowest GDP per head (PPS), accounting for 10% and 25%, respectively, of total population in the Union.

Source: European Commission (2001a), p. 6.

As indicated in Table 3, disparities at regional level within an enlarged Union of 27 members will double in magnitude. In an enlarged EU, the ratio of per capita GDP in the top regions to that in the bottom regions is around double the ratio for the present EU. The top 25 percent of regions in an enlarged EU would have an average per capita GDP 3.4 times larger than that of the bottom 25 percent, compared with the ratio of 2.0 in the present EU. After enlargement, the top 10 percent of regions would have an average per capita GDP 5.7 times that of the bottom 10 percent, compared with the present ratio of 2.6. The population living in regions with per capita GDP of less than 75 percent of present EU average will be more than double, from 71 million to 174 million, or from 19 percent of the EU-15 population to 36 percent of the EU-26[iii] population (excluding Malta).

The current state of the enlargement process

Soon after the fall of the Berlin Wall and the beginning of the political and economic transition of central and eastern Europe (CEE), the governments of the incumbent EU Member States promised that the Union would welcome the former socialist countries as new members. The Copenhagen European Council formally confirmed this promise in 1993. Turkey's status as a candidate for EU membership was recognized by the Helsinki Council in 1999. The Copenhagen Council also formulated the following requirements for membership:

- Political criteria: Stability of democratic institutions and of the rule of law, and respect for and protection of minorities.
- Economic criteria: Functioning market economy capable to withstand competitive pressures in the European markets.
- Community *Acquis* criteria: Ability to fulfill the obligations of membership and to adhere to the goals of economic, monetary, and political union.

At the European Council in Essen in December 1994, the EU adopted a pre-accession strategy for the candidate countries. This strategy focused on the conclusion of *Europe Agreements* with each individual country and sectoral and legislative measures to facilitate the implementation of liberal trade regimes between the candidate countries and the EU. Europe Agreements provide the legal framework for association between the candidates and the EU. Importantly, they establish a free trade area for industrial goods between these countries and the EU by 2002. The implication is that, as far as industrial products are concerned, the trade effects of enlargement will already be largely in place by the time the first candidates become full members. Nevertheless, there will be important trade repercussions of membership in service industries and transportation. The Europe Agreements also provide the framework for policy dialogue and for the transposition of EU law into the national law of the candidate countries. While Malta, Cyprus, and Turkey have had Association Agreements since the early 1970s, the first Europe Agreement was concluded with Poland in 1991, and the last with Slovenia in 1996. The Essen Summit's Europe Agreements also made the Phare program as the key financial instrument to assist candidate countries in the accession process.

Accession negotiations were formally opened with the first six countries— Cyprus, Hungary, Poland, Estonia, the Czech Republic, and Slovenia—in 1998. To organize these negotiations, the European Commission drew up a list of 31 chapters that have to be negotiated and closed for a successful accession. Table 4 presents these chapters together with an indication of the progress achieved by the central and eastern European countries so far. Romania and Bulgaria currently the only country with fewer than 29 chapters open for negotiations. In all other candidate countries, the only chapter that has not been opened yet is the one dealing with Community institutions. Cyprus and Hungary were able to close the largest number of chapters so far—23 and 22, respectively. The Czech Republic and Slovenia are closely behind, while the number of chapters closed is only 18 for Poland.

As indicated by the number of countries for which a chapter has been closed, the chapters dealing with the free movement of goods, services, and capital, as well as those dealing with industrial policy, small and medium-sized enterprise, education and research as well as consumer and health protection have been closed with almost all candidate countries by now. The stickier chapters, relating to competition policy, agriculture, transport and taxation policy, regional policy, cooperation in justice and home affairs, and financial and budgetary provisions are still under negotiation with almost all candidate countries.

Table 4. Current state of negotiations

Chapter	Cyprus	Czech Rep	Estonia	Hungary	Poland	Slovenia	Bulgaria	Latvia	Lithuania	Malta	Romania	Slovakia
1. Free movement of goods	X	X	X	X	X	X	*0	*X	*X	*X	—	*X
2. Free movement of persons	X	X	(X)	X	(X)	(X)	**0	*X	*(X)	*X	—	*X
3. Freedom to provide services	X	X	(X)	X	X	X	*0	X	X	*X	—	X
4. Free movement of capital	X	X	X	X	(X)	X	X	X	X	0	*0	X
5. Company law	X	X	X	X	0	X	X	X	X	X	*0	*X
6. Competition policy	0	0	0	0	0	0	*0	0	0	0	0	0
7. Agriculture	0	0	0	0	0	0	—	*0	*0	**	—	*0
8. Fisheries	X	X	X	X	0	X	*X	X	*X	0	*X	X
9. Transport policy	X	0	0	0	0	0	*0	0	0	X	*0	0
10. Taxation	0	0	0	X	0	0	**0	*0	*0	*0	**0	*0
11. Economic and monetary union	X	X	X	X	X	X	—	X	*X	X	—	*X
12. Statistics	X	X	X	X	X	X	X	X	X	X	X	X
13. Social policy and employment	X	X	X	X	X	X	**0	*X	X	0	**0	*X
14. Energy	X	0	0	X	X	X	**	*0	*0	*X	—	*X
15. Industrial policy	X	X	X	X	X	X	—	X	X	X	—	X
16. Small and medium-sized enterprises	X	X	X	X	X	X	X	X	X	X	X	X
17. Science and research	X	X	X	X	X	X	X	X	X	X	X	X
18. Education and training	X	X	X	X	X	X	X	X	X	X	X	X
19. Telecommunications and information technology	X	X	X	X	X	X	X	*0	X	X	0	X
20. Culture and audiovisual policy	X	X	X	0	X	X	X	X	X	X	0	X
21. Regional policy and structural instruments	0	0	0	0	0	0	**	*0	*0	*0	—	*0
22. Environment	X	X	X	X	X	X	**0	*0	X	*0	—	*0
23. Consumers and health protection	X	X	X	X	X	X	X	X	*X	X	**X	X
24. Cooperation in justice and home affairs	0	0	0	0	0	0	*0	*0	*0	*0	—	*0
25. Customs union	X	X	0	X	X	X	*0	*X	*0	*0	*0	X
26. External relations	X	X	X	X	X	X	X	X	X	X	X	X
27. Common foreign and security policy	X	X	X	X	X	X	X	X	X	X	X	X
28. Financial control	X	X	X	X	X	X	*0	*0	*0	*X	—	0
29. Financial and budgetary provisions	0	0	0	0	0	0	**	*0	*0	*0	—	*0
30. Institutions												
31. Other												
Chapters opened	29	29	29	29	29	29	23	29	29	28	17	29
Chapters closed	23	21	19	22	18	21	12	18	18	18	8	20

0 = chapter provisionally closed.
X = chapter opened, under negotiation.
(X) = chapter for which the provisional closure proposed in the EUCP has not been accepted by the CC.
* = chapter opened to negotiations under the Swedish Presidency.
** = chapter to be opened to negotiations under the Belgian Presidency.
— = chapter not yet opened to negotiations.

Source: Report of the European Commission on the progress towards accession by each of the candidate countries, Nov 2001

A critical issue in the enlargement process is the adoption of EU law and regulations into the legislation of the new member countries. This has two aspects: the passage of appropriate legal acts by the prospective member countries and the effective enforcement of these acts by the national authorities. The latter is particularly important, since the EU relies entirely on national administrations in the implementation and enforcement of its regulations. Although violations of EU law by national administrations can be challenged before the European Courts, court cases take a long time. The lack of a legal tradition compatible with, and an administration experienced with, a market environment in the central and eastern European countries is a major difficulty in this context. Even if the proper legislation exists, administrations in these countries have no reputation or track record in implementing and enforcing it. The EU and individual Member States have extended considerable technical assistance to the prospective members in recent years, improving their administrative capacities in this regard. Still, there is a risk that countries would use weak implementation and enforcement to gain competitive advantages for their industries.

From an economic point of view, this is perhaps less significant than it might seem at first glance. After all, the weaker administrative capacity in the new Member States also creates higher bureaucratic costs, and many Single Market regulations that are appropriate for the more advanced economies of the incumbent members are probably overly tight and costly for the transition economies. Thus, weaker enforcement may just balance out competitive disadvantages of these economies. Nevertheless, the perception that unequal implementation of EU legislation would distort competition in the European markets could easily produce political barriers against enlargement. For the smaller accession countries, this creates an incentive to join the EU together with Poland, Hungary, and the Czech Republic, whose greater political weight will tend to persuade Europe's political leaders to push forward their accession even if a full implementation of EU legislation is not yet assured.

Institutional consequences of enlargement

Enlargement will cause additional stress on the institutions governing the EU, which were once designed for six Member States. These institutions are already criticized for the lack of efficiency in decision-making. The sheer increase in the number of members of the European Commission, the European Council, and the European Parliament will add to the difficulties these bodies will face while trying to act efficiently and in a timely manner.

Facing this challenge, the EU leaders committed themselves to reforming the institutions in order to ensure their efficiency, while preserving its legitimacy as a union of states and people.[iv] To accomplish this, the agenda for the Treaty of Nice focused on changes of:

1. The distribution of votes in the European Council,
2. The scope of qualified majority voting in the Council,
3. The size and composition of the Commission and the European Parliament, and
4. The rules for enhanced cooperation.

The result is the Treaty of Nice, which is due to be adopted by Member States by 2002 and which should take effect in 2005. Its recent rejection by the Irish referendum has created some uncertainty, however, whether the Treaty will be ratified in its current form under the current timetable.

Current institutional questions

Institutional reforms of the EU are difficult because of two critical issues.[v] The first is the unresolved question of the EU's "finality": Is the EU a group of sovereign nations committed to free mobility of goods, services, capital and people, or is the EU the stepping stone to a European federation of states? The first view implies that nations remain the most relevant decision-making units in Europe and delegate only limited aspects of their sovereignty to the EU. The second view implies that the EU itself gradually becomes the most relevant decision-making unit and that the Member States subject themselves to the decisions of a majority among them. Enlargement makes the issue even more difficult, as decisions based on veto rights, unanimity, and large majorities (which are the essence of the first view) become ever more difficult with the growing number of countries.

In the past, the members of the EU have avoided defining the EU's finality mainly because different members have pursued different agendas, and leaving the question open was a way to accommodate that fact. Importantly, some countries wished to deepen and widen European integration further—that is, to develop further and more powerful Community institutions and increase the scope of authority of the existing ones—while others were reluctant to relinquish more of their national sovereignties. The often complicated and opaque legal structure of the EU is in fact the result of a sensitive balance of these different agendas. Enlargement by a large number of new members whose political agendas within the EU are still unknown will almost surely upset this balance. Specifically, some countries now fear that the central and eastern European countries would often side with Germany in matters relating to the further development of the EU, thus creating a new center of influence and weakening the old "axis" between Germany and France. The new political debates over (a need for) a European Constitution and the assignment of political competences between the EU and its members reflect the growing wish to clarify these issues before the new members come in. Doing so will be a complicated and time-consuming political process, but not developing an answer also makes enlargement more difficult, because any enlargement needs unanimous agreement of all incumbent Member States.

The other critical issue is the conflict between large and small states in the EU. As in many international organizations and federal constitutions, the small states are, in terms of population size, overrepresented in EU decision-making bodies. The resulting tendency of EU decisions to be dominated by the interests of small states will increase with enlargement, as all current candidates except Poland are "small." This, in turn, raises the desire of the large states to protect themselves against being overruled in majority decisions. The difficulty here is that any change in the rules upsets the balance of power between large and small states even before enlargement. As long as the number of new entrants is still uncertain, the small states will be reluctant to agree to a shift in power toward the larger ones.

These underlying conflicts imply that accession might become ever more difficult for countries joining later rather than sooner. Anticipating this increase in difficulty creates an important incentive for the current candidate countries to be in the first wave of accession, fearing that the next round may take a long time and raise the economic and political requirements even further.[vi] The obvious alternative, namely a "big-bang" enlargement bringing in all candidate countries at once, could, in fact, be easier, since the EU institutions would have to be renegotiated only once, that option could postpone the entire enlargement process, which would seem intolerable for the more advanced candidate countries. The Commission recently acknowledged that ten countries should be ready for joining in 2004, a statement suggesting that this is the most preferred scenario in Brussels.

Institutional reforms

The following section looks at the impact of enlargement on the institutional status quo and according to the institutional reforms foreseen by the Treaty of Nice.

1. Council of Ministers

The Council of Ministers consists of a minister from each Member State. In 80 percent of all its decisions, including all Single Market issues, a qualified majority is required for a resolution to pass (Yataganas 2001). Although the larger Member States have a greater number of votes in the Council, the distribution of votes gives the smaller states more relative power than what is suggested by the size of their populations.

The Treaty of Nice changes the Council's decision rules. The new rules should be implemented regardless of whether new members have joined the EU or not.[vii] The main changes are:

1. New weighting of the voting rights;
2. An increase in the qualified majority threshold from currently 71 percent of the votes to 74 percent (for the EU-27);
3. Two additional criteria for a winning majority: a majority must represent at least 50 percent of the number of EU Member States and at least 62 percent of the EU population. The reasoning behind this last point is that Council majorities representing less than 50 percent of the EU population would be possible otherwise.

Table 5: Voting weights in EU institutions according to the Treaties of Amsterdam and Nice

| | COUNCIL | | | | | | EUROPEAN PARLIAMENT | | | EUROPEAN COMMISSION | |
| | Voting weights | | NICE TWO ADDITIONAL CRITERIA: Population | | | No. of states | No. of seats | | | No. of Commissioners | |
	actual	Under the Nice Treaty	inhabitants (millions)	in % EU–15	in % EU–27		EU-15	EU-27	change	actual	from 2005 on
Germany	10	29	82.04	21.86%	17.05%	1	99	99	0	2	1
United Kingdom	10	29	59.25	15.79%	12.31%	1	87	72	−15	2	1
France	10	29	58.97	15.71%	12.25%	1	87	72	−15	2	1
Italy	10	29	57.61	15.35%	11.97%	1	87	72	−15	2	1
Spain	8	27	39.39	10.50%	8.19%	1	64	50	−14	2	1
Poland		27	38.67		8.04%	1		50	50		1
Romania		14	22.49		4.67%	1		33	33		1
Netherlands	5	13	15.76	4.20%	3.28%	1	31	25	−6	1	1
Greece	5	12	10.53	2.81%	2.19%	1	25	22	−3	1	1
Czech Republic		12	10.29		2.14%	1	20	20		1	
Belgium	5	12	10.21	2.72%	2.12%	1	25	22	−3	1	1
Hungary		12	10.09		2.10%	1		20	20		1
Portugal	5	12	9.98	2.66%	2.07%	1	25	22	−3	1	1
Sweden	4	10	8.85	2.36%	1.84%	1	22	18	−4	1	1
Bulgaria		10	8.23		1.71%	1		17	17		1
Austria	4	10	8.08	2.15%	1.68%	1	21	17	−4	1	1
Slovakia		7	5.39		1.12%	1		13	13		1
Denmark	3	7	5.31	1.42%	1.10%	1	16	13	−3	1	1
Finland	3	7	5.16	1.37%	1.07%	1	16	13	−3	1	1
Ireland	3	7	3.74	1.00%	0.78%	1	15	12	−3	1	1
Lithuania		7	3.70		0.77%	1		12	12		1
Latvia		4	2.44		0.51%	1		8	8		1
Slovenia		4	1.98		0.41%	1		7	7		1
Estonia		4	1.45		0.30%	1		6	6		1
Cyprus		4	0.75		0.16%	1		6	6		1
Luxembourg	2	4	0.43	0.11%	0.09%	1	6	6	0	1	1
Malta		3	0.38		0.08%	1		5	5		1
TOTAL		345	481	100%	100.00%	27	626	732	106	21	27
Threshold	96	255		233	298	14	313	366			
Threshold (in %)	71%	74%	62%	62%	62%	50%	50%	50%			

Table 5 reports the old and the new distribution of voting weights in the EU Council under the Nice Treaty. Out of a total of 345 votes in an EU-27, the qualified majority is set at 255 votes and the blocking minority at 88. The latter would rise to 92 with the accession of the 27th Member State.

The Treaty of Nice gives proportionally more votes to large nations than they had before, protecting them somewhat more from being outvoted. But the rise in the majority threshold from 71 percent to 74 percent also creates many more possibilities for the formation of blocking coalitions. The two new criteria make it more difficult to reach a winning majority, although their practical impact has been estimated to be small.[viii]

2. European Commission

The Commission is the Community's executive. As the guardian of the European Treaties, it takes enforcement action, implements the EU budget, and manages Community policies. The Commission also has an important role as the agenda setter in the Council, where it has the monopoly right initiating Community legislation.

Today, small EU states have one Commissioner each, while large states have two. Although Commissioners are supposed to take a EU perspective of their activities and policies and have no mandate to represent national interests and views, this rule promotes such an understanding of their role. Keeping this rule would have resulted in a very large Commission after enlargement. The Treaty of Nice limits the number of Commissioners to one per country and the total number of Commissioners to 27. Note that this is still very large compared with the size of the executive in national governments. Moreover, the Treaty increases the power of the president with respect to internal organization and the allocation of portfolios.

3. European Parliament

The number of members of the European Parliament and its composition will change after the next European elections in June 2004, with reductions in the number of seats in all current Member States (total reduction from the current 626 to 535 for EU-15) except for Germany and Luxembourg, which will retain their present numbers (see Table 5.) The final figures are based primarily on each country's population, with a certain bonus for the smallest countries to allow for the representation of a broad range of political groups.

Most EU legislation must be approved by both the Council and the European Parliament (co-decision procedure). The Parliament takes its decisions by simple majority.

4. Extending the scope of qualified majority voting

Although majority voting was in fact introduced in several areas already by the Treaty of Rome in 1958, the EU operated for a long time on the working assumption that veto rights were in effect if national interest were at stake (Yataganas 2001). With the Single European Act in the mid-1980s, the Council shifted to qualified majority voting (QMV) on matters related to legislation implementing the Single European Market. The Maastricht and the Amsterdam Treaties extended QMV further. After Amsterdam, 75 Treaty provisions remained subject to unanimity vote. Of those, the Commission proposed in Nice to switch 50 to become subject to QMV, though in the end, only 27 of those 50 proposed provisions became subject to QMV. Some of the legislative measures that have been moved to qualified majority voting will now be subject to Parliamentary approval under the co-decision procedure. The co-decision procedure will apply to seven provisions (Articles 13, 62, 63, 65, 157, 159, and 191, Treaty on European Union).[ix]

The final negotiations in Nice centered around five sensitive areas where the transition to QMV was particularly important for the enlarged Union, but where different national preferences among current members made this transition difficult. The relevant provisions concerned the coordination of social security schemes for cross-border workers and minimum requirements in social policy (Articles 42 and 137); visas, asylum, and immigration issues (Article 67); taxation (Article 93); the services and industrial property aspects of the common commercial policy (Article 133); and the financing of economic and social cohesion policy (Article 161).

5. Enlargement and decision-making efficiency

Enlargement poses a potential dilemma between the EU's "ability to act" and the preservation of its democratic legitimacy. As the number of Council members, Commissioners, and Members of the European Parliament (MEP) increases with enlargement, the probability that a country is overruled by a majority in these bodies increases. The democratic legitimacy problem arises, because the Commissioners are not accountable to an EU electorate, the Council's accountability to national parliaments is weak due to the opaqueness of its decision-making procedures, and the European Parliament has only very limited powers.

Even if Member States agree on important issues in principle, the sheer increase in the number of members will make the administration and management of decision making more complex; this complexity increases as the majority requirements become more stringent. As a result, the decision-making process in the EU could slow down. Unanimous decisions would then be taken only if a Member State believes the issue under consideration to be unimportant or if the Member State is more than compensated for consenting by concessions from other Members on other issues.[x] With QMV, the "vote trading" possibilities increase with the number of possible coalitions to block a decision, which rises exponentially as the number of EU members grows.

The implications of enlargement for the EU's decision-making capacity can be illustrated with the help of quantitative indicators (for an overview of the recent literature, see Baldwin et al 2001). A first indicator measures the likelihood of being able to form a winning coalition supporting a policy proposal in the Council. This indicator is called the *passage probability*. Technically, this is the ratio of all possible winning coalitions in the Council to all possible coalitions. This can be interpreted as the likelihood of a randomly chosen proposal being passed by the Council.[xi] The passage probability depends on the number of members, the distribution of voters, and the majority threshold.[xii] Under the rules of the Nice Treaty, enlargement by 12 countries reduces the passage probability from a currently already low level of 7.8 percent to 2.5 percent (It was 21.9 percent in the Community of 6.) That is, only 1 in 40 proposals would have a chance to be passed by the Council. The new distribution of votes and the new threshold for QMV of the Treaty of Nice contribute to this reduction. Baldwin et al (2001) conclude that the Nice Treaty failed to meet the goal of maintaining the efficiency of EU decision-making after enlargement

These estimates are necessarily rough approximations. For an exact measure, we would need detailed information about the decisions that will arise and the preferences and voting behavior of all current and future members. Furthermore, the estimates disregard the possibility of bundling proposals to facilitate vote trading and improve the chances of finding winning coalitions. Finally, the indicator does not distinguish between policy issues subject purely to national responsibility (for example, labor market issues) and issues raised by the existence of a common institution such as the monetary union or the single market.[xiii] The passage probability is likely to be higher in the latter domain.

How easily can Council decisions be blocked in an EU of 27 members? To develop an answer, we may look at the smallest possible coalition under a given threshold. One question discussed here is whether the new members have enough votes to form an alliance that can efficiently block Council decisions. Another natural alliance is among current and future potential net recipients of transfers in the negotiation over the distribution of EU budget appropriations (agriculture and structural funds). A measure can be blocked by any of the three criteria defined by the Nice reform. According to Table 5, a coalition among the current cohesion countries plus the 12 new members will represent two more states than the 14 needed for a

blocking minority. Under voting right criteria, this alliance has 75 votes more than the 91 needed for a blocking minority, while a coalition of new members alone has 17 more votes. Thus, both coalitions will be able to block decisions in the Council under QMV. A coalition between Germany and the Visegrad-5 (Poland, Czech Republic, Slovakia, Hungary, and Slovenia) representing only 6 members and 148 million people can block decisions because the total number of votes equals the 91 needed for a veto.

A country's ability to influence EU decisions depends importantly on its ability to make or break a winning coalition in the Council. This is measured by the *Banzhaf Index*. This index estimates the likelihood that a Member State will be in a position to turn any losing coalition into a winning one by joining it. Bobay (2001) calculates Banzaf Indexes for the EU-27 under the current system and the Nice provisions. He shows that the Treaty of Nice raises the influence of the large Member States, including Poland, although the losses in influence incurred by the incumbent smaller states are rather small (see Figure 1).

Figure 1: Power to turn coalitions into winning ones under the actual system and under changes implied by the Treaty of Nice

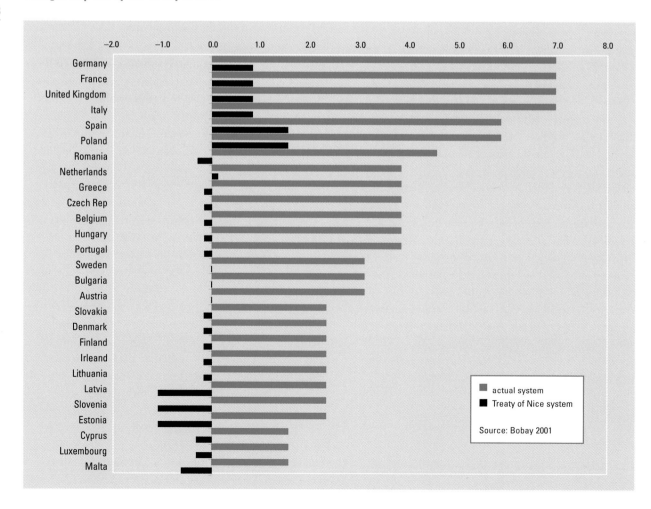

Enhanced cooperation: The way out?

The main conclusion of this analysis is that the sheer increase in the number of member countries will make the governance of the EU much more complicated than it is already today. The Nice Summit clearly did not fulfill the hope that the EU would be able to reform its institutions and clear the way for effective governance with a larger number of members. The implication is that EU policymaking will become more and more rigid and driven by vote-trading rather than economic rationale. The result could be an increasing inability to adapt EU market regulations to changing environments in global markets.

Yet the Treaty of Nice also introduced a potential way out of this problem. This is the strengthening of policy coordination in limited policy fields and among subgroups of countries under the label of *enhanced cooperation*. Under enhanced cooperation, Member States can form subgroups committed to the development of new forms of integration, allowing for deeper integration or a broader scope of cooperation within the subgroup. Under the Treaty of Nice, Member States can no longer veto the formation of enhanced cooperation arrangements in economic affairs and justice and home affairs (ie, the first and third pillars of the EU.) Enhanced cooperation arrangements can now be formed also involving security issues (second pillar) except those with defense implications. Any enhanced cooperation arrangement needs at least eight members. The Commission plays an important role in the creation and development of enhanced cooperation arrangements, as it can refuse proposals for the formation of arrangements concerning the first pillar and it controls their further development. In the other two areas, the Commission's role is less significant. The Council must approve enhanced cooperation arrangements by qualified majority and, in issues involving the co-decision procedure, the European Parliament must also agree.

Enhanced cooperation has the potential to overcome some of the decision-making problems of the EU, as it gives Member States the option to pursue new forms of integration in smaller, more manageable, and more homogeneous groups. The shift of the right of initiative from the Commission to the Member States implied by the process is a significant departure from EU traditions, where this role has always been the monopoly of the Commission. While the option for enhanced cooperation promises to improve the dynamics of EU policy making, its greatest risk is that the development of multiple subgroups could become divisive for the EU as a whole.[xiv]

Labor market effects and migration

Post-enlargement East-West migration is emerging as one of the most controversial issues pertaining to the enlargement process. Among the current EU members, the prospect of an inflow of migrants from the accession-candidate countries is met with a variety of attitudes. On the one hand, countries such as the Netherlands and Ireland, which currently enjoy low unemployment and even experience labor shortages in some professions, see it as an opportunity to attract a skilled workforce and fill gaps in their labor markets. Others, most notably the two frontline countries, Austria and Germany, perceive East-West migration as a threat, fearing it will have adverse effects on their labor markets. These differences in attitudes have been reflected in the official positions taken by the EU and the individual countries. Thus, the Commission announced it would impose transitional periods of restricted labor mobility on the new members. Nevertheless, a number of countries (Denmark, Ireland, the Netherlands, and Sweden) indicated they would grant the new entrants the same labor-market privileges as currently enjoyed by the other EU members immediately upon their entry to the EU.

The discussion on the prospects and implications of post-enlargement migration has been replete with emotional arguments (ranging from xenophobia on the one hand to appeals for solidarity and European unity on the other), but it has remained relatively detached from economic arguments. This section discusses the available estimates of the post-enlargement migration potential and surveys theoretical arguments and empirical evidence relevant for assessing the labor-market effects of post-enlargement migration inflow to the current member countries.

Migration flows respond to expected wage differentials (ie, wage differentials adjusted for the probability of finding employment, see Todaro 1969; Harris and Todaro 1970). The earnings differentials between the EU and the candidate countries are indeed considerable. For the Czech Republic, Estonia, Hungary, Poland, and Slovenia, per capita GDP evaluated at purchasing power parity ranges between 34 and 67 percent of the level attained by Germany. In addition, the accession countries are currently stricken also by relatively high unemployment. Hence, given these economic realities, it is reasonable to expect a net immigration to the current EU member countries.[xv]

Forecasting post-enlargement migration flows

Forecasting the future migration inflow is inherently difficult and requires a combination of sound econometric technique and qualified guesswork. An obvious problem is that future migration cannot be estimated simply by extrapolating past data, as the removal of barriers to labor mobility will obviously dramatically change the pattern of East-West migration, introducing a structural break into the underlying econometric model. Analysts attempting to construct predictions of future East-West migration flows typically deal with this problem by means of double extrapolation—that is, they estimate a model of migration (where migration is explained by per capita incomes and unemployment in the source and destination countries, as well as dummies for EU membership and/or other institutional arrangements that facilitate labor mobility) for a sample of western and southern European countries. They then extrapolate this model in time as well as in space to the accession-candidate countries (which are not included in the original data set because migration levels before the end of the Cold War was negligible). Post-enlargement East-West migration is then assumed to follow the same pattern as migration among current EU members (often taking migration in the wake of the southern enlargement as an explicit benchmark).

Bauer and Zimmermann (1999) estimate a model of migration from Greece, Spain, and Portugal to the other EU countries for the period of 1985 through 1997. Based on the model's parameters, their forecast of net immigration from Slovenia, Slovakia, the Czech Republic, Hungary, and Poland is approximately 0.9 million persons (2.6 million if Bulgaria and Romania are also included), or between 0.2 percent and 1.8 percent of the sending countries' populations (3.2 percent and 6.5 percent for Bulgaria and Romania, respectively). Brücker at al (2001; see also Boeri and Brücker 2000), on the other hand, use the migration experience of Germany. They estimate a model of migration from 16 European countries, Turkey, and the United States to Germany from 1967 through 1998. Their results suggest that the total net immigration inflow from all 10 post-communist candidate countries (assuming migration to the rest of the EU will follow a pattern similar to that to Germany, and that Germany will receive the same share of the inflow as its share in the stock of migrants from accession countries in 1998[xvi]) will be 3.5 million, or approximately 3 percent of the candidate countries' population (Bulgaria and Romania, because of their low incomes, account for more than a third of this inflow). Annual migration inflow is predicted to peak at around 300,000 shortly following the enlargement, and then decline continuously (and eventually turn into a net outflow for the more affluent accession countries).

Sinn et al (2001) follow a similar approach to that of Brücker et al (covering migration from Italy, Greece, Portugal, Spain, and Turkey into Germany from 1974 through 1997). Their results, however, envisage a considerably higher number of migrants: between 3.2 and 4 million, or 4 to 5 percent of the sending counties' population, arriving in Germany alone (moreover, their analysis includes only the Czech Republic, Hungary, Poland, Romania, and Slovakia). If this estimate is extended to the entire EU (under the same assumptions as those made by Boeri and Brücker and Brücker et al), the resulting number of migrants is between 5 and 6.5 million, or 6 to 7.5 percent of the sending countries' population. However, their results may be biased upward because of their omission of fixed effects (see discussion below). Indeed, Fertig and Schmidt (2000), who incorporate country-specific fixed effects into their analysis (in addition, they control for demographic effects), predict much lower migration than either of the studies discussed above. Specifically, their forecasted immigration from the Czech Republic, Estonia, Hungary, and Poland to Germany is between 300,000 and 400,000 (ie, 500,000 to 700,000 for the EU as a whole) when assuming that candidate countries display *average* migration patterns, and between 0.9 and 1.3 million in the high-migration scenario (1.5 to 2 million to the EU as a whole).

Thus, available forecasts of post-enlargement migration, despite somewhat different methodologies, yield rather similar results: long-term net immigration is forecasted as approximately 1 to 2 million (3 to 4 million if Bulgaria and Romania are also included), or between 2 and 4 percent of the accession countries' population. Annual migration flows will peak around 300,000 and then decline. To put these figures into perspective, Brücker at al (2001) report that annual immigration into the EU averaged 1.5 million over the last decade (2 million if estimates of illegal migration are also included). Hence, the enlargement of the EU to include the post-communist accession-candidate countries will not bring about anything close to a dramatic increase in immigration.

These estimates can be criticized, however, because they are based on models that do not include the post-communist accession-candidate countries (the only eastern European country included in Brücker at al's analysis is the former Yugoslavia). Moreover, readiness to migrate differs across countries. Indeed, as Alecke, Huber, and Untiedt (2000) show, inclusion of country-specific effects in migration models can change the estimated coefficients dramatically. Hence, the migration behavior of workers from the accession countries can be quite different from the predictions discussed above because those predictions do not account for country-specific migration patterns (an exception is Brücker et al, who attempt to impute country-specific fixed effects for the candidate countries based on the human development index and regional dummies). To shed some light on migration patters in transition economies, Fidrmuc (2001) looks at determinants of internal (ie, interregional, not international) migration in a number of post-communist countries (Czech Republic, Hungary, Lithuania, Poland, and Slovakia) and compares them with results obtained for EU countries (Italy, Netherlands, Spain, and Portugal). He finds that migration in the accession-candidate countries responds only weakly to interregional differentials in wages and unemployment rates, and the pattern of this response is not consistent with migration facilitating regional adjustment (in particular, his findings indicate that high wages encourage overall migration, inward and outward, and unemployment similarly discourages overall migration). Moreover, even when significant, the effect of wages and unemployment on net migration flows is economically small. Hence, he concludes that workers in the accession-candidate countries are generally not very mobile and respond reluctantly to economic incentives for migration. As most of migration occurs among areas with relatively high wages, it appears that high-wage earners (presumably workers with above-average skills) are disproportionately represented in migration flows. Therefore, EU enlargement is likely to lead primarily to an inflow of skilled labor (and a brain drain from the point of view of the source countries).

In summary, estimates of future migration inflow from the accession countries indicate that the inflow will be far from overwhelming, especially when compared with current immigration flows into the EU. Empirical evidence on migration patterns in accession countries indicates, moreover, very low labor mobility, despite sizeable interregional differentials in wages and employment prospects. Hence, although the future enlargement of the EU will bring about immigration into the current EU Member States, the size of the inflow does not beget great concern.

Labor-market implications for the destination countries

The conventional arguments concerning labor-market effects of migration rest on standard textbook demand-and-supply considerations in a closed-economy setting (see, for example, Friedberg and Hunt 1995; and Bauer and Zimmermann 1999). Accordingly, immigration pushes out the supply of labor (assuming migrant workers are substitutes rather than complements for native workers), which, as long as demand for labor remains intact, results in lower wages and unemployment. Unemployment rises either because the local workers reduce their supply of labor as wages fall, or because wages may be downwardly rigid. In addition, as the capital-labor ratio falls as a result of immigration, the return to capital rises.

In an open-economy framework, this line of reasoning does not hold. Although migration may have adverse labor-market repercussions in the short run, the economy absorbs the inflow of migrant workers in the medium and long term. First, higher interest rates bring about higher investment. In an open economy, this increase in investment will be financed by external borrowing rather than by a reduction of current consumption. Second, as stipulated by the Heckscher-Ohlin model of international trade, a change in factor endowments (in this case an increase in the supply of labor) will not affect factor prices in the long term but rather will be absorbed by changes in the composition of output. Hence, as a result of immigration, the economy will produce—and export—more labor-intensive products than before.

To gauge the labor-market repercussions of post-enlargement migration on the current EU member countries, it is instructive to consider other instances of large-scale migration flows. The case of Russian immigration to Israel appears particularly relevant, because it is likely to be similar in nature (though not in scope) to East-West migration in the wake of the next EU enlargement (immigration from formerly communist countries to a developed western country). During the 1990s, Israel admitted hundreds of thousands of ethnic Jews from eastern Europe, especially the former Soviet Union. Between 1990 and 1997, approximately 700,000 immigrants arrived, swelling Israeli population by 11 percent and the labor force by 15 percent (see Gandal et al 2000; Cohen and Hsieh 2000). Almost half of this inflow occurred within a span of two years: 1990 through 1991. In relative terms, this is an unprecedented event that dwarfs even the most *pessimistic* predictions concerning East-West migration in the EU.

91

The short-term impact of such a massive immigration was in line with the textbook demand-and-supply analysis described above: average wages of native Israelis fell and interest rates rose sharply during 1990 through 1991. However, the initial adverse effect quickly dissipated and, by 1997, real wages and interest rates returned to their pre-1990 levels (Cohen and Hsieh 2000). Moreover, the Israeli labor market quickly absorbed the immigrants so that, by 1997, unemployment and labor-force participation among Russian immigrants were not dramatically out of line with those of native Israelis (nonetheless, the immigrants were subject to substantial, though in part temporary, skill downgrading; see also Friedberg 2000). The medium-term adjustment to immigration was in line with theory's predictions. Cohen and Hsieh (2000) show that the initial increase in interest rates led to an investment boom financed largely by external borrowing. The investment boom in turn brought about rising real wages and falling interest rates. Gandal et al (2000) argue that global technological change generating greater demand for skilled labor also helped smooth away the effects of immigration. However, both studies conclude that changes in the composition of output in line with the Heckscher-Ohlin model did not account for much of the overall adjustment—possibly because adjustment via trade may take longer than adjustment via capital inflow and technological change.

Other studies of labor-market effects of massive immigration episodes, where the recipient countries were open economies, surveyed by Borjas (1994) and Friedberg and Hunt (1995) also suggest that immigration has negligible or no adverse effects on natives' wages and employment in the long term. Hence, based on arguments founded in economic theory as well as empirical evidence from immigration episodes that were much more massive than the envisaged post-enlargement East-West migration, there appears little cause for concern in the current EU member countries.

Summary

Economic theory and available empirical evidence indicate that enlargement of the EU to include post-communist countries of central and eastern Europe will result neither in massive immigration inflow nor in a dramatic upsurge of unemployment and a collapse of average wages in the current Member States. In fact, as Bauer and Zimmermann (1999) show, immigration may have a positive overall welfare effect on the recipient countries, especially if the migrants are predominantly highly skilled.[xvii] Moreover, even if immigration were indeed to have adverse repercussions for EU labor markets, imposing barriers to labor mobility may not be of much help. With free trade and free capital mobility, jobs can be easily moved to where labor is cheap. Indeed, Konings and Murphy (2001) find evidence that wage differentials induce relocation of jobs among subsidiaries of multinational enterprises, especially those operating in the manufacturing sector. Although they find that this effect currently applies only to parent and daughter companies located in the EU, it is likely that, following enlargement, it will extend also to the new member countries.

In fact, barriers to labor mobility may discourage immigrant workers already resident in the West from considering returning to their home countries, because they would typically lose residence and employment rights in the host country. This was apparently the case of many Spanish and Portuguese immigrants in western Europe, who chose to return to their home countries only after the EU extended unrestricted labor mobility to Spain and Portugal. Similarly, Brücker at al (2001) find that migration from countries that enjoyed free labor mobility with Germany was considerably lower than that from countries that had *only* guest-worker agreements with Germany (after controlling for relative incomes and employment rates). Indeed, the *option to emigrate* may be an important factor keeping the potential migrants at home (Burda, 1995, shows that the value of such an option is unambiguously positive, and applies this argument to explain the unexpectedly low East-West migration in the wake of German re-unification).

Regional effects and cohesion

The ongoing debate about the EU enlargement highlights concerns about increasing disparities in a European Union of 27 members and the budgetary consequences of extending the current EU cohesion policy to the new members. Although these issues are not new, there are at least three reasons that make the upcoming enlargement and its impact on cohesion different from previous enlargements:

- The number of the current applicant countries (AC) is larger than that it has been in any of previous enlargements.[xviii]

- Ten of the applicant countries are still transition economies and despite the success of market reforms in the more advanced ones, structural differences, including income differentials, compared with the current European Member States and EU averages are significant.

- Solidarity among the incumbent EU members has probably decreased during the last two decades, and the current net contributors to the EU budget are less willing to pay the bill for the less-developed Member States and regions. Meanwhile, the current net beneficiaries of financial assistance are reluctant to accept cuts in their transfers.

Although diversity of cultures, languages, traditions, and history are considered part of Europe's richness, disparities in the level of development of regions and living standards are potential sources of instability and economic inefficiency. The Commission motivates the EU cohesion policy as an expression of Europe-wide solidarity and as a precondition for economic efficiency and global competitiveness.

The Treaty of Rome already made an explicit reference to "harmonious development," the need to consolidate economic unity among Member States and reduce disparities between regions (Article 158). However, regional policies formulated at European level and the Structural Funds[xix] spent to reduce inequalities between regions and social groups gained significance only later and in response to the increasing diversity and disparities resulting from successive enlargements. The first policy response came with the creation of the European Regional Development Fund (ERDF) in 1975, which aimed at helping to reduce socioeconomic imbalances between regions following the accession of Denmark, Ireland, and the United Kingdom. The ERDF is based on the principle of redistribution between richer and poorer regions of the Community. The first multi-annual coordinated regional development actions, the Integrated Mediterranean Programmes, followed the accession of Spain and Portugal in 1986. The focus on cohesion was strengthened with the Single European Act agreed in 1987, which added Title V "Economic and Social Cohesion" to the Treaty of Rome. The new Articles 130(a) and 130(e) link the "harmonious development" of the Community to the coordination of the Structural Funds.

The principle of multi-annual programming was reinforced in 1989 with the first reform of the Structural Funds. On this occasion, priority development objectives were established, as well as a system of partnership with the Member States and the economic and social partners. The Maastricht Treaty recognized the risk that the European Monetary Union could worsen regional disparities, and it established the Cohesion Fund with the aim of financing projects in the fields of environment and trans-European transport networks in the four Member States with a GDP per capita less than 90 percent of the Union's average (Greece, Portugal, Spain, and Ireland). The second reform of the Structural Funds was adopted at the Berlin Council in 1999. Priority objectives were redefined and financial provisions better targeted toward the most disadvantaged regions and groups. However, some argue that regional policy is nothing else than side payments to applicants and the Member States, ensuring support for deepening integration (Preston 1997).

The remainder of this section is structured as follows. First, we discuss the expected impact of enlargement on particular EU regions, namely the less-developed, industrial, and border regions. Second, convergence prospects for the applicant countries are outlined. Third, we investigate options for cohesion policy in an enlarged Union of 27 members. Fourth, we present an overview of estimated enlargement costs, including the cost of extending the current policies in the areas of agriculture and structural operations to the new members.

The impact of enlargement on EU regions

Less-developed regions

The accession of 12 applicant countries will change the composition and relative levels of income of the regions belonging to the least affluent category today. In particular, that category will include only a few regions from current Member States. The inclusion of countries with a lower per capita GDP will result in a reduction of the EU average GDP by 15 percent. As a consequence, 27 of the regions in the current EU will find themselves above 75 percent of the EU-27 average (for instance, among the current 11 regions of Spain that receive Structural Funds, only 3 will remain eligible). The bottom 10 percent of regions (in terms of population) in an enlarged EU consists of regions in eastern parts of Poland, Bulgaria, and

Romania together with Lithuania and Latvia (European Commission 2001a, p. 9).

As a result, after the enlargement the needs for structural assistance will become concentrated in the new members, which will become net recipients of EU transfers, while the needs in the current net beneficiary countries will not completely disappear.

Industrial regions

The share of employment in industry in AC-12 (32 percent) is comparable with the average for EU-15 (30 percent). There are concerns in industrial regions of current EU Member States about growing import penetration from goods originating in the new members, increasing unemployment due to low wage competition from the new Member States and increased investment diverted from the current EU industrial regions to the new Member States. The impact on industrial regions in the EU will depend on structural characteristics of these regions. An index of the regional impact of enlargement constructed by Gretschmann (1999) can be used to identify potential winners and losers. This index is based on the following criteria: (1) the proportional size of the manufacturing sector in the industrial region (MFR), (2) the proportional size of the tradable service sector in the industrial region (TSS), (3) the unemployment rate, (4) gross value added (GVA) per capita, (5) the annual change in GVA, (6) the distance from the new Member States, and (7) the importance of inward investment.

The above-mentioned study finds that regions such as West of Scotland, Nord Pas de Calais, North Rhine Westfalia, and Toscana are expected to benefit from enlargement, while regions such as Sachsen–Anhalt and Asturias are likely to be among losers, as shown in Table 6.

Border regions

Border regions are seen as potentially most affected by enlargement. A study conducted for the European Commission[xx] argues that the effects will differ, depending on the competitiveness of enterprises and sectors located in those border regions having competitive enterprises and sectors are expected to gain from the proximity of new markets and the supply of wider selection of inputs. Increased competition along the EU/CEE countries border will result in losses in less competitive regions. At the EU/CEE border, GDP per capita and productivity (excluding commuters) is lower in all border regions of CEE compared with that of their EU neighbors, except in the case of Bratislava and neighboring Austrian regions of Niederösterreich and Burgenland. On the other hand, unemployment is higher in German border regions compared with neighboring Polish and Czech regions, but the situation is reversed in the Austrian, Greek, and Italian border regions with their neighbors in CEE countries.

Table 6: Winner and loser regions from EU enlargement

	MFR	TSS	Unemployment	GVA per capita	GVA change 1991–1997	Distance	Inward investment	Winners/Losers
West of Scotland	+	+	–	+	+	–	–	+
Nord Pas de Calais	–	+	–	–	+	+	–	+
North Rhine Westfalia	–	+	+	+	–	+	+	+
Sachsen–Anhalt	+	–	–	–	+	+	–	–
Toscana	–	+	+	+	+	+	+	+
Asturias	+	+	–	–	–	–	–	–

	Extent of import penetration	Export of tradable services	Vulnerability caused by labor price	Labor efficiency to respond to competition	Economic resilience to respond to competition	Proximity to the CEE-5*	Dependency on FDI	Winers/ Losers
West of Scotland	low	high	low	high	high	low	high	+
Nord Pas de Calais	high	high	low	low	high	high	high	+
North Rhine Westfalia	high	high	high	high	low	high	low	+
Sachsen- Anhalt	low	low	low	low	high	high	high	–
Toscana	high	high	high	high	high	high	low	+
Asturias	low	high	low	low	low	low	high	–

*the Czech Republic, Estonia, Hungary, Poland, and Slovenia

+ = winners; – = losers
MFR < 20% = + ; > 20% = – ; TSS < 35% = – ; > 35% = +; Unemployment < 10% = +, > 10% = –; GVA per capita < 11,000 EUR = –, > 11,000 = + ;
GVA change (1991–1997) < 1.5 = – ; > 1.5 = + ; Distance < 600 km = + ; > 600 km = –; Inward investment: high dependency = –; low dependency = +.

Source: Gretschmann (1999)

Convergence scenarios

The catching-up experience of the cohesion countries (Ireland, Greece, Portugal, and Spain) suggests that a trade-off might exist between national and regional convergence.[xxi] High growth rates at the aggregate level in Ireland and Spain have been accompanied by a widening of regional disparities, while regional convergence in Greece has been associated with low national growth.

A recent study on the impact of EU enlargement on cohesion (Weise et al 2001) has simulated several scenarios of convergence for the applicant countries at both national and regional levels. The preferred scenario—assuming investment rates and population growth in the CEE countries equal to the mean values of the European market economies in the post-war period—suggests that the CEE countries would achieve a per capita GDP between 50 and 83 percent of the EU-15 average in 2037. At the regional level, assuming a convergence rate of 2 percent for the GDP per capita to the EU-15 average (which is the standard estimate in international research on convergence), this study finds that initially more rapid growth of already "rich" regions does not necessarily harm cohesion if the poorer ones catch up at a later stage. The results of these simulations suggest that economic disparities within CEE countries, will persist however, and thus they will probably remain a task for European and national regional development policies in the long perspective.

Options for the cohesion policy in an enlarged European Union

According to the European Commission,[xxii] enlargement imposes the following three challenges on the EU's cohesion policy: first, the disparities in levels of development will increase; second, the needs for assistance will be concentrated in Eastern Europe; and third, the current inequalities in EU-15 will not disappear, although the relative positions of some less-developed regions will be improved due to the entry of less affluent regions.[xxiii]

In order to answer these challenges, the current EU cohesion policy needs to be reformed. The Commission plans to present its proposals for a reformed regional policy in 2004 or 2005—that is, after enlargement. In order to prepare the EU's financial plan for the 2007 through 2013 period, a decision on financing the EU regional policy should be made in 2006. However, the debate on the future of the cohesion policy in an enlarged Union has already started. In this respect, three questions have been put forth:[xxiv] (1) Are disparities in development acceptable? (2) Is a European policy for the regions necessary? (3) Is a real convergence useful?

While less-developed regions will remain the number one priority for the EU regional policy, the Commission plans to act throughout the territory of the Union including the less-favored regions such as urban areas in difficulty, regions affected by industrial restructuring, border regions, and depopulated rural areas. Meanwhile, the contribution of the other Community policies to the cohesion objective should be reinforced. The Commission is also considering the change of the rules on which the Structural Funds are allocated. The possibilities considered include: (1) raising the eligibility threshold for Structural Funds from 75 to 90 percent of the EU average GDP; (2) setting two thresholds; (3) using unemployment levels as a basis for calculation instead of relative wealth; and (4) raising the ceiling for regional aid from the current 0.45 percent to 0.66 percent of EU GDP.[xxv]

The former Italian Prime Minister Giuliano D'Amato[xxvi] has proposed the following as possible changes to EU regional policy: (1) small amounts of aid to be distributed amongst all members of the enlarged Union; (2) different criteria for eligibility to receive aid; and (3) a new formula for the calculation of aid for all the members.

In its opinion on the future European regional policy in an enlarged Union,[xxvii] the Committee of the Regions proposes the introduction of further criteria alongside GDP thresholds in order to classify the relative needs of the different regions. Thus, a system of criteria should also include, for example: remoteness/accessibility and demographic trends/sparsity of population, and sectoral and regional deficits relevant to development, inter alia in the area of training, innovation, research and development and industrial restructuring. The creation of a new crisis intervention instrument is also suggested. Such an emergency aid would make it possible to use EU resources other than those earmarked for structural measures to react to unexpected, serious structural crises, which could not be resolved by the affected regions alone.

Estimated enlargement costs

Estimates of enlargement costs are not easy since several uncertainties remain. Among these uncertainties are how many countries will enter the EU, when, and in which order. In addition, the quality of such estimates depends on the quality of estimations of the GDP growth of EU-15 and of the applicant countries (AC), as well as of the absorption capacity of AC regarding the Structural Funds. Neither the budgetary aspects of individual accessions nor the financial impact of the Common Agricultural Policy (CAP) and Structural Policy (SP) have been yet discussed during the accession negotiations. The inclusion of direct aid in the agriculture package, the moment of the full participation in the EU's own resources system, and the modalities of transfers with respect to Structural Funds remain still open questions.

The current working basis for the budgetary implications of enlargement is the Financial Framework EU-21 agreed by the Berlin Council of March 1999, which aimed at preparing for the accession of six candidate countries in 2002.[xxviii] The planned expenditure for enlargement amounts to 6.45 billion euros in 2002 and increases to 16.78 billion euros in 2006. The foreseen expenditure for CAP was 1.6 billion euros in 2002, rising to 3.4 billion euros in 2006. For structural operations, 3.7 billion euros were foreseen in 2002, increasing to 12.08 billion euros in 2006. These estimates are based on the assumption that the new Member States will not receive full agricultural and structural support. In the total EU budget, the foreseen enlargement spending looks small ranging from 4.2 percent in 2002 to 13.7 percent in 2006. In comparison, the payments planned for agriculture and structural operations in the current Member States represent in the total EU budget 76 percent in 2002 and 68 percent in 2006, respectively.

The situation has changed with the Nice Summit. The Commission now assumes that 10 new Member States could enter the EU in 2004 (all current candidate countries apart from Romania and Bulgaria). The current negotiating position of EU-15 on CAP is that farmers in the new Member States will not receive direct income support because they have not suffered from farm price reductions. This would put a limit on agricultural expenditure for the new Member States. However, the Commission acknowledges that some concessions on direct income support or equivalent measures might be made in order to settle the agricultural negotiations. Hence, the estimates for the cost of enlargement with respect to CAP could follow a high-cost scenario with direct income support, or a low-cost scenario, without. The latest estimates of the Commission are based on the assumption that annual growth rates would average 4 percent in the new Member States and 2.5 percent in the

EU-15 after 2002. Transfers under Structural Operations are limited to 4 percent of national GDP a year.

According to a Working Document of the European Parliament,[xxix] the Commission estimates that the expenditure for enlargement for 10 countries in the year 2004 will be in the range of 10.1 billion euros (low-cost scenario) to 13 billion euros (high-cost scenario, in 2005 from 14.9 billion to 23 billion euros, and in 2006 from 18 billion to 25.6 billion euros.

The above-mentioned Working Document estimates that, in the case of a rapid accession without direct support, the agricultural transfers will amount to 2 billion euros in 2004 and 5.2 billion in 2013. Under the same assumption about the speed of accession but with direct support, the estimates suggests that the new Member States would receive 3.6 billion euros in 2004 and 17.1 billion in 2013. Compared to the ceilings set by the current Financial Framework, enlargement is affordable in respect to agriculture expenses without direct aid even if ten countries join instead of six. Otherwise, depending on the outcome of the CAP reforms, the Financial Framework must be adapted. The European Parliament report supports the phasing-in method with respect to agricultural transfers, arguing that this way the EU budget would be better in control and dramatic income differences between farmers and other sectors in the new Member States could be avoided.

The European Parliament's estimates of the cost of structural operations are made first for the case of a maximum annual transfer of Structural Funds (4 percent of the recipient GDP) and second for the case of phasing-in transfers, taking into account the absorption capacity of the applicant countries. In the latter case, the estimated scenarios start at 1.5 percent of GDP in the first year of accession increasing annually by 0.5 percent. This report argues that if the phasing-in method is used, the transfers from Structural Funds will be affordable within the Financial Framework even if ten countries join in 2004. In this case the EU-budget transfers for Structural Operations in the applicant countries are estimated at 6.1 billion euros in 2004, increasing gradually to 26.0 billion euros in 2013. In the case of immediate transfers of 4 percent of GDP to the six new Member States, these transfers will be much larger than accounted for in the Financial Framework.

Summary

This section has discussed the expected impact of EU enlargement on economic cohesion. Although concerns such as increasing disparities in an enlarged Union and the need to allocate greater financial resources for the extension of the EU cohesion policy to the new members are not new, the fifth enlargement differs from the previous ones at least for three reasons: first, the larger number of the applicant countries with which the negotiations are under way; second, the magnitude of structural differences involved, including income differentials between the transition countries and the current Member States; third, a declining feeling of solidarity in the current Member States.

Enlargement will increase disparities within a EU-27 at both national and regional levels. What is new is the magnitude of these disparities. Some EU regions will be more affected than others. Specifically, a number of less-developed regions will improve their relative position due to the accession of less affluent regions and countries. As a consequence they will no longer qualify for assistance under the current rules for Structural Funds, although they will continue to have structural difficulties. Industrial regions may benefit or lose from enlargement depending on their particular structural characteristics, such as their share of manufacturing, their share of tradable services, the unemployment rate, dependency on inward investment, their proximity to the new Member States, and the gross value added per capita and its annual change. The impact of enlargement on border regions will differ depending on the competitiveness of enterprises and sectors located in those regions. Existing simulations of the convergence prospects in the applicant countries suggest that, assuming growth rates in applicant countries higher than in the current Member States, the catching-up process will take two generations.

The cohesion policy will face new challenges and greater needs in an enlarged Union of 27 members. Although the applicant countries expect to be treated under the same rules as the current Member States, the current net beneficiaries of structural transfers fear losing their benefits. The debate over reforming cohesion policy includes both the change of eligibility criteria and the call for a greater contribution to the cohesion objective of the other Community policies. Existing estimates of the costs of expenditures for CAP and structural policies in an enlarged Union suggest that enlargement is affordable if both policies are reformed. A phasing-in method for transfers seems to be in line with the current absorption capacity of the applicant countries.

Conclusions

This paper has discussed several aspects and perspectives of the upcoming enlargement of the European Union. Although the economic effects, including the costs, of this enlargement can be expected to be moderate at the aggregate level of the incumbent EU, there are important consequences of a distributional nature. Enlargement shifts the intricate balance of power within the EU decision-making bodies and raises the need for reforms. Enlargement will have labor-market effects through migration flows, which are welcomed by some regions and sectors and feared by others. Enlargement will change the economies of current border regions and change the direction and flows of transfers within the EU.

The biggest problem with the enlargement is perhaps that it does not create large and immediate payoffs to the incumbent members that could be used to compensate those socio-economic groups that lose out due to enlargement. One implication is that, despite frequent lip-service to their support of the project, the governments of the incumbent EU countries can be expected to be careful about risking their re-election chances on it. This makes the process rather vulnerable to being taken hostage by interest groups. The German government's insistence on long transition periods before new members are granted full labor mobility reflects this: It is paying a favor only to unions in the construction industry, and this despite the current scarcity of labor in many other parts of the German economy.

An important implication of this payoff problem is that the enlargement—if it proceeded in waves—would become more complicated for the countries in the later waves than for those in the earlier waves. That is, the candidate countries have a strong incentive to join at the earliest possibility. This puts pressure on them to speed up reform. But at the same time it also creates incentives for focusing on passing laws and adopting formal rules more than on implementing them effectively. There is, therefore, a risk that accession will result in weak and uneven implementation of the rules of the Single Market. In view of this, the Commission emphasizes the need for proper implementation of EU laws and regulation by the accession candidates, but, in the end, it will find it hard to monitor their implementation, given that it has no administrative branches of its own for this purpose. Should the first wave of the enlargement produce difficulties and disappointments with the functioning of the Single Market, the result could well be a much longer accession process for the remaining countries.

While its economic implications for the EU as a whole seem to be moderate or small, the current enlargement does serve as an engine of institutional change that was long overdue. At the same time, EU membership will contribute to the consolidation and stabilization of the new democracies in the Central and East European countries, with important pay-offs in terms of political stability and peace in the regions. These pay-offs are difficult to quantify, but there is no doubt that they will be significant for the current EU members as well.

References

Alecke, Björn, Peter Huber and Gerhard Untiedt (2000). "What a Difference a Constant Makes: How Predictable are International Migration Flows?" WIFO and GEFRA, mimeo.

Baldwin, R. E., J. Francois, R. Portes (1997), "The Costs and Benefits of Eastern Enlargement: The Impact on the EU and Central Europe." Economic Policy April, 125–170.

Baldwin, Richard, Erik Berglöf, F. Giavazzi, and Mika Widgrén (2001). Nice Try: Should the Treaty of Nice be Ratified? CEPR Monitoring European Integration 11, June.

Barnier, M. (2001). "Cohesion in the Enlarged European Union," Speech to the European Forum on Economic and Social Cohesion, Brussels, 21 May.

Bauer, Thomas and Klaus F. Zimmermann (1999). Assessment of Possible Migration Pressure and its Labor Market Impact Following EU Enlargement to Central and Eastern Europe. IZA, Bonn.

Frédéric Bobay (2001).Émergence d'un nouvel équilibre européen à Nice, Analyse de la réforme du Conseil de l'Union européenne à partir de la théorie des jeux. Paper presented at the Forum Franco-Allemande.

Boeri, Tito and Herbert Brücker (2000). The Impact of Eastern Enlargement of Employment and Labor Markets in the EU Member States, Berlin and Milan, mimeo.

Breuss, F. (2001), "Macroeconomic Effects of EU Enlargement for Old and New Members." Mimeo: Austrian Institute for Economic Research (Wifo).

Borjas, George J. (1994). "The Economics of Immigration." Journal of Economic Literature 32 (December):1667–1717.

Brücker, Herbert, Gil Epstein, Barry McCormick, Gilles Saint-Paul, Alessandra Venturini and Klaus Zimmermann (2001), "Managing Migration in the European Welfare State," presented at The Third European Conference of the Fondazione RODOLFO DEBENEDETTI: Immigration Policy and the Welfare State in Trieste, Italy on June 23, 2001.

Burda, Michael (1995)."Migration and the Option Value of Waiting." Economic and Social Review 27: 1–19.

Cohen, Sarit and Chang-Tai Hsieh (2000), "Macroeconomic and Labor Market Impact of Russian Immigration in Israel," Bar-Ilan University, mimeo.

Committee of the Regions (2001). Opinion on the Structure and Goals of European Regional Policy in the Context of Enlargement and Globalisation: Opening the Debate. Brussels.

Dewatripont, Mathias, David Begg, Francesco Giavazzi, Jürgen von Hagen, Ian Harden, Torsten Persson, Andre Sapir, and Guido Tabellini (1996). Flexible Integration. Monitoring European Integration 6, London: CEPR.

European Bank for Reconstruction and Development (2001). Transition Report Update 2001.London: EBRD.

European Commission (2000). Adapting the Institutions to Make a Success of Enlargement. COM (2000) 34.

European Commission (2001a). Unity, Solidarity, Diversity for Europe, its People and its Territory. Second Report on Economic and Social Cohesion. Luxembourg: Office for Official Publications of the European Communities.

European Commission (2001b). Summary of the Treaty of Nice, Memorandum to the Members of the Commission, SEC (2001) 99.

European Commission (2001c). "The Economic Impact of Enlargement," Enlargement Papers No. 4.

European Commission (2001). "Spring Forecast." European Reform Monitor, Issue 2001/2, April.

European Parliament (2001). Working Document on the Financial Implications of EU Enlargement, Committee on Budgets, 11 April 2001.

Fertig, Michael and Christoph M. Schmidt (2000). Aggregate-Level Migration Studies as a Tool for Forecasting Future Migration Streams. IZA Discussion Paper 183, Bonn.

Fidrmuc, Jan (2001). "Migration and Adjustment to Shocks in Transition Economies." Working Paper. Center for European Integration Studies (ZEI), University of Bonn.

Friedberg, Rachel M. (2000). "You Can't Take It with You? Immigrant Assimilation and the Portability of Human Capital." Journal of Labor Economics 18(2): 221–251.

Friedberg, Rachel M. and Jennifer Hunt (1995). "The Impact of Immigrants on Host Country Wages, Employment and Growth." Journal of Economic Perspectives 9(2): 23–44.

Gandal, Neil, Gordon H. Hanson, and Matthew J. Slaughter (2000), "Technology, Trade and Adjustment to Immigration in Israel," mimeo.

Gretschmann, K. (1999). Managing Industrial Change after the Year 2000: The Impact of EU Enlargement on Industrial Regions in Europe, Final Report. Aachen: RWTH Aachen.

Haensch, K. (2001), "Maximum des Erreichbaren—Minimum des Notwendigen? Die Ergebnisse von Nizza." In: integration 2/01, 94-102.

Hallet, M. (2001). "Real Convergence and Catching-Up in the EU," paper presented to the workshop "Structural Funds and Convergence," The Hague, 12 June.

Harris, J. R. and M. P. Todaro (1970). "Migration, Unemployment and Development: A Two Sector Analysis," American Economic Review 60 (1): 120–142.

Heinemann, Friedrich (2000), "The Political Economy of EU Enlargement and the Treaty of Nice." Mimeo, ZEW Mannheim

Inter-Governmental Conference 2000: Report on the Inter-Governmental Conference, June.

Konings, Josef and Alan Murphy (2001). Do Multinational Enterprises Substitute Parent Jobs for Foreign Ones? Evidence from European Firm-Level Panel Data. CEPR Discussion Paper No. 2972, September 2001.

Organization for Economic Cooperation and Development (2001), Transition at a Glance, Paris, www.oecd.org

Petrakos, G. and Y. Saratis (2000). "Regional inequalities in Greece," Papers in Regional Science 79: 57–74.

Preston, C. (1997). Enlargement and Integration in the European Union. London: Routledge.

Quah, D. (1999). "Models of explicit distribution dynamics," European Commission, The Socio-Economic Impact of Projects Financed by the Cohesion Fund: A Modelling Approach. Luxembourg: Office for Official Publications of the European Communities.

Sinn, H.W., G. Flaig, M. Werding, S. Munz, N. Düll, H. Hofmann, A. Hänlein, J. Krusse, H.J. Reinhard, and B. Schulte (2001). EU-Erweiterung und Arbeitskräfte-migration: Wege zu einer schritt-tweisen Annäherung der Arbeitsmärkte. Munich: IFO.

Todaro, Michael P. (1969). "A Model of Labor Migration and Urban Unemployment in Less Developed Countries." American Economic Review 59 (1): 138–148.

Von Hagen, Jürgen and Susanne Mundschenk (2001). The Functioning of Economic Policy Coordination, ZEI Working Paper, B08.

Weise, C., J. Bachtler, R. Downes, I. McMaster, K. Toepel (2001). The Impact of EU Enlargement on Cohesion, Final Report. Berlin and Glasgow: German Institute for Economic Research and European Policies Research Centre.

Yataganas, Xenophon A. (2001). The Treaty of Nice: The Sharing of Power and the Institutional Balance in the European Union—A Continental Perspective; Havard Jean Monnet Working Paper 03/01.

Notes

[i] The effect will be different for an enlargement bringing Turkey into the EU. In this paper we assume that Turkey's EU membership is still further away than the membership of the 12 accession countries. This assumption is justified on the basis of the Copenhagen criteria listed below.

[ii] Authors' calculations based on data provided in C. Weise et al (2001), p. 196–198.

[iii] EU-26 is without Malta.

[iv] Presidency Report on the Inter-Governmental Conference, June 2000.

[v] For a detailed discussion, see Dewatripont et al (1996).

[vi] It has been noted that EU membership is a moving target. Entry requirements were much less stringent in the 1970s, when they were limited to the common market and EC obligations, than in the 1990s and today, when they include economic and monetary union as well as cooperation in home affairs and foreign policy.

[vii] Because it is not yet known exactly when and in what order the applicant countries will join the EU, the new definition of qualified majority within the Council, as well as the new composition of the Commission and the new distribution of seats in the European Parliament, are determined by the Treaty of Nice for a Union of 15 Member States. The Treaty restricts itself to setting out the principles and methods for changing this system as the EU grows: they are listed in the Protocol on Enlargement and attached declarations.

[viii] There are in total 3 million possible combinations for forming coalitions. Of those, only 16 coalitions are affected by the simple majority criteria and only 7 by the population criteria (Bobay 2001).

[ix] The Nice provisions foresee the co-decision procedure for the following EC Treaty Articles: 13 (incentives to combat discrimination), 65 (judicial cooperation in civil matters), 157 (specific industrial support measures), 159 (economic and social cohesion actions outside the Structural Funds), 191 (statute for European political parties), and 62 and 63 (visas, asylum and immigration).

[x] Negotiations are often in line with the principle of a quid pro quo. In the Intergovernmental Conference (IGC) for example, Germany gave up additional votes in the Council in return for 27 more MEPs than the other large countries; France had to give concessions on the common commercial policy to ensure parity with Germany in the decision-making process; the small Member States had to accept a reduction in their relative weight in the Council to safeguard their equal representation on the Commission, and so on (Yataganas 2001).

[xi] *Random* in this context means that no member knows in advance whether it would be for or against the proposition.

[xii] The passage probability under unanimity for a random proposal may be calculated assuming a 50/50 chance that a country votes "yes." In an EU-15, the passage probability with unanimity is already small, with, and even smaller in the EU-27 where the probability is practically 0.

[xiii] See von Hagen and Mundschenk (2001) for further discussion.

[xiv] See Dewatripont et al (1996) for further analysis.

[xv] Nevertheless, the two most affluent accession countries—Slovenia and the Czech Republic—have had a negative net migration balance with eight EU countries (Belgium, Denmark, Finland, Germany, Luxembourg, Netherlands, Sweden, and the United Kingdom) over 1992 through 1997 and 1993 through 1997, respectively (see Boeri and Bruecker 2000, Table A.16). Both countries have also had a negative balance with Germany alone.

[xvi] This assumption, however, is not innocuous. Germany has had a high number of foreign nationals among its residents, but that reflects not only the attractiveness of Germany as a destination country, but also the stringency of its naturalization law.

[xvii] Indeed, the accession-candidate countries differ from the traditional source countries of Europe's immigrants in that they have a relatively highly skilled labor force.

[xviii] Previous enlargement negotiations included no more than four countries.

[xix] The four Structural Funds used to channel the financial assistance for the European economic and social cohesion policy are: the European Regional Development Fund (ERDF), The European Social Fund (ESF), The European Agricultural Guidance and Guarantee Fund (EAGGF), and the Financial Instrument for Fisheries Guidance (FIFG).

[xx] C. Weise et al (2001), *The Impact of EU Enlargement on Cohesion, Berlin and Glasgow*, The German Institute for Economic Research Berlin (DIW) and European Policies Research Centre, Glasgow (EPRC).

[xxi] See, for instance, evidence provided by Quah (1999), Petrakos and Saratis (2000), and Hallet (2001).

[xxii] "Cohesion in the Enlarged European Union," Speech of Michel Barnier, European Commissioner for Regional Policy and Institutional Reform, to the Second European Cohesion Forum, Brussels, 21 May 2001.

[xxiii] Michel Barnier, ibid.

[xxiv] Michel Barnier, ibid.

[xxv] Euractiv, Dossier on the Cost of Enlargement, 14 May 2001.

[xxvi] Ibid.

[xxvii] Opinion of the Committee of the Regions on "The Structure and Goals of European Regional Policy in the Context of Enlargement and Globalization: Opening the Debate," 15 February 2001.

[xxviii] The six countries with which the EU was negotiating at that time: the Czech Republic, Estonia, Hungary, Poland, Slovenia, and Cyprus.

[xxix] Working Document on the financial implications of EU enlargement, European Parliament, Committee on Budgets, 11 April 2001.

Economic Consequences of Poland's Accession to the European Union

WITOLD M. ORŁOWSKI, Independent Centre for Economic Studies (NOBE)

General remarks

The negotiations on Poland's entry into the European Union (EU) are approaching the most critical stage, at which the most sensitive issues are going to be put on the table. Despite all the problems that may appear, it seems possible that the negotiations will be concluded by the end of 2002, and the membership may be granted as early as in 2004. Obviously, nothing can be taken for granted. The compromise necessary to pave the way for an early membership can be difficult to achieve. Rather, the difficulty is to arrive at a set of various compromises among the most important actors of the game: the EU as a whole, EU member states, Poland, and various groups within the Polish society. Nevertheless, EU membership in the near future becomes an increasingly feasible scenario.

In this paper I try to summarize the most important economic consequences of Poland's accession to the EU. The paper focuses on: (1) the likely conditions of accession (the outcome of negotiations), (2) the macroeconomic challenges and opportunities presented by admission, including both the problems of the real and nominal convergence, and (3) consequences for the enterprise sector. Obviously, these topics are related one to another and cannot be really separated.[i]

However, before starting a discussion on various consequences of the accession, a few important points should be kept in mind while assessing challenges and opportunities of the accession.

First, Poland joins the EU after almost half a century of the communist rule that led to the peripheralization, separation from the mainstream of the economic and technological development of the world, destruction of its market institutions, and cutting its natural economic links with western Europe. For a few decades, Poland could not join the European integration process due to the political reasons. If we had been free to choose during the 1950s, probably we would have joined the European Economic Commission (EEC) from the beginning. Unfortunately, it was not possible. We did not participate actively in shaping the European Communities, the single market, nor the European Monetary Union (EMU). Nevertheless, today we are determined to join the EU, because in our view the economic and legal framework created by the EU, despite some shortcomings, serves economic stability and economic development well.

Second, Poland joins the EU as a relatively poor country. The distance between Poland and western Europe, although resulting from 300 years of economic history, is bigger today than any time in the history. The distance increased dramatically during the times of the communist economy in Poland. In 1950, GDP per capita in Poland was 10 percent less than the GDP in Italy, and close to that in Spain; in 1989 was slightly more than a fourth of the Italian level, and a third of the Spanish level

(Figure 1). The only way to reduce this distance is to maintain for several decades the high rate of growth of the Polish GDP, much higher than in the EU. Therefore, we do not join the EU to get infinite access to the development assistance, nor to help our workers to emigrate to the richer western European countries. We want to join the EU as the membership will contribute to the faster economic and social development of Poland.

Third, there seems to be no reasonable alternative to joining the EU. Western Europe is the only big market close to Poland, and the force of the economic gravity will inevitably push Poland in the direction of the integration (Figure 2). Already today, the level of integration and dependence on the EU markets—measured for example by the share of the EU trade in the total foreign trade—is much higher than it was in the Club-Med countries in the 1980s. This is also particularly visible in the case of the financial markets, jealously protected by the southern Europeans for long years after the membership was granted. A high level of integration results also from the Europe Agreement (the association agreement) between Poland and EU. Under this Agreement, not only is trade basically free (with the exception of food), but also the financial markets are pretty liberalized and EU market regulation policies are adopted in many fields. Therefore the full economic integration of Poland with the EU is an inevitable fact. The only remaining question concerns the economic, legal, and institutional framework in which the integration is going to proceed. As the full EU member-

ship creates an environment much more favorable to Poland (to understand that this is the case, it is it enough to point out to the generous development assistance granted to Poland once the country joins the EU) the country is determined to proceed with the accession.

Finally, it is necessary to acknowledge that membership in the EU is a challenge for our economy and society. Poland is well prepared to face such challenges, however. The real shock that Poland had to absorb in 1990–1991 was much more dangerous. In 1989, the Polish economy was close to collapse, Polish firms did not have the ability to adjust, and Polish products could not compete on the world markets. Despite this, Poland has undertaken a radical program of reforms in central and eastern Europe, a program that bore fruit quite quickly. The liberalization shock connected with EU membership is not on the same scale.

The real challenge for Poland will be to maintain, after joining the EU, fast and sustainable economic growth. That requires the conclusion of the structural reforms undertaken during the 1990s, such as privatization and restructuring of enterprises, structural reforms of the public sector, enhancement of the market institutions and public administration, and liberalization of the labor market, which will make it more flexible. The burden of taxation should be lowered, and the state should pull back from its extensively high role in the economy to leave more resources in the private sector. Economic and legal stability should be secured to attract long-term foreign capital.

103

Figure 1: GDP per capita in Poland, Germany, and Spain, 1918–1999

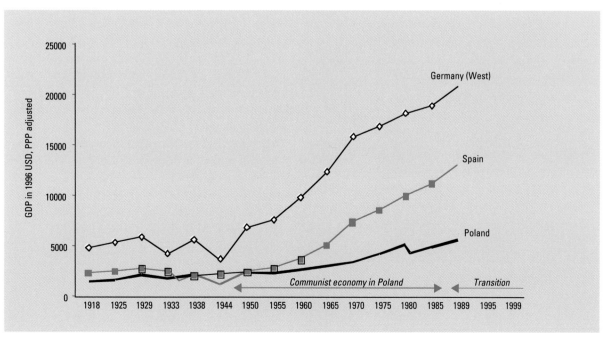

Figure 2: Relative size of economies of Poland, the EU-15, and CEE countries (GDP in PPP terms, EU-15 = 100, 1999)

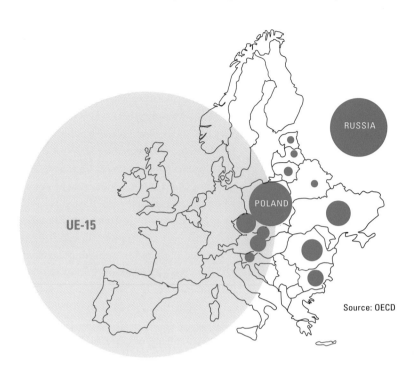

Source: OECD

Negotiations and entry conditions

Based on the Copenhagen criteria, Poland made an official application to join the EU in 1994. Three years later, the European Commission issued a favorable opinion on the Poland's application (European Commission 1997), and the negotiations of the conditions of entry started in March 1998. Currently, after having closed 16 out of 29 chapters, and finalizing the agreement on the next 4 chapters, negotiations are approaching the most critical stage at which the most sensitive issues are to be discussed.

Some specific features of the negotiation process

First, the negotiations are not between two competitors but among the present and future members of the same union. For this reason, both sides are interested in Poland's successful entry into a uniform market. If, in the future, Poland shows poor economic results such as difficulties with the balance of payments, the EU would be forced to provide financial support (as was the case with Greece in the 1980s).

Second, the negotiations are not "negotiations" in the traditional sense of the word. To enter the EU, Poland basically has to accept the full *acquis communautaire* (the pre-accession requirements; the possible concessions would be minimal and extremely difficult to obtain). The issues that can be negotiated include the possibility of transition periods in implementing some parts of the *acquis communautaire* (particularly the most costly ones); the possibility of introducing transition periods during which Poland will take full advantage of some of the membership rights; procedures regarding Poland's involvement in certain common policies of the Union; the size of financial support for Poland resulting from participation in the sharing of the structural funds.

Despite the fact that the negotiations are expected to be difficult, it is possible that Poland will be accepted as a Member State relatively soon. The target date, as currently set by both sides, is to finish the negotiations by the year 2002 and to enter the EU in 2004. However, meeting such a timetable (called "very ambitious" by the EU) would require a huge adjustment effort from both sides, and a strong political commitment to solve the problems. In the absence of any of the items, the negotiations may last for much longer.

Likely economic conditions required for Poland's entry into the EU

- Acceptance of the internal market rules, including the full liberalization of flows of goods and services and full acceptance and implementation of EU market regulation policies. The elimination of frontiers between Poland and the old EU will obviously require the adoption of the whole internal market product–related *acquis*. There may be some transitionary restrictions on the freedom to deliver selected types of services (eg, the construction services), mainly caused by German and Austrian concerns about the effects for the labor markets. On the Polish side, an effort will be made to gain a transition period for the phasing-out of the privileges given to investors in the special economic zones, and for implementation of some costly intellectual property regulations (eg, in the pharmaceutical industry).

- Full liberalization of the capital flows. The only temporary restrictions that may apply—these are of only minor importance—concern the sale of agricultural land to foreigners (due to social and political rather than economic considerations).

- Relatively long-term transition periods (no more than 7 years) for the freedom of movement of labor.

- Covering the Polish agriculture by the Common Agricultural Policy (CAP) of the EU. Given the technical and financial constraints of Polish agriculture, it is most likely that Poland will be covered from the day of the entry by the price-support mechanisms of CAP, while the country will only gradually get full access to the direct-income support for farmers (the initial extreme negotiation positions of Poland, demanding full access immediately, and the EU, excluding Poland from this part of CAP, are likely to lead to some compromise). It is worthwhile noticing that the current form of the CAP is far from being optimal from the point of view of Polish development needs, and in fact may actually lead to some slow-down of the restructuring of the rural areas while failing to satisfy the financial expectations of farmers (Orłowski 1998). Nevertheless, the strength of the agricultural lobbies in both the EU and Poland seems to be a decisive factor in shaping the entry conditions of Poland.

- Broad access to the EU structural funds, with a cap of 4 percent of GDP on the maximal financial allowances available for the country. One may note, however, that the actual absorption abilities of Poland, as well as the other central and eastern European (CEE) countries may create a bigger obstacle to using the available funds than the 4 percent cap, particularly during the first years of the membership.

- Relatively long transition periods in the implementation of various costly environmental EU regulations (especially those that do not interfere directly with the competitive market position of Polish firms, such as the drinking water treatment directive assessed in Hughes and Bucknall 2000).

Poland's rationale for the enlargement

Despite all the transition periods, such entry conditions mean that Poland will have to adopt, on the day of the membership, the bulk of the *acquis communautaire*, while getting the major part of the membership rights. Although the impact of taking over the Internal Market *acquis* is likely to impose certain additional costs on enterprises and on the government, gaining entry to the internal market of the Union is the great prize. The exclusions from this rule, albeit politically sensitive, seem to have a minor importance for the Polish economy. The rationale for the enlargement for Poland is the following.

First, as an EU member, Poland will get irrevocable unlimited access to the western European market. Given the huge differentials in wage levels between Poland and its western neighbors, that should create the tremendous business opportunities for national and foreign investors. Second, EU membership will greatly reduce investment risk, encouraging long-term capital flow to Poland (Baldwin et al 1997). Third, EU membership will help Poland in developing a stable, market-friendly legal framework that will encourage long-term investment. Fourth, Poland, as an EU member, will be entitled to generous financial transfers from the structural policy and CAP.

Membership in the EU means adjustment costs for Poland as well. Polish producers should adjust to the Internal Market. On the one hand, that means fulfilling the product norms of the EU, to ensure that a product manufactured in Poland satisfies consumer protection rules of the Union (as it can be sold everywhere in the EU). On the other hand, competition pressure will greatly increase, and the freedom to support domestic firms with public assistance will be severely restricted. Both phenomena will require an adjustment on the part of Polish firms—increasing investment and enhancing productivity—if the firms are to survive. To make the situation even more challenging, Polish firms will have to make additional investments to ensure fulfilling of the EU environmental or social protection norms.

Costs

The costs for Poland may be threefold. First, the accelerated restructuring and modernization of the economy reinforced by enhanced competition may lead to a hike in unemployment, particularly if the adjustment abilities of the enterprises are low and the flexibility of the labor market poor. The problem has got its regional dimension, as some regions—particularly those with the ailing industries—may be hurt much more severely than others. Second, Poland may be forced to introduce some costly legislation that will be counterproductive to the long-term growth of competitiveness and productivity. An example of this type of cost is the high level of the social protection that leads to higher labor costs and less market flexibility, or a protectionist policy in the field of agriculture that slows down structural changes. Finally, Poland may have to adopt some costly regulations that do not fit with the current preferences of Polish society. A good example of this sort of regulation is found in the area of the environment. The rich EU countries run very costly environmental policies. Although a need to spend more on the environment in Poland is obvious, at its current level of income, Polish society would probably prefer to have less costly environmental policies than those of the EU. Some policy factors may be also come into play: the environment in Poland is more polluted than in the EU, and Polish environmental policies, which put more stress on the concentration of resources and which are more market-based, seem to suit Poland's needs better than the EU environmental *acquis*.

The adoption of the *acquis* will obviously add constraints to the freedom of the government to make policy, and it will put new constraints on enterprise management and lead to the creation of new institutions or changes in existing ones. These additional constraints should not be seen only as costs: the process of accession and adoption of the *acquis* will also bring clear benefits. Poland's loss of control of its trade policy, for instance, will be offset by participation in trade policy decisions in the Union (whether this is an advantage or not will of course depend on the nature of EU trade policy in the future) and by the well-known benefits coming from the general liberalization of the trade regime. Costs of implementing environmental regulations will partly be recouped by lower spending on health over the longer term. Additional constraints will clearly be applied to macroeconomic policy, monetary policy, and structural policies.

Macroeconomic effects: The challenge of real convergence

As stated earlier, the main challenge for Polish economic policy connected with the accession is to see EU membership as a vehicle for accelerating economic growth. The key issue for the country is whether EU membership will generate "real economic convergence"—that is, the ability of a less-developed country to grow more quickly so that, over time, the initial gap in GDP per capita diminishes. From the point of view of the neoclassical economy, this can be easily explained by the following mechanism: in poor regions, labor is cheap and capital relatively expensive because it is scarce (poor regions have low income, and, therefore, small savings). If the capital is expensive, the marginal return resulting from its use—equal to its price—is high. That means that capital investments in a poor region bring higher returns than they do in a rich region, where the capital is relatively cheap and abundant. This constitutes an incentive to move the capital from rich regions to poor regions, which, in turn, leads to higher growth rates in poor regions.

In fact, high growth rates in poor regions do not require imports of capital. In the traditional models of economic growth, the neoclassical production function—representing the process of transforming production factors (labor and capital) into goods and services—shows that marginal productivity of production factors diminishes as they increase in amount. This means that, in an economy that does not have much capital, each saved and invested unit of capital gives higher production growth than it does in a developed economy. There is therefore no need to borrow capital from abroad; given the same savings rate, a less-developed economy will be growing faster than a well-developed economy.

Table 1 shows the distance between Poland other CEE countries, and EU-15 countries, measured both in the GDP per capita terms (adjusted for PPP) and in the terms of the GDP growth rate needed over the next 25 years for the economies of these countries (CEEs, Poland, and EU-15) to converge. This rate varies from 4 percent in Slovenia to 9 percent in Bulgaria (for the current poorest EU Member States from 3.4 to 4.2 percent). In the case of Poland, the required rate is 6.5 percent annually.

At first glance, the required annual percent rate does not look terribly high. On closer inspection, it does. A growth of over 6 percent, albeit not beyond reach, is extremely difficult to maintain over the longer period of time (it has been achieved by South Korea in the period 1972 to 1997, that is, until the crisis; however, the poorest EU countries had average growth rates in that period ranging from 2 to 4 percent). Moreover, a characteristic feature of the real convergence process is that the growth of a country is faster the lower the development level (obviously, this is true only if the right policies are

Table 1. Distance between CEE and EU-15 countries, 1998

	GDP per capita	GDP growth rate	
	in PPP terms (EU-15 level = 100)	Average observed 1995–1999	Necessary to achieve convergence in 25 years*
Poland	38	5.8	6.5
Hungary	50	3.4	5.4
Czech Republic	60	1.6	4.6
Slovakia	49	5.2	5.5
Slovenia	70	4.2	4.0
Romania	28	-0.6	7.9
Bulgaria	22	-2.2	8.9
Lithuania	31	3.4	7.4
Latvia	28	2.1	7.9
Estonia	37	4.0	6.7
Greece	66	2.8	4.2
Portugal	75	3.4	3.7
Spain	81	3.4	3.4
EU-15	100	1.8	

*Assumed EU-15 GDP growth rate of 2.5 percent
Sources: OECD, EBRD, and author's calculations

Table 2. Investment in human capital in Poland and selected EU countries

	Full-time students enrolled in tertiary education per 100 persons in the 5–25 age bracket			Spending on R&D as percent of GDP (1994)
	1990	1994	1996	
Greece	—	8.6	—	0.49
Ireland	4.4	6.2	—	1.41
Portugal	—	7.6	—	0.63
Spain	7.5	10.1	—	0.85
EU-15 average	7.6	9.1	—	1.95
Poland	2.9	5.1	6.5	0.82

Sources: GUS, OECD.
Note: "—" indicates not available.

applied). That leads to a slowdown—over time—of growth rates as the underdeveloped countries approach the level of the developed countries. Therefore, even faster growth is necessary during the first years if a 5 or 6 percent growth is to be obtained over 25 years. Ireland is, until now, the only example of a success in the real convergence process in the EU.

To what extent the adoption of the EU's legal framework and market regulation may contribute to Polish economic growth? Generally speaking, the *acquis communautaire* is a package of regulations governing the functioning of the EU's single market, where barriers to the free flow of goods, services, and production factors (labor and capital) are lifted, and where uniform principles of market organization are introduced (competition law, state aids, consumer rights, environmental protection, support for regions, and so on). Independently of how critical one can be about some market-unfriendly elements of the *acquis* (CAP in particular), *acquis* represents a well-developed coherent set of laws that support economic development. Implementing the *acquis* in Poland may contribute to speeding up real convergence (Barbone and Zalduendo [1997] suggest that the combination of the acceptance of the EU legal order, correct macroeconomic policies, and high saving rates may shorten the process of real convergence for Poland to around 20 years).

Modern growth theory suggests that the most important single factor contributing to real convergence is human capital. Investment in human capital (learning and experience) plays a crucial role in fostering long-term growth. Human capital in Poland, as well as in the other CEE countries, is not as highly developed as is often assumed. If Poland wants to maximize its chances for real

convergence, then this type of investment should be strongly promoted. Table 2 indicates the scale of investment in human capital (in a broad sense) in Poland compared with that of selected EU members.

Despite the fast progress observed in Poland during the 1990s, the proportion of students in the population in the mid-1990s was still much lower than in the majority of EU countries (although, surprisingly, it was close to that of Ireland). Polish R&D spending as a proportion of GDP, albeit lower than the EU-15 average, was comparable with that of Spain. The quality of education and scientific research is another important issue, as the educational patterns inherited from the communist times did not fit the needs of the market economy. In-depth reforms in education and research, as well as securing sufficient funds to finance them, will play a crucial role in maximizing Poland's chances for real convergence.

Of course, some positive role may be also played by the EU structural policy. Poland, as an EU member, will be entitled to development assistance that reaches probably as much as 7 to 8 billion euros annually by the year 2006 (up to 4 percent of GDP). These funds may help in developing infrastructure, in promoting rural development, and in creating new jobs. The EU experience to date shows, however, that even the most generous structural fund transfers cannot solve a country's problems unless the right economic policies are pursued and markets are flexible. The most striking example of the failure of transfers to improve economic performance (due to a lack of appropriate domestic policy) is Greece, a country that received one of the highest levels of transfers in relation to GDP. Structural funds may help a country to enter the path of real convergence, but by no means will it guarantee it.

All of this means that the economic policy that can promote Poland's chances of convergence should focus on maintaining responsible macroeconomic policy aimed at creating a stable framework for economic activities. This focus would also include promoting domestic savings, in particular reducing the public-sector deficit; diminishing the role of the state in the economy by reducing the tax burden; privatizing state-owned companies; demonopolizing, restructuring, and liberalizing the economy; promoting the development of efficient financial markets; and creating incentives to invest in human capital.

In the history of EU enlargement to date, one can make only one strong case for real convergence having occurred: the case of Ireland. The Irish Republic joined the EU (at that time it was called the EEC) in 1973 when its GDP per capita was 60 percent of the EU-15 average. During the 1970s and 1980s, its GDP increased only slowly, and in 1989 it reached 68 percent of the EU average. But in the 1990s, Irish GDP growth accelerated in relative terms and in only 8 years it managed to reach the EU-15 average (1997). On the other hand, a counterexample can be found in the case of Greece. Greece joined the EEC in 1981 when its per capita GDP was close to the Irish at 66 percent of the EU-15 average. But in the years that followed, Greek GDP per capita did not change a great deal in relation to the EU-15, and it remained at 66 percent of the EU average even in 1997. It is evident that in this case no real convergence occurred.

Careful analysis of the historical experience gives an interesting insight into the problem of Poland's chances of maintaining high growth after the accession as well as the policies needed to promote it. Several factors can explain the difference in the performance of Greece and Ireland. One should start by noticing that success was not related to the size of support received from the EU budget (both countries were obtaining a similar scale of support, as a percent of GDP; see Orłowski 1998). Interestingly, transfers from the EU to Ireland reached high levels already in mid-1970s; however, indications of real convergence did not emerge until the 1990s.

The dramatic difference between Greece and Ireland can be seen in macroeconomic and structural policies. In Greece, the fiscal expansion program realized during the 1980s led to an increase of the budget deficit, from 3 percent to over 18 percent of GDP, and destabilization of the economy. In Ireland—after a period of high deficits in the 1970s, reaching 15 percent of GDP—the deficit was brought down close to zero (the process started in mid-1980s). Compared with Greece, Ireland had much lower level of government spending (in relation to GDP) and a lower level of public-sector companies in GDP. In the mid-1980s, in Greece the level of share of public sector companies in GDP increased to 23 percent of GDP according to World Bank data. Greece was the only country within the EU that, instead of privatizing, nationalized some sectors of economy in the 1980s (a consequence of populist policies at the beginning of 1980s). Unlike Greece, Ireland created very good climate for investments, particularly for foreign investors. Furthermore, Greece displayed a total inability to create a stable framework for economic growth. Greece's indecisive economic policy, which led to an increase of the state budget, money supply, and salaries, resulted in a relatively high level of inflation, between 14 and 22 percent in the 1980s. It was not until the mid-1990s that inflation was gradually reduced to a one-digit level, the result of a coordinated action of fiscal and monetary policies. Lack of stable prices has an adverse effect on long-term decisions regarding savings and investments. In contrast, Ireland reduced inflation to 2 to 3 percent during the 1980s. Generally speaking, Greece's lack of success can be explained with her failure to comply with the principles of the Washington consensus; Ireland's success with her very strict adherence to those same principles.

The long-term economic performances of Greece and Ireland in the EU sheds some light on what are likely to be key determinants of real convergence also in the Polish case.

European Union accession brings more resources to the country (more inflows of foreign direct investment [FDI] and more EU transfers). The key issue is to use these resources to finance additional investment expenditure rather than using them to finance consumption. The main challenge, therefore, is to resist strong pressures for a rapid increase in consumption once large EU development assistance and private capital begin to flow. The simplest mechanism conducive to boosting consumption works through greater public spending—both increased government consumption and higher transfers to households—and deficits. Obviously, one can use the additional external resource to finance public-sector fall in savings level (Figure 3).

As Figures 3 and 4 suggest, the main macroeconomic factor behind the Greek failure was the use of the foreign financing for maintaining consumption, while the radical change of a similar policy by Ireland in the mid-1980s helped to boost Irish economic growth.

Nevertheless, one should take into account the fact that the temptation to increase consumption rapidly in a relatively poor country joining the EU may be quite strong. Given the relatively cheap and easily available financing of the fiscal deficit post-EU accession, those pressures may be hard to resist. Clearly, a prudent macroeconomic policy that encourages saving and long-run investment is at the core of success. The inability of Greece to maintain high saving resulted in sluggish economic growth and general social disappointment with the integration process.

Figure 3: The use of external resources to finance spending of the government

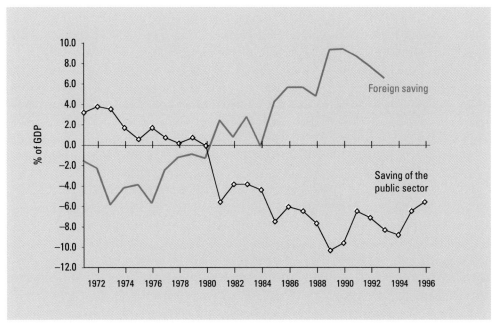

Source: Orłowski, 1998

Figure 4: The use of external sources to finance saving of the government

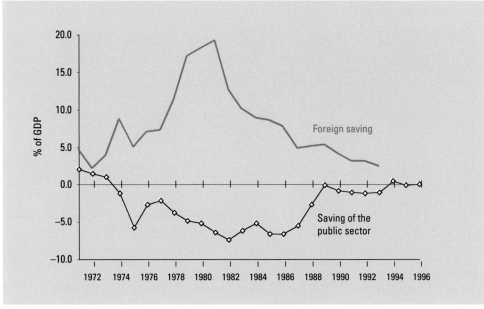

Source: Orłowski, 1998

Macroeconomic challenge: Nominal convergence

The nominal convergence—that is, fulfilling the requirements of the Economic and Monetary Union (EMU)—is another challenge for the Polish economy. As the EMU requirements became part of the *acquis*, the membership of Poland must also entail it (a permanent "opt-out" is not an option). Although a country does not have to accept the principles of EMU at the very moment of accession, it is assumed that new EU members will accept them over time (European Commission 1997). But it is obvious that, so far as a country remains outside the euro area, some room for maneuver in fiscal and monetary policy, albeit restricted, will still exist.

The Maastricht criteria are generally considered to be a set of orthodox rules for the conduct of fiscal and monetary policy. The final objective of the EMU is to create a stable macroeconomic framework with very low inflation, no exchange rate risk, sustainable fiscal positions of governments, and totally free movement of capital. The main benefits of monetary union include elimination of exchange rate risk (an incentive for long-term EU-wide economic ventures), price stability, elimination of unjustified price differences between markets, lower foreign exchange reserves needs, and dynamic growth effects due to improved microeconomic efficiency.

Despite the generally positive impact that hardening the macroeconomic environment may have on the Polish economy, some dangers clearly exist.

First, the low adjustment capabilities of economic agents—typical for transition economies—may impose high adjustment costs (for example, in dealing with external shocks). If factor markets are not flexible enough, social costs may also be excessive and expressed in a sharp increase in unemployment. All these factors may be eliminated, or at least limited, by the continuation of appropriate structural policies and reforms.

Second, albeit the low inflation is likely to help long-term growth, the costs of disinflation (bringing down inflation to the EMU required levels) may be very high. This is particularly true due to the possible existence of a strong Balassa-Samuelson effect. The effect, stemming from the difference in the growth productivity between the tradable and nontradable sector, leads to higher inflation in the fast-growing economy than in the economy with slow growth, even if the exchange rate between both economies is fixed. This phenomenon is due to the fast increase of prices of nontradables (the tradable goods' inflation is equal in both countries), and may be additionally strengthened by "corrective" inflation, for example, the increase in previously suppressed prices of energy or social services. If a strong nontradable goods inflation prevails, achieving the desired average level of the consumer price index (CPI) inflation may require deflation in the tradable sector, and therefore may lead to the recession. Moreover,

as the Irish example of the late 1990s shows, the Balassa-Samuelson effect leads to the real appreciation of the currency (going, in the case of the fixed exchange rate, through the increase in the wage and CPI inflation). Such a phenomenon undermines the competitiveness of the tradable sector and may lead to the increase in unemployment (either through the loss of jobs in the tradable sector intended to keep the unit labor costs low, or due to the economic slowdown).

Third, if the fulfillment of the inflation criterion can be achieved only under the condition of a major economic slowdown, it becomes more difficult to fulfill the fiscal criterion. Although the Polish public debt to GDP ratio remains rather low, the fiscal crisis witnessed in 2001 suggests that, without a deep reform of the public sector, it is not possible to keep the deficit at the required level when the economy slows down.

Therefore the question for Poland, as well as for other CEE countries, is not whether to join EMU but rather how to join, given the above-mentioned restrictions. It is clear, that appropriate structural policies, labor market policies, and public-sector reforms de facto create a new set of the EMU criteria for the new member states.

The effects for enterprises

Adoption of the *acquis* is likely to place additional adjustment burden on the domestic firms. In particular, meeting the EU product-related norms and other internal market regulations, and meeting the environmental and work safety standards may prove very costly, while the enhanced market competition will make it more difficult for firms to keep their market shares and profitability. Clearly the availability of foreign financial assistance and the general fall of the price of capital may help in meeting the challenge.

Although the cost of adopting the *acquis* in horizontal policy areas such as environment, social policy, the internal market, and transport will be very considerable, the benefits in many cases will be even higher in terms of reduced health costs, lives saved, and better transport facilities. In the first place, however, it is the gross costs that will affect enterprises in the relatively short-term, the benefits arising generally in the longer term. Many of the costs will, however, not result from regulations that impose new or different standards, but simply from the need to upgrade infrastructure and equipment to remain competitive in liberalizing markets. Moreover, in the majority of cases these costs will have to be carried independently, whether Poland joins the EU or not. Membership in the EU will mean, however, an acceleration of the restructuring process. More restriction put on the public aid to enterprises and more market competition means also more restructuring pressure, leading to possible job losses in various parts of the economy. Clearly, different sectors of the economy will suffer cost increases—partly related to the horizontal costs but also because of specific sectoral regulation that exists.

The costs of adopting EU regulations will vary depending on the initial situation of branches. Moreover, a likely increase in costs of some production inputs—unit cost of labor (expressed in the common currency), or energy costs, just to give a few examples—will hurt, to various degrees, the competitiveness of the Polish enterprises.

Changes in competitiveness will depend on several main elements (Mayhew and Orłowski 2000):

- costs of adopting the Internal Market standards and regulations (horizontal or sector-specific);
- costs of adopting the EU Social Chapter;
- costs of adjustment to the enhanced competition, mainly in the form of the additional restructuring and investment needed;
- changes in the cost of labor (effect of real wage growth and productivity changes), which may be strengthened by the real appreciation of the currency stemming from the Balassa-Samuelson effect; and
- elimination of remaining tariffs and other barriers to the free flow of goods.

The last element, considered crucial in the standard trade liberalization analysis, will have only a reduced impact on the post-accession situation of Polish firms. Tariffs on exports of Polish industrial goods to the EU have already disappeared, and tariffs on EU exports have are being progressively phased out. Some effects can be expected from the introduction of the Common External Tariff and from adopting the Common Trade Policy (relatively small given the modest share of non-EU trade in Polish exports and imports). It seems also that the expected impact of the Social Chapter is likely to be smaller than generally perceived (with the exception of a few costly work safety regulations). However, the costs of meeting the environmental requirements are likely to be very high.

Concluding remarks

EU accession is likely to create big challenges, but also big opportunities for the Polish economy. The bulk of adjustment is likely to fall on the Polish enterprises, exposed to the stronger market competition, facing additional costs of meeting the EU Internal Market requirements, and dealing with the increased pressure of the wage costs. The path of restructuring will be accelerated while the rules of granting public aid seriously restricted. However, these are mainly pure adjustment costs, aimed at bringing the future benefits.

Poland's economic policy should concentrate on the concluding the program of structural reforms aimed at enhancing the adjustment abilities of enterprises and making the markets—particularly the labor market— more flexible.

The real test for the success of the EU membership of Poland is connected with unemployment. Poland needs the economic growth that promotes job creation and solves the problem of unemployment. The problems of Spain show that the link between growth and unemployment is not automatic. On top of demographic pressure, Poland will have to absorb huge outflow of employees from the ailing industries and from the agriculture. On the EU market only the high productivity and competitiveness can guarantee sufficient job creation. Enhancement of both, through higher saving and investment, should be the main target of Poland's economic policy.

111

References

Barbone, L. and J. Zalzuendo. 1997. "EU Accession of Central and Eastern Europe. Bridging the Income Gap," World Bank Policy Research Working Paper No. 1721, Washington DC.

Barro, R., X. Sala-i-Martin. 1995. *Economic Growth*. New York: McGraw-Hill.

Baldwin, R. E. 1994. *Towards an Integrated Europe*. London: Centre for Economic and Policy Research.

Baldwin, R. E., J. F. François, and R. Portes. 1997. "The Costs and Benefits of Eastern Enlargement: The Impact on the EU and Central Europe," *Economic Policy* (United Kingdom), No. 24: 125–176.

European Commission. 1997. "Agenda 2000—Commission Opinion on Poland's Application for Membership of the European Union." Brussels: European Commission.

Golinowska, S. et al. 2000. "*Skutki integracji Polski z Unią Europejską*, Warsaw: Fundacja Edukacji Ekonomicznej/Fundacja Eberta.

Hughes, G. and J. Bucknall. 2000. "Poland: Complying with EU Environmental Legislation," World Bank Technical Paper No. 454. Washington DC: World Bank.

Mayhew, A. and W. M. Orłowski. 2000. "The Impact of EU Accession on Enterprise Adaptation in the EU-Associated Countries in Central and Eastern Europe," Falmer: Sussex University Working Papers in Contemporary European Studies, No. 44.

Orłowski, W. M. 1998. "The Road to Europe," Łódź: Instytut Europejski.

Orłowski, W. M. 2000. *Produkt Krajowy Brutto Polski 1900–2000* Łódź: NOBE.

Orłowski, W. M. 2000a. *Koszty i korzyści z członkostwa w Unii Europejskiej. Metody-modele-szacunki*. Warsaw: CASE.

Sachs, J. and A. Warner. 1996. *Achieving Rapid Growth in Transition Economies of Central Europe*, Cambridge, Massachusetts: Harvard Institute for International Development.

World Bank. 1996. *From Plan to Market, World Development Report 1996*. Oxford: Oxford University Press.

European Union Enlargement and the Balkans

VLADIMIR GLIGOROV, The Vienna Institute for International Economic Studies

Introduction

The enlargement process for eastern and southeastern Europe has been designed as one of guided convergence of countries in transition that are already partially or potentially integrated with the European Union (EU).[i] To judge that a country can be fully integrated into the EU, one must judge that it has satisfied a number of conditions that are either necessary or sufficient or something in between. One is that a country is European, which is not just a geographical criterion but a value criterion too, that is, the country should share with the EU the same set of fundamental values (whichever those might be). Another condition is that there is, actually or potentially, an economic integration, that is, that the EU is or is going to be the predominant economic, (eg, trade), partner of the country in question.[ii] The third condition is the country's political integration, which means that the potential EU member either has or is developing political and social institutions that are to be found in the EU (democracy, rule of law, civil society, and the like).[iii] The actual enlargement can be negotiated at some point when it is judged that the conditions have been adequately met and that the process of convergence is on track and is irreversible.

Thus, there are essentially two issues to discuss. One is the interplay of these conditions in the process of their fulfillment, and the other is the process of convergence itself. In the canonical case, a country would, actually or potentially, fulfill the main conditions for becoming a member and would also be judged capable of sustainable convergence to the evolving EU norm. However, there are cases in which a country could be judged as satisfying, actually or potentially, one or the other of the conditions but in which that country's complete convergence may still not be deemed sustainable. A number of countries in the Balkans,[iv] and indeed the region as a whole, are arguably such cases. The question, then, is how this process of enlargement of the EU in the Balkans can be guided. The EU has been groping for an answer, rather unsuccessfully, for a decade now.

The reason that the Balkans is an issue when it comes to EU membership is that the region is economically integrated with the EU, actually or potentially. Most of the countries in the region are small and potentially quite open, though the actual level of openness is significantly below its potential. Their main markets are in the EU. In addition, most of their financial resources in the form of transfers and investments come from the EU. However, their economic integration is not necessarily accompanied, or accompanied in a sustainable way, with those of the EU in terms of values and politics. The region is also quite underdeveloped, and there is a serious issue of whether the convergence with the EU can really be a sustainable process within the prevailing approach of EU enlargement.

Economic integration

From the EU side, the region as a whole is not unimportant, though at the moment its economic significance is rather small. The GDP of the region as a whole is below US$ 100 billion at current (ie, 2000 or 2001) exchange rates (which is less than the GDP of Greece or Portugal). However, there are about 55 million people in the Balkans,[v] and their production as well as their consumption is intricately connected with the EU, which is already the main trading partner for almost all the Balkan economies. In addition, EU countries are a natural destination for the majority of the migrants from this region. Also, modernization has been historically associated with the West, especially when it comes to the spread of science, research, and knowledge in general. Finally, EU is already present in the Balkans through Greece, which is a member country, and Turkey, which has a long-standing relationship with the EU and is now a candidate for membership.

Thus, economic integration of the Balkans with the EU can only increase as the countries in the region and the region as a whole start to grow. Calculations of the potential for trade based on the gravity model (which predicts potential trade between states, depending on their size and distance from each other) show that there is quite a lot of room for the countries in this region to increase their trade with the EU.[vi] This refers more to exports than to imports, as the region runs a significant trade deficit, especially in its trade with the EU. Some of this increase in trade with the EU would take the form of trade diversion at the expense of the regional markets. But some would be clearly trade creation, as the current barriers to trade are removed.

Financial integration is also significant. There are at least two aspects to it. On one hand, private and public transfers from the EU are very important. In a number of countries and territories, remittances play a very significant role (though the official statistics do not always capture the real extent of that role). Aid and lending from the EU or the EU Member States also play a significant role. Finally, what foreign investment there is comes mainly from firms and individuals residing in the EU. The potential for foreign investments based on gravity model estimations show the same characteristics, as do those for potential trade: there is significant potential for growth of investments from the EU into the region.

On the other hand, most Balkan countries are using the euro (mostly in the form of the German mark), actually or potentially, much more than they use their domestic currencies. Thus, in most cases, the foreign reserves of the local central banks will be higher than the domestic money in circulation. If foreign currency savings, in the banks and at home, are added, it can be concluded that currency substitution is quite significant. This is partly because of the devaluation risk and partly because of the default risk. The two together make it difficult to put up a sound domestic banking system without significant participation of the foreign banks. Indeed, foreign-owned banks dominate the financial markets in Croatia, Bosnia, and Herzegovina and Macedonia, and they will soon extend their dominance in Yugoslavia, Bulgaria, and Romania. Although the reasons for these developments are not the same in every country, the consequences are.

If other trade and financial dealings with the EU are taken into account, the extent of actual and potential integration of the Balkans with the EU increases. Thus, a number of Balkan countries depend significantly on tourism and on trade in other services, and most of it is with the EU. The Adriatic Coast and the Black Sea are popular destinations for tourists from the EU. The same goes for transit services, which are quite important for a number of countries. If attention is paid to financial flows, it is obvious—from the fact that trade and current accounts of most of the Balkan countries are highly negative—that these countries will have to import savings for a long time. Most of those savings will be coming from the EU, as they have in the past.

There are other aspects of economic integration of the Balkans with the EU that have great potential for growth. These are: technology and transfers of knowledge, as well as business connections of all kinds. Thus, it is fair to say that the Balkans is potentially integrated with the EU as much as any region in Europe, if not more.

The actual and potential integration is bound to increase with the process of enlargement itself. Some of the neighboring countries, such as Hungary and Slovenia, are certain to be included into the first wave of EU enlargement. As they play an increasingly important role in the Balkans, the enlarged EU will be an even more dominant economic space for the Balkan region than it is now. Indeed, in economic and political sense, the EU will practically encircle the Balkans or the southeastern Europe.

Table 1: Economic indicators in southeastern European countries, 2000

	ALB	B&H [1]	BUL	CRO	MAC	ROM	YUG
Population							
Area in km²	28,750	51,130	110,910	56,540	25,710	238,390	91,296
Population, 1,000 persons	3,401	3750[2]	8,150	4,500	2,030	22,443	8,380
Population per km²	118	73[2]	73	80	79	94	92
Gross domestic product (GDP)							
GDP, real growth, in percent	7.8	9.0	5.8	3.7	5.1	1.6	7.0
GDP at exchange rate, US dollars (millions)	3,811	4,140	11,989	19,023	3,291	36,719	10,000
GDP/capita (US dollars at exchange rate)	1,120	1104[3]	1,471	4,227	1,621	1,636	1,193
Output							
Industrial output, real growth, in percent	6.4[2]	8.8/5.6	5.8	1.7	3.5	8.2	12.2
Agricultural output, real growth, in percent	5.0[2]	—	−16.0	10.2[4]	−6.5	−14.1	−19.7
Retail trade turnover, annual change in percent (real)	—	—	0.7	14.4	11.9	−3.8	7.7
Employment							
Employment total, 1,000 persons, end of period	1,067	639	2,943	1,341	550	8813[4]	2,238
Employment, annual change in percent	−1.8	−2.4	−4.7	−1.7	0.8	−2.3[4]	−2.6
Unemployment registered, 1,000 persons, end of period	215	415	683	379	262	1,007	812
Unemployment rate in percent end of period	16.8	38.9/40.2	17.9	22.3	32.2	10.5	26.8
Wages and prices							
Average monthly gross wage (US dollars at exchange rate)	107[8]	174[5]	112	588	155[5]	133	69[5]
Consumer inflation, percent per annum	0.0	1.2/13.6	10.3	6.2	10.6	45.7	85.6
Producer prices in industry	—	—	17.2	9.7	8.9	53.4	106.5
General government budget							
Government balance, percent of GDP	−11.0	−7.2[2, 6]	0.7[7]	−3.9[7]	3.5	−3.6[7]	−6.1[4]
Foreign Trade							
Exports total, fob, US dollars (millions)	256	742	4,812	4,432	1,319	10,366	1,723
Annual change in percent	−6.9	14.3	20.1	3.0	10.7	21.9	15.0
Imports total, fob, US dollars (million)	1,070	2,899	6,494	7,923	2,085	13,055	3,711
Annual change in percent	14.1	15.9	17.7	1.6	17.4	25.6	12.6
Trade balance	−814	−2,157	−1,682	−3,491	−766	−2,689	−1,988
Trade balance percent of GDP	−21.4	−52.1	−14.0	−12.5	−23.3	−7.3	−19.9
Current account							
Current account, US dollars (million)	−129.7[2]	963	−701	−531	−113	−1,400	−1,300
Percent of GDP	−3.4[2]	23.3	−5.9	−2.8	−3.4	−3.8	−13.0
Gross reserves excl. gold, US dollars (millions)	608	499	3,155	3,525	429	2,470	1,229[4]
Gross foreign debt, US dollars (million)	1,067	2,584	10,364	10,810	1,436	9,843	12,500
Money Supply							
M1, percent of GDP	20.3[2]	16.0	14.3	11.4	10.3	5.8	9.3
M2, percent of GDP	47.4[2]	28.1	36.5	46.5	18.8	23.2	46.1[2]
Refinancing rate percent per annum, end of period	17.8[2]	—	4.7	5.9	7.9	35.0	26.8

[1] Where two figures are given, the first refers to the Federation, the second to Republika Srpska
[2] 1999 data
[3] Calculated using 1999 population data
[4] 1998 data
[5] Net wages
[6] Consolidated government budget
[7] Central government budget
[8] Budget institutions only

Source: WIIW database incorporating national and international statistics, IMF, CBBH

Integration and underdevelopment

Among the potential new members of the EU, the Balkans hosts the least-developed countries. Gross Domestic Product (GDP) *per capita* is less than US$ 2,000 at current exchange rates (in 2000 or 2001). At Purchasing Power Parity (PPP), GDP *per capita* may be somewhere between US$ 4,000 and 5,000 currently (see Table 1).[vii] The share of agriculture is, as a rule, high, whichever way it is measured. The share of industry, with some exceptions, tends to be small. Services play significant role, as does the informal economy. Unemployment tends to be high or very high, with some exceptions. Poverty rates are high, as is social inequality. Exports are low, while imports tend to be much higher. States have serious fiscal problems, both on the revenue and on the expenditure sides.

The region would have been less-than-developed even had it not grown negatively in the last 10 years or so. Unfortunately, the drop in GDP and in industrial production has been significant in all cases, and has been dramatic in a number of cases. Thus, Yugoslavia has lost more than 50 percent of its GDP since 1989, and the same is true for Bosnia and Herzegovina. In other cases the loss has been smaller, but is still significant. Thus, the Balkans has experienced the period of retardation in the last decade or so.[viii]

This negative growth has had consequences for economic relations with the EU. Looking into the trade structure, it can be seen that, unlike some central European countries in transition, the Balkans has developed the foreign trade structure typical of a backward economy. Export is dominated by raw materials, where they exist, and heavy industry products; by labor-intensive goods, most often connected with outward processing trade; and by some agricultural products. Also, exports are rather concentrated, in most cases, in few products. Imports are by contrast diverse, as the region needs to buy almost everything.

As most of the Balkan countries export almost the same products, the intraregional trade is not very developed, though there are exceptions. Almost invariably, the EU is the main trading partner. In most cases, the EU countries that participate are Germany, Italy, Austria, and Greece. Some countries in the region do not trade with each other at all, while some trade a great deal. Thus, Macedonia and Bosnia and Herzegovina trade a lot within the region, while Croatia and Bosnia and Herzegovina do not really trade with Bulgaria and Romania, for instance. In general, it could be said that the intraregional trade is still somewhat distorted, with trade flows between countries often being below as well as above potential. Tables 2a and b give the shares of imports and exports of all the countries in the region.

Trade with the EU is the most important trade and tends to take a high share, though not high levels, almost irrespective of the exchange rate and tariff regimes. Imports are constrained by the ability to pay for them, while exports have shown the tendency to stagnate, sometimes after the initial increase that occurred due to often very low pre-1989 trade integration with the EU. In some cases these rates respond to the acceleration or deceleration of growth in the EU, but in a number of cases they show little change, at least in dollar terms. Thus, exports are constrained by competitiveness in terms of price, quality, diversity, and the like.

Though there are no estimates, it is reasonable to expect that the elasticity of imports is low while that of exports is quite high (though not in all cases, because some of the exports, such as exports of raw materials and grain, sell at world prices). This is because imports have no domestic substitutes, while exports have to compete in price rather than in quality or in special market characteristics, as very few differentiated products are in fact exported.

Trade regimes in the Balkans differ a great deal. Bulgaria and Romania have Europe Agreements with the EU that have liberalized their trade of manufactured goods. As for the rest of southeastern Europe (called *the Western Balkans* by the EU), the EU has unilaterally lifted almost all tariff and nontariff restrictions to imports from these countries. These countries in turn have committed themselves to signing bilateral free trade agreements till the end of 2002. However, the trade regimes do not reveal the real extent and level of barriers to trade within the region and between the region and the EU. Borders, security systems, legal uncertainties, and sheer political animosities present formidable obstacles to intra- and interregional trade and business activities in general. The Balkans remains a region in which a number of states are characterized as having illiberal economic regimes and where there are political entities that do not rely exclusively or effectively on the rule of law. This interferes with the economic developments in the region as a whole.

Table 2a. Southeastern European trade: Share of exports with a specific country as a percent of total exports (2000)

TO:	OF:															
---	ALB	B&H	BUL	CRO	MAC	ROM	YUG	AUS	GER	GRE	HUN	ITA	RUS	SLO	TUR	EU
Albania	—	0.1	0.5	—	1.3	0.1	0.1	0.0	0.0	2.3	0.1	0.1	0.0	0.1	—	0.0
Bosnia & Herzegovina	—	—	0.2	11.6	1.7	0.1	—	0.2	0.1	0.2	0.7	0.1	0.1	4.4	—	0.0
Bulgaria	0.0	0.0	—	0.1	1.8	1.8	2.4	0.3	0.1	4.2	0.2	0.2	0.6	0.3	0.7	0.1
Croatia	0.1	10.2	0.1	—	3.7	0.2	—	0.9	0.2	0.2	0.6	0.6	0.3	7.9	0.1	0.2
Macedonia	1.7	1.3	2.3	1.4	—	0.1	—	0.1	0.0	3.5	2.0	1.0	0.1	0.6	1.1	0.4
Romania	0.0	1.0	1.8	0.1	0.2	—	—	0.7	0.4	3.5	2.0	1.0	0.9	0.6	1.1	0.4
Yugoslavia*	—	—	7.8	—	22.4	—	—	0.3	0.1	1.1	0.3	0.2	0.2	0.2	—	0.1
Austria	0.6	5.8	1.4	6.4	0.4	3.1	4.2	—	5.3	0.8	11.2	2.2	0.7	7.5	1.4	2.1
Germany	6.9	13.5	9.1	14.6	17.3	17.2	20.3	33.4	—	12.3	33.5	15.1	9.0	27.2	18.9	12.0
Greece	16.2	1.4	7.8	2.4	7.6	2.4	8.8	0.5	0.8	—	0.4	2.0	1.2	0.3	1.3	0.9
Hungary	0.0	0.4	0.6	1.4	0.3	3.0	1.5	5.0	1.7	0.5	—	0.9	2.3	1.9	—	1.2
Italy	57.1	31.3	14.3	21.6	12.1	21.1	27.6	8.9	7.6	9.2	5.3	—	7.0	13.6	6.7	5.9
Russia	0.2	3.0	2.5	1.4	0.7	0.7	—	0.9	1.1	2.3	1.4	1.0	—	2.2	1.1	0.8
Slovenia	0.3	7.6	0.6	10.9	3.4	0.7	3.5	1.7	0.4	0.2	1.0	0.8	0.1	—	0.2	0.3
Turkey	0.5	—	10.2	0.8	0.8	5.3	—	0.7	1.4	5.1	0.3	1.8	3.0	0.8	—	1.3
EU	85.4	67.2	51.2	54.9	46.4	61.7	75.9	61.7	55.8	43.6	70.0	54.9	33.1	63.9	51.3	60.8
BALKANS	1.9	12.6	12.6	13.1	31.1	2.3	2.4	2.5	1.0	15.9	4.0	2.4	2.0	15.3	1.9	0.9
SEE–1	2.2	20.6	13.8	25.4	34.8	6.1	7.4	9.2	3.1	16.6	5.0	4.2	4.5	17.2	2.1	2.4
SEE–2	18.9	22.0	31.8	28.7	43.1	13.8	16.2	10.4	5.3	21.7	5.7	8.0	8.7	18.3	3.3	4.5
Total, US dollars (billions)	0.3	0.7	4.8	4.1	1.3	10.2	0.9	66.6	548.8	10.7	26.9	236.6	103.0	8.7	27.6	2240.7

All exports: f.o.b.

* Exports are to Federal Republic of Yugoslavia, except exports from Macedonia, Russia, and Slovenia where not specified.

EU includes: Austria, Belgium, Denmark, Finland, France, Germany, Greece, Ireland, Italy, Luxembourg, Netherlands, Portugal, Spain, Sweden, and the United Kingdom.

BALKANS includes Albania, Bosnia and Herzegovina, Bulgaria, Croatia, Macedonia, Romania, and Yugoslavia.

SEE–1 (Southeastern Europe–1) includes BALKANS plus Hungary and Slovenia.

SEE–2 (Southeastern Europe–2) includes SEE–1 plus Greece and Turkey.

Source: IMF Direction of Trade Statistics Quarterly June 2001

Table 2b. Southeastern European trade: Share of imports with a specific country as a percent of total imports (2000)

TO:	OF:															
---	ALB	B&H	BUL	CRO	MAC	ROM	YUG	AUS	GER	GRE	HUN	ITA	RUS	SLO	TUR	EU
Albania	—	—	0.0	—	0.2	—	0.1	0.0	0.0	0.1	0.0	0.1	0.0	0.0	—	1.1
Bosnia & Herzegovina	0.0	—	0.0	1.0	0.5	0.1	—	0.1	0.0	0.0	0.0	0.1	0.1	0.6	—	2.2
Bulgaria	2.5	0.4	—	0.1	5.4	0.6	14.3	0.1	0.1	1.4	0.1	0.3	0.3	0.5	1.0	0.1
Croatia	1.0	19.3	0.1	—	2.8	0.0	—	0.4	0.1	0.1	0.2	0.3	0.2	—	0.1	0.1
Macedonia	2.0	0.9	0.4	0.7	—	0.0	—	0.0	0.0	0.2	0.0	0.1	0.0	0.5	—	0.0
Romania	0.7	0.5	3.6	0.2	0.5	—	—	0.5	0.4	1.1	0.8	1.0	0.2	0.6	0.9	0.3
Yugoslavia*	—	—	0.4	—	9.6	—	—	0.1	0.0	0.3	0.0	0.1	0.2	0.1	—	0.0
Austria	1.0	6.7	2.3	6.7	2.5	3.9	6.7	—	3.9	0.9	10.7	2.3	1.2	8.2	0.9	1.6
Germany	5.7	13.8	14.1	16.4	13.3	18.8	17.3	45.6	—	13.4	30.4	17.5	11.5	19.0	16.0	13.1
Greece	27.0	0.9	5.0	0.3	8.6	1.7	4.9	0.1	0.3	—	0.2	0.5	0.4	0.2	1.1	0.2
Hungary	1.0	7.6	1.0	2.3	1.1	3.6	3.4	4.8	1.9	0.4	—	0.7	1.2	2.9	—	0.9
Italy	35.9	12.8	8.6	17.1	11.4	20.5	18.6	7.2	6.8	13.5	7.1	—	3.6	17.4	8.9	5.3
Russia	0.6	2.3	24.9	8.1	3.5	7.7	—	1.5	2.6	3.8	7.7	3.2	—	2.3	6.5	1.9
Slovenia	0.8	15.9	0.4	8.0	8.1	0.4	4.5	1.3	0.5	0.1	0.5	0.5	0.3	—	0.1	0.3
Turkey	5.4	—	3.4	0.3	2.8	2.0	—	0.6	1.1	1.4	0.4	0.9	1.0	0.5	—	0.7
EU	77.8	44.5	44.9	56.0	47.1	63.7	61.5	71.7	52.1	58.7	66.4	56.3	32.9	67.8	53.6	58.0
BALKANS	6.2	21.1	4.5	2.0	18.9	0.7	14.4	1.2	0.7	3.3	1.1	2.0	1.0	2.2	2.0	3.9
SEE–1	7.9	44.5	5.8	12.4	28.0	4.7	22.3	7.4	3.1	3.7	1.7	3.2	2.5	5.1	2.1	5.0
SEE–2	40.4	45.4	14.2	13.0	39.5	8.5	27.2	8.2	4.6	5.1	2.2	4.5	3.9	5.8	3.2	6.0
Total, US dollars (billion)	1.0	2.7	6.4	7.7	2.2	11.9	2.9	68.4	501.5	27.8	34.2	235.3	33.9	10.1	52.7	2328.3

All imports: c.i.f.

* Imports are from Federal Republic of Yugoslavia, except imports to Macedonia, Russia, and Slovenia where not specified.

EU includes Austria, Belgium, Denmark, Finland, France, Germany, Greece, Ireland, Italy, Luxembourg, Netherlands, Portugal, Spain, Sweden, and the United Kingdom.

BALKANS includes Albania, Bosnia and Herzegovina, Bulgaria, Croatia, Macedonia, Romania, and Yugoslavia.

SEE–1 (Southeastern Europe–1) includes BALKANS plus Hungary and Slovenia.

SEE–2 (Southeastern Europe–2) includes SEE–1 plus Greece and Turkey.

Source: IMF Direction of Trade Statistics Quarterly June 2001

Political disintegration

Economic integration has not been accompanied with political integration up to now. In fact, politics in the 1990s in the Balkans was almost all concerning disintegration. The disintegration was both intra- and inter-regional. Many causes contributed to that. One was the series of wars on the territory of former Yugoslavia, which are not even over yet. Another cause was the differentiated approach to the region by the European Union and by international institutions and organizations. Finally, international community got involved quite extensively in the region, but in most cases by setting up or supporting non-standard political and economic structures,[ix] which have been designed to deal with security rather than issues of integration. As a consequence, the region has emerged as a laggard in the process of EU enlargement.

One possible classification of political regimes in the region could go like this:

- Countries approaching an advanced stage of democratization:[x] Romania and Bulgaria.
- Countries in apparently sustainable process of democratization: Croatia.
- Countries in the process of democratization: Albania.
- Countries at the start of the process of democratization: Yugoslavia (Serbia and Montenegro).
- Countries in political crisis (breakdown of democratization): Macedonia.
- Countries with significant international security and political presence (quasi-protectorates): Bosnia and Herzegovina.
- Territories at the start of the process of democratization: Montenegro.
- Territories that are *de facto* international protectorates: Kosovo.

The political landscape is even more complicated and unstable than this rather general classification indicates. This schema does, however, get across the political complexity of the Balkans. Of course, often-difficult relations between the states in the region also have to be taken into account. The process of disintegration has yet to be finished, and normalization of the region is still an unfinished task.

Common values

Looking at the other main conditions for the membership in the EU, there are no openly expressed doubts that the Balkan nations historically share European values. However, there is an entrenched belief that these are also Balkan values, which could be perhaps identified with the European values that predominated in the nineteenth century, that is, in the age of nationalism. Indeed, in the last 10 years or so, ethnic homogenization has been one of the main political features in most, though not all, Balkan countries. Thus it is often believed that the Balkans need to modernize in order to become European in the contemporary sense of that word, which basically means that they should outgrow their preoccupation with nationalism and ethnic animosities.

Whether the analogy is the right one could be debated, but there is no doubt that ethnic nationalism is stronger than civic culture in many countries in the Balkans. Though elements of civil society do exist, those elements are under twin pressures from the lack of rule of law on one hand, and from ethnic discrimination on the other. Both account for institutional deficiencies that some have also taken to be the causes of the underdevelopment of the Balkans. Indeed, some have detected the lack of social capital in many Balkan countries.

These assertions should be treated carefully, however. It is, for instance when it comes to the availability of social capital, true that trust in the banking system is rather low, but that is not because there is generally low use of trust as an institutional device. If anything, the opposite is true. Trust in social relations is relied on more than either the legal system or the financial system. The reasons that, for instance, banks are not trusted are the same reasons that they would not be trusted anywhere. The same goes for the legal system, which is corrupt and biased and is generally not an instrument of the rule of law. Thus, it is not really the lack of social capital that is the problem, but the lack of legal capital that is influencing destructively the rather high social capital. In other words, it is the collapse of the state and formal institutions in general that are the root problem, rather than the collapse or nonexistence of civil society or of the informal norms.

However, there is no doubt that the EU has failed to anchor decisively the institutional and cultural developments in the Balkans during the process of transition in the last 10 or so years. Thus, there is an issue of convergence to European values in the Balkans or, in other words, there is still an issue of modernization of the whole region.

Inconsistent public preferences

These so-called Balkan values reveal an inconsistency in public preferences.[xi] More specifically, given the significant potential for economic integration and the propensity to political disintegration, it can be concluded that economic preferences contradict political ones in the Balkans. This contradiction is revealed in actual economic and political developments in the Balkans. It does not arise primarily from the relations with the EU, but rather from the intraregional problems and conflicts. The EU interferes, however, in two ways.

One potential interference of the EU is positive: it could push the prospect of enlargement up the regional and country-specific public agenda so that, for instance, nationalistic policies are not preferred to those of European integration. The EU has, however, failed to do this up to now. It has preferred to keep the Balkans effectively out.

The other interference of the EU can be negative: treating different Balkan countries differently and introducing incentives for intraregional competition that fuels disintegration rather than integration. This has in fact been in many ways what the EU has done.

Thus, the EU can either resolve the inconsistency in the Balkan public preferences or aggravate it. In the past, the EU has not been able to come up with a strategy and a set of policies that would contribute decisively to the resolution of the inconsistency of the public preferences in the Balkans. There is an understanding that a regional approach is necessary in this context, but the EU has been slow at developing a clear and workable regional strategy.

This inconsistency between economic and political preferences is sharper in some countries than in others. In the Balkans, there is a lot of diversity. On one hand, though none of the Balkan countries are very developed, there is significant difference between, for instance, Croatia and Albania, a difference that is probably larger in some sense than the difference between, for instance, Croatia and Austria. On the other hand, there are also significant political differences between countries because some political units in the region are not really states but rather provinces or territories or peoples in search of a state.

These diversities work for different mixes of economic and political preferences. In some cases, the political agenda almost completely dominates every other issue. In some other cases, economic preferences are emerging as the more important ones. From the point of view of the process of accession to the EU, it would be important if the issue of accession would structure both the political and the economic agenda. This, however, has not really happened in the Balkans because the regional and domestic political agenda have held dominant places in most countries and territories.

Converging economic policies

Economic integration is a fact either actually or potentially. The problem is that the levels of development of the EU and the Balkans differ so much. As a consequence, the question has arisen as to whether the policy integration with the EU is the best strategy for the development of this region. This is another level at which the inconsistency between economic and political preferences is revealed.

Initially, it may be doubted that trade integration, which is always the first element to come about in the process of integration with the EU, should be accompanied by the coordination of economic policies. Indeed, in cooperation and association treaties negotiated with the EU, trade integration is treated asymmetrically, with the EU markets being opened, at least in principle, much faster than the markets of the other countries. Also, candidate countries or other countries with contractual arrangements with the EU are not encouraged to join the monetary union or to adopt the euro before becoming the full members of the EU. Finally, though tax harmonization is fostered, mainly through the introduction of the value added tax (VAT), other aspects of fiscal policy are not. Thus, the countries outside the EU may diverge in their economic policies while integrating their trade and possibly their investments.

This divergence may also be the consequence of the different way in which the international financial institutions (IFIs) and the EU view the process of transition and enlargement. For instance, most countries in the Balkans have been advised by the International Monetary Fund (IMF) to adopt some version of a fixed-exchange regime. The problems with these regimes are well known, but an additional problem is that some very strict versions of fixed-exchange rate regimes, such as currency boards, are incompatible with the way EU sees the process of adoption of euro. In the Balkans, two countries have currency boards (Bulgaria and Bosnia and Herzegovina) and two territories have introduced the euro as their legal tender unilaterally (Kosovo and Montenegro). Most other countries, with the exception of Romania, have more or less fixed pegs (though nominally those are registered with the IMF as floats). Given that the EU prefers bands that keep narrowing as the country is converging to the euro, these exchange-rate regimes are inconsistent with that process; because of this, they may encounter a credibility problem in the foreign exchange and money markets.

The exchange rate regimes used are also biased against the use of monetary policy. This has the consequence that money is more expensive than it would otherwise be. Interest rates that are paid in the Balkans are far above those that would be compatible with the potential growth rate of the respective economies. Calculating the interest rates that would be consistent with the sustainable growth that ensures convergence with the EU, it becomes clear that interest rates in the Balkans are much higher than such growth would require. Thus, the lack of the appropriate monetary policy has negative effects for growth. It also leaves too much to fiscal policy, which is even more difficult to conduct in the Balkans than the monetary policy is.

Beyond economic policy, economic and political preferences may clash in the area of regulation and institution building in general. The adoption of the legal system of the EU (the *acquis communautaire*) may be difficult not only because it takes time and resources, which could be used elsewhere, but also because it may not be in accordance with the public preferences of the respective country's political public. Thus, as has already been noted, a country may adopt a law or a set of laws but fail to implement them, or may tend to implement them in an innovative way—that is, according to the politically desired spirit of the law rather than in accordance with the written letter.

Bilateralism or multilateralism

The EU has developed a regional approach to southeastern Europe unlike its approach to central Europe.[xii] It also has a regional approach to the Western Balkans. The two approaches are not always easy to distinguish. Initially, after the Dayton Peace Agreement on Bosnia and Herzegovina in 1995, the region of the *Western Balkans* was defined in order to encompass the countries that were involved in two separate but related crisis points: those around Bosnia and Herzegovina and Kosovo. The guiding idea of this approach was that the countries in this region could not expect to improve their relations with the EU unless they upgraded their mutual relations. After the Kosovo crisis in 1999, the region of *southeastern Europe* was distinguished, which was to be given special attention by the international community as a whole and by the EU in particular. The guiding idea was to work for liberalization of regional trade and for regional approach to investments and development. However, the two regions were never completely integrated because Bulgaria and Romania became candidates for full membership in the EU while the countries from the Western Balkans were offered a new instrument of integration with the EU, the so-called Stabilisation and Association Agreement (SAA), recently renamed the Stabilisation and Association process (SAp), as an interim step to the Europe Agreement and to the status of the candidate for membership.

Indeed, looking at the southeastern Europe region as a whole, the current situation as to the contractual relations with the EU is as follows:

- Candidates for membership: Bulgaria and Romania.
- SAAs: Macedonia and Croatia (signed with the EU and in the process of ratification by the individual member states).
- Cooperation agreement: Albania, SAA negotiations to start soon.
- No contractual relations: Bosnia and Herzegovina and Yugoslavia with the SAAs to be offered some time in the future.

In the wider regions of the Balkans and southeastern Europe, Greece is a full member of the EU, Turkey is in the currency union with the EU and is a candidate for membership, while Slovenia and Hungary are candidates that are expected to be in the first wave of EU enlargement. Thus, it is easy to see that EU has quite diverse relationship with the various countries in the region.

SAA process, or SAp, as the enlargement process itself, is a bilateral affair between the EU and the applicant country. The EU takes the initiative in the sense that it has to judge that the country in question is ready to start to negotiate the contract of membership. No appropriate instrument or procedure for a multilateral approach really exists. After the war in Kosovo, an organization called the Stability Pact (SP) was launched. It had the explicit aim of fostering regional integration and, thus, regional advance toward the EU. However, the SP is not an instrument of the EU alone. Apart from the SEE countries, it includes all the G8 countries as well as all the international institutions and organizations. Its main aim is to coordinate regional cooperation and financing of regional projects (not only economic but also those in the area of state, civil society, and security building and strengthening).

Both the SAp and the SP process present problems. The SAp treats different countries in the region differently and thus introduces distortions and diversity in the region in which it also wants regional liberalization and homogenization. The SP process suffers from a potentially lethal problem of many principals working with many agents (the multiple principal-multiple agent problem). This arrangement can be credited with the less-than-stellar performance of either the SAp or the SP. But the main problem with respect to the process of EU enlargement is that it is not clear how the SP process is related to the process of enlargement, that is, how is the multilateral body of the SP related to the bilateral process of joining the EU? Thus, though the EU has a regional approach to the SEE, it does not have an efficient instrument of regional policy.

Weak states

The accession of the Balkans to the EU has been hampered by developments that are different in different countries, but which have one consequence that is similar in all of these countries. They all have weak states, and some are state-like or nonstate political entities. By *weakness of the state* it is not meant that the state has few resources, financial or legal, at its disposal; in fact, the contrary is often the case. Rather, a state is weak if:

- it demonstrates a weakness of political will (what can be called political akrasia),
- it cannot be said that it exhibits the rule of law, and
- it faces periodic crisis of one type or another.

In the Balkans, the weakness of political will is a pervasive fact. One aspect of this fact is present in the conflict between the economic and political preferences of the publics in Balkan countries, which was discussed earlier. Another aspect is evident from the fact that the various publics in the Balkans are not ready to face the necessary tradeoffs, especially the tradeoffs between whatever is required by the transition and development and the catering to special interests that would prefer nothing to change, at least as far as the changes would affect their vested interests.

As a consequence of the weakness of the will, in a number of cases, nonstandard political entities have been created with decisive involvement from the international community, part of which was the EU—though perhaps the EU was not its most influential member. Clearly, Bosnia and Herzegovina has a very weak central state and also weak regional states, of which one is really an underground or shadow state. It is also, to a large extent, governed by the international bodies, of which the Office of the High Representative, who is an EU representative, is the most powerful. Yugoslavia is also a very weak state with a complex internal political setup (Serbia and Montenegro, the two federal states, are essentially independent; Kosovo, constitutionally a province in Serbia, is a de facto international protectorate). Macedonia has also shown serious weaknesses lately and is slipping into a very shaky *modus vivendi*.

In these cases, political weakness is essentially a constitutional one. In other cases in the Balkans, political weakness has to do with the distorted process of representation of public preferences, sometimes referred to as *state capture*. This distortion is impeding the process of enlargement because the necessary institutional changes cannot be introduced or, when formally introduced—for instance through an appropriate legislation—cannot be implemented, or are interpreted in such a way by the administration and the courts that their implementation amounts to the reality appearing exactly the opposite of the formal norm.

This political weakness is connected also with the lack of rule of law. It is generally recognized that the rule of law is not very strong in the Balkans. Indeed, legal systems are often quite contradictory or ambiguous so as to leave ample room for arbitrary and discretionary interpretation. As the interpretation by the governments and the courts is subject to influence according to private supplies of appropriate incentive schemes, the result is a high level of corruption. That corruption supports various forms of second economy as well as outright criminal activities. It is not necessary to emphasize how damaging this is to the process of joining the EU.

Finally, the states in the region manage economies with deep macroeconomic problems that make their economic policies unsustainable. Thus, for instance, in many cases fiscal balances are very strained and would not be sustainable without foreign aid and assistance. In addition, external imbalances are also large and ultimately unsustainable. Finally, unemployment is high and employment is low.

Because of persistent macroeconomic imbalances, there are periodic recessions or crisis in the region. Here is an overview of recent (since 1995) economic crises in the Balkans:

- 1996–1997: Albania's economy collapses; hyperinflation in Bulgaria.
- 1998: Croatia's banking system collapses and the economy goes into a recession.
- 1998–1999: Romanian economy goes into prolonged recession.
- 1999: Bosnia and Herzegovina experiences serious slowdown in economic activity; the slowdown is even sharper in 2000, with similar prospects for the year 2001.
- 1999: Yugoslavia collapses.
- 2001: Macedonia comes to the brink of civil war.

The early 1990s were even worse. Indeed, after a torturous decade, only in the year 2000 did the whole region post positive growth. This will not be repeated in the year 2001, however, because of the crisis in Macedonia and the significant slowdown in Bosnia and Herzegovina. In other cases, the accumulation of imbalances sounds a warning to the need for either external balance or fiscal adjustment that may not be possible without some cost in the slowdown of growth. Thus, the states in the Balkans have shown no sustained resolve to stabilize their economies; this has been also related to their approach to transition, which was often indecisive and inconsistent.

The future role of the European Union in the Balkans

The EU experience with the Balkans has highlighted the problems of enlargement itself as well as that of the ability of the EU to act in somewhat unusual circumstances.

The problem with enlargement is that it cannot be easily applied to countries or regions that are dependent on the EU, but are at a very different level of development. In other words, the process of enlargement has not revealed itself as a substitute for, or even as a complement of, development policy.

The EU has become aware of this problem, and has set up a Community Assistance Programme (CARDS), which should assist the Balkan countries in their reconstruction and development efforts. The program should channel money in support of the SAp, which is EU's main instrument for supporting regional cooperation and integration with the EU. In October 2001, the EU released a regional strategy document that should be supported with country strategy documents and aims primarily and explicitly at issues of regional importance.

However, the EU has not found the right way to interfere positively into the public agenda of countries that are economically integrated with the EU, but that have political problems either within their region or with the EU or both. Balkan countries display these characteristics, though not all in the same degree, and the EU has not yet found the way to anchor the development of their public agenda into the process of accession.

The SAp process should address this issue through the signing of association agreements and an increased monitoring by the EU somewhat similar to the monitoring that is applied to the candidate countries in central Europe. The SAp process is at the very start at this point, because Macedonia signed the agreement only in April 2001, and the process of ratification has been very slow because of the deteriorating security situation in the country, while Croatia signed its agreement only at the end of October.

The problem is that the the EU has only one instrument—its offer of integration—but it does not necessarily work effectively on security and deep constitutional problems. Thus, there is a mismatch between the goals and instruments. Economic prospects do not necessarily elicit necessary political changes. This is aggravated by the fact that the international community, with significant contribution from the EU, has assisted in the emergence of nonstandard and weak political structures that are not performing well either as agencies of transition or for political reform and integration.

This is the key problem, and not much has been done in this area. It is to be expected that the EU will take a larger role in these matters because of the changing priorities in the United States and in the international community after the September 11 terrorist attack on the United States. At this moment, however, it is not clear what that strategy might be.

As security is one of the main problems in the Balkans, the EU has adopted a regional approach, which indeed is appropriate in such a case. However, the EU lacks the instruments to implement this approach because the process of integration and enlargement is a bilateral one. This is also the reason that the Stability Pact has not lived up to expectations: it has not found the proper instruments to make a difference in the region.

This dilemma between bilateralism and multilateralism will be resolved, in all probability, in favor of the bilateral approach. Regional integration and cooperation will be urged, but the real strength of the approach is in the bilateral negotiations and that is where the main stress will be. This is somewhat unfortunate because probably the best result so far has come out of the bold decision by the EU to lift most of the tariff and nontariff barriers for the exports from the Western Balkans, which has induced these countries later on to sign a multilateral agreement within the framework of the Stability Pact to liberalize trade throughout the region. These kinds of initiatives and policies from the EU are badly needed, but will probably be overshadowed by the bilateral process of association and integration.

Finally, the enlargement process depends on the existence of political will on both sides, that of the EU and that of the prospective member country or region. Both may fail to exist or may be weak. There may be no way to strengthen them, because the prospect may be too distant to make any difference and the benefits may be too small to mobilize enough interest.

There is little that can be done in this respect now, because the Balkan countries have been relegated to the slower process of enlargement and are thus too far from the date of accession for that to play a decisive role in the internal political process. Ways may be found to remedy that, but it is not clear what those might be at this moment.

In conclusion, it could be said that the EU has learned from its failures in the Balkans. But the situation that has emerged precludes some quick fixes. Thus, there is a long and tortuous road to Europe ahead for the Balkans.

References

Astrov, V., E. Christie, and V. Gligorov. (2001). *Balkans and Europe: Trade, State, Money and Politics.* Final Report of the WIIW Countdown Project.

Gligorov, V. (2000), "Delaying Integration", WIIW Working Paper.

IMF Direction of Trade Statistics Quarterly June 2001.

WIIW (2001). *Southeast Europe: Economic Statistics.*

Notes

[i] That is, that they are either *ex ante* (actually) or *ex post* (potentially) integrated where the judgment about the level of the former is an important indication about the expectation of the latter. More can be found on this subject in Gligorov (2000).

[ii] Other, more specific, criteria of economic integration boil down to the coordination of business cycles, to the ability to withstand the pressures of increased competition within the single EU market, and to harmonize institutions and economic policies with the EU.

[iii] In particular, this means the ability to implement the so-called *acquis communautaire*, that is, the fundamental legal order of the EU.

[iv] Southeastern Europe (SEE) now usually includes seven countries in transition: Albania, Bosnia and Herzegovina, Bulgaria, Croatia, Macedonia, Romania, and Yugoslavia (Serbia, Montenegro, and Kosovo). *Balkans* and *southeastern Europe* will be treated as synonymous here, and will be meant to include these seven countries.

[v] The population of the Balkans is not much smaller than the population of the four front-runners for EU integration from central Europe (Poland, the Czech Republic, Hungary, and Slovenia).

[vi] More on the gravity model in Astrov et al (2001).

[vii] For basic data, see Table 1. Detailed information can be found in WIIW (2001) and in Astrov et al (2001).

[viii] This retardation had followed the economic dead-end in which the Balkans found itself with communism after World War II.

[ix] These structures are protectorates, quasi-protectorates, non-viable political entities, and aid-dependent economies. There is further discussion of this in the following sections.

[x] By *democratization*, the process of building democracy is meant. It is taken to include at least two or three more or less free and fair elections and at least one orderly change of the parties in government.

[xi] There is further discussion on this point in Gligorov (2000).

[xii] Three names are in use, not always clearly distinguished. I use the *Balkans* interchangeably with *southeastern Europe* as the latter term is used now (see Note 4 above). Since 1995, the EU has also introduced the term *Western Balkans*, which refers to Albania, Bosnia and Herzegovina, Croatia, Macedonia, and Yugoslavia (Serbia, Montenegro, Kosovo), that is, to what was later, after 1999, to be called *Southeast Europe minus Bulgaria and Romania*. Confusingly, these two regions are subject to two different though overlapping regional approaches, as explained in the text.

Can Russia Compete?

THIERRY MALLERET, World Economic Forum

FIONA J. PAUA, World Economic Forum

PETER K. CORNELIUS, World Economic Forum

Three years ago, few had expected that Russia—then mired in a severe financial crisis—would, by 2001, outpace the economic growth of many of the world's leading economies. At a time when economic growth in several countries has slowed to a standstill, it is remarkable that Russia has posted a 5 percent year-on-year real GDP gain for the first half of 2001. Although lower than in 2000, when output expanded by more than 8 percent for the year as a whole, this rate of growth appears particularly impressive in light of the substantial contraction of around 5 percent of GDP in 1998 in the wake of Russia's financial crisis. This performance has been achieved amid a striking improvement of its macroeconomic environment. Foreign exchange reserves, which were nearly depleted in August 1998, stood at near record levels of about US$ 38 billion at end-September 2001. The fiscal budget, which had been in deficit on the order of about 7 percent of GDP in the 6-year period up to 1998, ended 2000 with a surplus equivalent to 2.5 percent of GDP. Likewise, the current account registered a surplus of around US$ 46 billion, or 18 percent of GDP, in 2000, compared with only US$ 683 million in 1998. Finally, the rate of inflation fell to around 20 percent in 2000 from almost 85 percent in 1998.

The improvement of Russia's economic fundamentals has not gone unnoticed by investors. Foreign direct investment flows for the first half of 2001 surged by 40.5 percent, while portfolio investments soared by 370 percent. The latter is partly reflected in the 50-percent surge (January to mid-October 2001) of the RTS index in dollar terms, making the Russian bourse one of the best performing stock markets in the world. Rating agencies have also noted the improvement in Russia's prospects, with Standard & Poor's having upgraded the risk rating of Russian debt from the CCC rating with a "negative outlook" rating of its foreign currency debt on August 17, 1998, to the current B rating with a "stable" outlook.

Such optimism surrounding Russia's prospects stands in stark contrast to the short-term prognosis of the rest of the global economy, triggering skepticism as to whether such optimism is well founded. Indeed, while Russia has posted positive growth rates for the last 2 years, this expansion comes after a decade of negative, and at best, flat growth rates. Moreover, Russia's impressive economic performance over the last 2 years has happened in the context of a drastic devaluation of the ruble and highly favorable prices in the international markets of Russia's main export items—specifically oil, gas, and metals. But with the recent appreciation of the ruble and the declining trend in the market price of oil and other commodities, the question arises: can Russia sustain its growth trajectory?

The present paper approaches this question from the viewpoint of Russia's competitiveness, that is, through an assessment of whether the country has the structures, policies, and institutions in place to enable it to maintain the momentum of the medium- and longer-term growth of its economy. The first part of the paper discusses the events of August 1998 and the factors that triggered the financial crisis, which is now widely perceived as a turning point in Russia's transition to a market economy. The second part of the paper assesses Russia's competitiveness based on the findings of the *Global Competitiveness Report 2001–2002* (WEF 2001). Finally, the paper draws a number of policy conclusions regarding key areas that need to be addressed if Russia is to sustain its recent growth record over the medium and longer term.

The 1998 financial crisis and its roots

Russia's financial crisis of August 1998 is widely perceived as the beginning of a new era for the country's transition to a market-oriented economy. To be sure, the turmoil in the foreign exchange and capital markets was dramatic: on August 17, the Russian government announced that the exchange rate band was to be devalued from Rub 5.3–7.1 per US dollar to 6.0–9.5 per US dollar. At the same time, a 90-day moratorium was placed on principal payments on private external obligations (including payments on forward contracts), and it was announced that a compulsory restructuring of the domestic government debt would take place. The details on the debt restructuring were announced the following month, and they provided domestic debt holders with two options: these options entailed 5 percent of the bond principal paid in cash, with the rest converted into either ruble-dominated or US dollar–denominated bonds, with coupons substantially lower than prevailing market rates. Trading in GKOs (ruble-denominated discount instruments) and OFZs (ruble-denominated coupon bonds, and, like GKOs, issued by Russia's Ministry of Finance) was suspended.[i]

Amid the economic and political turmoil and central bank credit expansion, the market exchange rate fell through the Rub 9.5 level on August 26, and, faced with a progressive loss in confidence, the government was forced to abandon the exchange rate band altogether. In the wake of the crisis, Russia's economic performance deteriorated sharply. Over the remainder of 1998, consumer prices rose by more than 75 percent, and the ruble depreciated by more than 70 percent against the US dollar. Mirroring the severe financial pressure during the run-up of the crisis and the worsening of the economic situation in the post-crisis period, real output shrank by around 5 percent in 1998. Real investment fell by about 10 percent, while foreign direct investment collapsed to 1.2 billion US

dollars, a fraction of the 6.2 billion US dollars that flew into the country in 1997. Moreover, government revenues tumbled to less than 10 percent of GDP, resulting in a massive increase in the federal government deficit to 6 percent of GDP in 1998.

At the surface, Russia's financial crisis had its origins in the huge fiscal deficit and the associated increase in holdings of Russian government debt by domestic and foreign investors. Until late 1997, the government was relatively successful in selling GKOs and OFZs, with nonresident investors holding about one-third of domestic treasury securities (around US$ 20 billion valued at the current exchange rate) by May 1998. However, a number of external shocks, including weakening oil prices, and a series of domestic political events led to increased difficulties in selling ruble-denominated debt in the first half of 1998. Yields on ruble-denominated securities thus rose markedly. In June, the government decided to increase the issuance of US dollar–denominated debt in the Euromarkets, which, however, was absorbed only at successively higher interest rates.

Increasingly, it became clear that the government faced a pronounced bunching of amortizations in the treasury bill market during the second half of 1998. In fact, GKO/OFZ redemptions and coupon payments were estimated to average over US$ 1 billion a week through 1999. In the event, efforts to stretch the maturity structure of the debt in the context of an IMF-supported program and a voluntary domestic debt restructuring failed to restore market confidence, in part because only a relatively small amount was involved. Selling pressures thus increased in the financial markets, and with rising fears of bank failures, liquidity in the interbank market dried up. In the foreign exchange market, pressure on the ruble was amplified when Russian banks had to meet margin calls on their foreign currency debt-repurchase operations with foreign counterparts.

Of course, the factors that caused Russia's financial crisis are rooted far deeper. As suggested by numerous studies, slow progress in implementing structural reforms, especially in the enterprise and banking sectors, has played a particularly important role.[ii] Although inflation was brought down quickly in the framework of the government's stabilization programs since 1995, many important problems remained ignored, with program after program being poorly implemented, in part thanks to the opposition of strong vested interests (IMF 1999). At the same time, rapidly falling costs of borrowing in both the domestic treasury bill market and international financial markets due to a strong foreign appetite for Russian securities further undermined the government's incentives to implement far-reaching reforms.

In retrospect, it appears that the 1998 crisis was the result of a mutual reinforcement of fiscal and structural problems. Thanks to implicit and explicit subsidies, widespread *de facto* tax exemptions, and the tolerance of tax arrears and payments-in-kind, budget constraints remained soft. While fiscal policy thus failed to provide proper incentives for the restructuring of the corporate sector, social safety net arrangements, generally provided by the employer, discouraged labor mobility. The situation was aggravated by distortionary tax structures and arbitrary tax administration, which hampered the development of new small and medium-sized enterprises. Moreover, incentives for taxpayer compliance were seriously discouraged by the willingness of the federal and local governments to run up expenditure arrears, together with the tolerance of tax arrears and the practice of offsetting such arrears with expenditure arrears. In turn, inadequate progress with structural reforms continued to hamper economic growth and hence the expansion of the tax base, while government expenditures burdened the budget far more than it would have been otherwise the case.

Following the August 1998 crisis, Russia's problems deepened, at least initially. Weakening tax discipline, together with payments problems in the banking sector, resulted in a sharp decline in federal government cash revenue in the second half of 1998. This shortfall was financed primarily by central bank credit and a further build-up of budgetary arrears. As a result, inflation continued to rise and the foreign exchange market remained under severe pressure. At the same time, the structural reform program effectively came to a halt, and in several areas the government backtracked on specific measures. For instance, oil companies were obligated to supply non-paying domestic refineries, while tariffs for energy and other utilities were administratively frozen or reduced. Several other price controls were re-introduced, and bankruptcy procedures were suspended. Progress in implementing the bank-restructuring program announced in October 1998 remained slow, with no firm action taken against major insolvent banks. Finally, initiatives to normalize relations with foreign creditors met with little success, and the government announced at the end of 1998 that it would be unable to meet its 1999 obligations on Soviet-era debt to London (private) and Paris Club (official) creditors.

Against this background, few expected at that time a quick turnaround in Russia's economic growth. On the contrary, most observers agreed with the IMF (1999, pp. 34–38) that "Russia faces the prospect of protracted high inflation and prolonged recession unless determined and coherent efforts are made to address the country's underlying fiscal and structural problems and the additional challenges arising from the August 1998 crisis."

Assessing Russia's competitiveness

Two-and-a-half years later, it appears that Russia has achieved what may be perceived as an economic miracle. Output not only expanded after several years of contraction, but Russia has actually outperformed most other economies in 1999–2000 in terms of economic growth (Figure 1). Even in the first half of 2001, when global economic growth began to falter, Russia's economy continued to enjoy a rapid increase in economic activity in the range of 5 percent year on year.

The question is, of course, whether Russia's miraculous performance is explained by a fundamental improvement in its competitiveness thanks to structural reforms or instead by improvements in the economy's

Figure 1: Russia: GDP growth, 1991–2000 (annual percentage change)

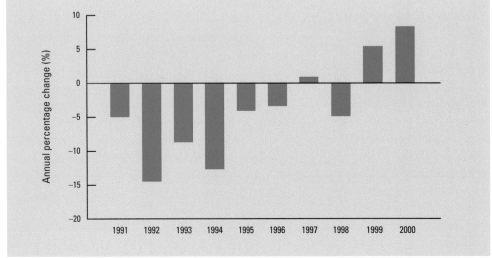

Figure 2: Russia: Structure of output, 1991–1998

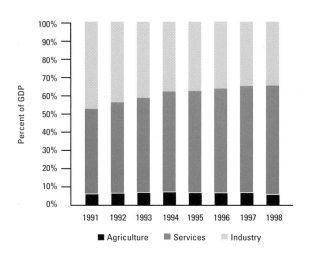

Figure 3: Gross industrial output by sector, 1998 versus 1999 (percentage change)

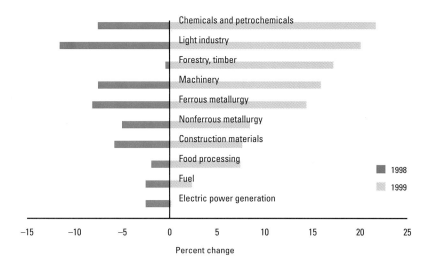

price competitiveness resulting from the massive depreciation of the ruble combined with the increase in Russia's
terms of trade driven by a substantial rise in energy prices.
This question is indeed critical, for in the latter case
Russia's fortune would appear highly susceptible to external shocks, such as a continued decline in energy prices.
To be sure, the industry sector, which includes the extraction industries and accounts for around one-third of GDP
(Figure 2), posted a much higher growth rate in 1999 than
the rest of the economy. Indeed, within the year after the
crisis, nearly all industries showed a marked turnaround,
suggesting that the exchange rate did play an important
role (Figure 3). Moreover, further support is provided by
the fact that the export sector expanded from 30.7 percent of GDP in 1998 to 45.8 percent in 2000. Mineral
fuels account for over 50 percent of exports and combined with metals, they comprise about 70 percent of total
export earnings (Figure 4).

Figure 4: Composition of merchandise exports, 2000

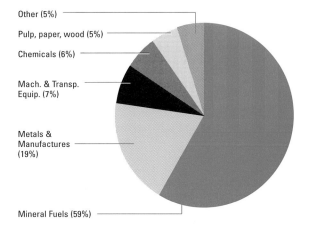

In the following, therefore, we examine Russia's competitiveness employing the analytical framework of the *Global Competitiveness Report 2001–2002* (GCR).

The GCR defines competitive countries as those that have the underlying economic conditions to achieve rapid economic growth for a number of years, taking into account their starting level of income. Whether or not such conditions are met, the conditions necessary to achieve growth must be distinguished from an analysis of a country's current level of economic prosperity. It is quite possible to have a rich country—approximated by its per-capita income—that is likely to grow slowly in the future (high capital stock and current technology, but low propensity to save and innovate). Conversely, it is also possible to have a poor country that is likely to grow rapidly in the future (low capital stock and current technology, but high propensity to save and to adopt new technologies from abroad). Of course, economies can also be rich and fast growing or poor and slow growing.

Given that, at least in theory, a distinction can be made between the circumstances that contribute to the *level* of income per capita and those that contribute to the *change* in income per capita, or *growth*, the GCR develops two different indexes (Porter et al 2000). Focusing on factors determining income levels, the Current Competitiveness Index (CCI) essentially looks at the sophistication of company strategy and operations and the quality of the national business environment in which companies operate. The Growth Competitiveness Index (GCI) ranks countries according to three sets of factors: (1) technology, (2) the quality of public institutions, and (3) the macroeconomic environment. For Russia as a *non-core innovator*—defined as a country with fewer than 15 utility patents registered in the United States per one million inhabitants—the three factors are attached equal weights of one-third.

In practice, of course, some of the same institutions, regulations, attributes, and practices affect both level and growth, though sometimes through different mechanisms. For instance, the presence of capable local suppliers benefits current efficiency, but also supports innovation. Similarly, the intensity of rivalry in an economy and the sophistication of local customers drive current productivity, but also foster productivity growth. Not surprisingly, therefore, there exists a relatively close correlation between the two indexes.[iii]

However, given this paper's primary objective of examining Russia's medium- and longer-term ability to sustain economic growth, the rest of it focuses especially on the GCI.

Overall, the GCI ranks Russia 63rd out of 75 countries, employing both a vast amount of publicly available information (ie, "hard data") and information contained in the World Economic Forum's Executive Opinion Survey ("soft data"). Russia's position reflects the following subrankings: (1) 60th on the technology index, (2) 61st on the public institutions index, and (3) 57th on the macroeconomic environment index. Although the individual rankings seem to suggest that the challenges facing Russia are nearly indistinguishable with regard to their respective importance, a closer examination reveals that in some areas more progress has already been achieved than in others. In the following, we focus on the three major subindexes in turn.

Technology

As the *Global Competitiveness Report 2001–2002* (Porter et al 2001) explains in great detail, technology matters at all stages of development and represents a key driver of competitiveness. At the Factor-Driven stage, firms produce commodities or relatively simple products of long-standardized technology designed in other more advanced countries. Technology is assimilated through imports, foreign direct investment, and imitation. In this stage, firms compete primarily on price, and given their usual focus on assembly, labor-intensive manufacturing and resource extraction, their economies are particularly sensitive to commodity price trends and world economic cycles.

As development proceeds, efficiency in producing standard products and services becomes a dominant source of global competitiveness. While in the second, Investment-Driven stage, technology still largely comes from abroad and is accessed through licensing, joint ventures and foreign direct investment, country increasingly develop the capacity to improve on it. Finally, in the Innovation-Driven stage, competitiveness is based on a country's capacity as a core innovator. Typically, this entails high rates of public and private investments in R&D and higher education, and improved capital markets and regulatory systems that support the start up of high-technology enterprises.

Countries in all three stages can achieve rapid economic growth, and, as a matter of fact, there exist several non-core economies that have enjoyed the world's very highest rates by rapidly absorbing the advanced technologies and capital of the core innovators. This process of "catch-up" growth has been extremely important for many emerging-market economies, but of course this process has its inherent limits. As a non-core economy narrows the income gap with the technology leaders, its ability to narrow the gap still further tends to diminish or even disappear. However, many countries have found the transition from technology-importing to innovation-based development the hardest in the process.

Where does Russia stand with regard to technology as a key driver of economic growth and competitiveness? Consistent with the *Global Competitiveness Report*, we look at three different factors: (1) Russia's level of innovation, (2) the country's ability to import and adopt new technologies from abroad, and (3) the quality of its information and communication technology (ICT) infrastructure. With a weight of one-eighth and three-eighth, respectively, the first two factors combined have the same weight as the third component.

Russia's innovative capacity indeed represents an important competitive advantage, as evidenced by the innovation subindex, which puts the country on the 28th position (of a total of 75 countries). The innovation subindex is composed of two different quantitative indicators and a number of Survey questions, with the hard and soft data having an equal weight of one-half (Table 1). As regards the former, Russian firms registered 1.3 utility patents in the United States in 2000, putting Russia on the 35th position on GCR scale. With a gross rate of tertiary enrollment of almost 43 percent, an indicator that is found to be closely correlated with economic development, Russia scores even better.

However, quantitative indicators of innovation have their limits. For instance, patents do not distinguish between minor innovations that are simply technological refinements and major innovations that revolutionize a field. Interestingly, Russian senior executives appear relatively skeptical with regard to the role of innovation in their country. With an average score of 4.5 on a scale ranging from 1 to7, Russia ranks only 70th concerning the importance of the role of innovation for generating revenue. According to their views, Russia lags significantly behind many other countries in terms of innovation, with a relative position of 56 out of 75 countries. One problem the Survey points to is the apparent lack of research cooperation between universities and companies.

The Survey reveals equally, if not more, important challenges with regard to adopting new technologies from abroad. More specifically, foreign direct investment appears to play only a minor role in this regard and appears even less important than foreign trade as a channel of access to foreign innovations. On the technology transfer index, Russia is thus ranked 49th among the 51 non-core innovators. Finally, important challenges remain in the field of upgrading Russia's ICT infrastructure, as suggested by hard data, such as the number of Internet hosts or the number of personal computers per capita, but also by the results of the Executive Opinion Survey.

Table 1: Determinants of Russia's GCI rank: Technology

Technology Index Components (non-core)	Score	Rank (out of 75)
I. INNOVATION SUBINDEX	**3.72**	**28**
Survey Questions	3.68	53
3.01 What is your country's position relative to world leaders?	3.2	56
3.02 Does continuous innovation play a major role in generating revenue for your business?	4.5	70
3.06 How much do companies in your country spend on R&D relative to other countries?	3.7	36
3.09 What is the extent of business collaboration in R&D with local universities?	3.3	52
Hard Data	3.73	27
3.16 US Utility Patents Granted per million population in 2000	1.3	35
3.19 Gross Tertiary Enrollment Rate in 1997	42.8	19
II. TECHNOLOGY TRANSFER SUBINDEX		
3.04 Is foreign direct investment in your country an important source of new technology?	4.0	73
3.23 Technology-in-trade residual	2.0	58
III. INFORMATION AND COMMUNICATION TECHNOLOGY SUBINDEX	**4.16**	**54**
Survey Questions	3.15	66
4.03 How extensive is internet access in schools	2.1	66
4.07 Is competition among ISPs sufficient to ensure high quality, infrequent interruptions and low prices?	3.7	65
4.08 Is ICT an overall priority for the government?	4.3	50
4.09 Are government programs successful in promoting the use of ICT?	3.1	65
4.11 Are laws relating to ICT (electronic commerce, digital signatures, consumer protection) well developed and enforced?	2.4	72
Hard Data	4.66	52
4.13 Number of mobile phone users	2.2	66
4.14 Number of internet users	211	52
4.15 Number of internet hosts	22.2	47
4.16 Number of telephone main lines	21.8	43
4.13 Number of personal computers	4.3	48

Source: WEF (2001).

131

Table 2: Determinants of Russia's GCI rank: Public institutions

Public Institutions Index Components	Score	Rank (out of 75)
I. CONTRACT AND LAW SUBINDEX SURVEY QUESTIONS	2.97	66
6.01 Is the judiciary independent from the government and/or parties to dispute?	2.9	62
6.02 Are financial assets and wealth clearly delineated and well-protected by law?	2.4	75
6.04 Is your government neutral among bidders when deciding upon public contracts	3.7	29
6.12 Does organized crime impose significant costs on business?	3.0	68
II. CORRUPTION SUBINDEX SURVEY QUESTIONS	4.38	53
7.01 How common are bribes paid in connection to import and export permits?	3.8	57
7.02 How common are bribes paid when getting connected to public utilities?	4.6	56
7.03 How common are bribes paid in connection with annual tax payments?	4.7	44

Source: WEF (2001)

Table 3: Determinants of Russia's GCI rank: Macroeconomic environment

Macroeconomic Environment Index	Score	Rank (out of 75)
MACROECONOMIC STABILITY SUBINDEX	4.52	30
Hard data		
2.28 Inflation in 2000	20.8	70
2.30 Lending-borrowing interest rate spread in 2000	17.9	70
2.29 Real exchange rate relative to the U.S. in 2000 (1995-95=100) 142.4		10
2.24 General government surplus in 2000	3.1	6
2.26 National savings rate in 2000	36.1	4.0
Survey		
2.01 Is your country's economy likely to be in a recession next year?	4.6	40
2.03 Has obtaining credit for your company become easier or more difficult in the past year?	4.3	31
COUNTRY CREDIT RATING SCORE	1.82	68
GOVERNMENT EXPENDITURE SCORE	3.69	44

Source: WEF (2001)

Public institutions

Although technology provides a key pillar of economic growth, the quality of public institutions is equally important. In the absence of an appropriate framework that ensures the protection of property rights, the objective resolution of contract and other legal disputes, efficiency of government spending in public services, and transparency in all levels of government, economic growth will remain severely hampered. All of these factors underpin the functioning of markets and therefore the efficient allocation of resources.

In several of these areas, Russia's perceived performance is comparatively poor. Bribes seem to have remained fairly common, especially in connection with import and export permits and in order to get speedier access to public utilities (Table 2). Notwithstanding important efforts to reform the tax administration, bribes also continue to represent an important problem with regard to tax payments.

However, an even more serious problem appears to exist in terms of enforcing the law and legal contracts. Organized crime is perceived to be widespread and the judiciary is seen as dependent from the government and the political system. However, the relatively worst performance concerns the protection of property rights, where Russia's score is the lowest among all countries covered by the *Global Competitiveness Report 2001–2002*. On the other hand, the bidding process for public contracts appears relatively less distorted, although in this area too much room for improvement continues to exist. With the contracts and law subindex and the corruption index having a weight of one-half each, overall Russia's public institutions are ranked 61st.

Macroeconomic environment

Finally, in the macroeconomic environment category, Russia has better rankings but not that much higher than it has in public institutions or technology categories. Examining the composition, however, reveals a mixed bag of results. On the positive side, Russia's macroeconomic stability subindex rank is 30th, reflecting the progress that has been made in recent years. Within the subindex, which has a weight of 50 percent, Russia belongs to the top ten in terms of national savings rate, general government surplus, and real exchange rate relative to the US dollar. Among its competitive disadvantages however, are both inflation and the lending-borrowing interest rate spread—where Russia is ranked 70th for both criteria.

Provided that further progress can be made in stabilizing the economy and putting in place a framework that is conducive to technological progress and economic growth, Russia's credit rating should also improve (Table 3). Currently, however, Russia is still perceived as a risky debtor, which is mirrored in the comparatively high premium on the cost of capital. Ranked 68th in terms of the country's credit rating, which carries a weight of one-fourth in the macroeconomic environment index, Russia's experience confirms that re-establishing confidence in the international investors' community requires sustained efforts over the long term.

Table 4: Regional division of foreign direct investment, 2000

REGION	TOTAL FDI (US$ MILLION)	PERCENT OF TOTAL
Moscow	4,037.0	36.8
St. Petersburg	1,159.9	10.6
Krasnodar Territory	979.5	9.0
Omsk Region	791.8	7.2
Chelyabinsk Region	595.7	5.4
Leningrad Region	305.6	2.8
Moscow Region	290.6	2.7
Sakhalin Region	250.6	2.3
Samara Region	236.3	2.1
Tyumen	184.3	1.7
Novosibirsk	157.2	1.4
Total Russia	11.0	100

Source: EBRD (2001)

Policy conclusions

For Russia to increase its competitiveness and thereby improve its medium-term growth prospects, it must work toward transitioning from a still largely Factor-Driven economy to an Investment-Driven economy. To make the transition successfully, the country must harness global technologies to local production, either though investment or trade, as well as increase overall domestic investment. Although levels of foreign direct investment have increased, particularly last year, to US$ 11.0 billion, this is considerably lower on a per capita basis than it is in other transition economies. Cumulative foreign direct investment flows per capita at the end of 2000 was only around US$ 160, compared with US$ 2,130 in Hungary, US$ 1,950 in the Czech Republic, and US$ 1,950 in Poland (EIU 2001). Equally important, most of the investment is unevenly spread, and skewed towards the western part of the country (Table 4).

To facilitate investment, domestic and foreign, Russia must work on improving the country's business environment that is conducive to entrepreneurship and private risk taking. This entails further efforts on the macroeconomic front. Equally, if not more important, however, are sustained structural reforms. The following areas appear particularly critical:

- *Public and corporate governance*
  While the government has begun to initiate reforms in public and corporate governance, there remains a need to ensure successful implementation. On the issue of public governance, in August 2000, President Putin created a commission charged with designing a plan for reforming the entire state service and administration. The first set of laws resulting from this initiative has just been passed this year (2001) and it will be interesting to see if the perception regarding its impact will be reflected in next year's Executive Opinion Survey results captured in the annual *Global Competitiveness Report*.

  Similar strides have also been made in the area of corporate governance, but there remains an equally important need to ensure rigorous implementation. Transparency and disclosure still needs to be improved, and awareness of shareholder rights still needs to be enhanced. The cost of poor corporate governance to investors is estimated at about US$ 50 billion, with the Russian state bearing about a quarter of this total loss.[iv] Reforms in this arena are fairly recent, with the national *Code of Best Practice for Corporate Governance* published on September 2001 by the Federal Commission for the Securities Market (FCSM).

- *Strengthening the legal framework*
  Russia's low ranking in the contracts and law subindex highlights the need to strengthen the legal framework. To the Duma's credit, several significant legislative initiatives have been passed in the last year, spanning the criminal, tax, and civil codes as well as legislation concerning production-sharing agreement. There remains an urgent need, however, to establish the framework for property rights.

  Given the importance of technology for the country's medium- and long-term competitiveness, there must be a clear legal framework for the use and application of information and communications technologies. Intellectual property legislation, as well as a law governing electronic commerce, needs to be passed and properly enforced.

133

• *Reform of the financial sector*

Access to credit is critical to supporting the growth of companies in Russia, and it is imperative that financial markets in general be reformed to ensure proper functioning and adequate regulation. The banking sector, specifically, requires reform. The sector's aggregate lending volume is small at 11 percent of GDP. Equally important, the issue regarding minimum capitalization needs to be resolved, as only a fraction of Russia's 1,300 banks appears to be sufficiently capitalized. There are also lingering concerns resulting from the 1998 crisis that insolvent banks are still operating and have not undergone adequate restructuring. Current discussions in Russia of reform of this sector also include other relevant issues such as the extent of foreign participation, the introduction of international accounting standards, and a deposit insurance scheme.

• *Restructuring large monopolies and state-owned enterprises*

The government also needs to advance its transition to a Market-Driven economy by continuing liberalization and privatization. Large monopolies such as the Railways, UES, and Gazprom need liberalization to curb implicit subsidies. Although the situation is improving slightly, the Russian economy continues to operate on implicit subsidies derived from below-market domestic commodity prices and tariffs. Gazprom and UES alone provide US$ 13 billion in subsidies to domestic consumers through artificially low prices.[v] The tremendous challenge the state is currently facing is to conceive how to liberalize the market without sacrificing consumer welfare. This will have to be done rapidly: accident-prone assets require massive investment, which is unlikely to come unless reforms are implemented.

Privatization presents a mechanism to eliminate arrears and foster modernization for the large monopolies. It can also be instrumental for restructuring state-owned enterprises. According to the United Enterprise Register, there were 367,400 organizations with state or municipal ownership and 114,500 with mixed ownership. The stronger market and efficiency orientation ushered by privatization is bound to increase the productivity of these enterprises and unleash further growth momentum into the economy.

• *Investments in education and research & development*

In order to facilitate the country's transition to an Investment-Driven economy (and, eventually, to an Innovation-Driven economy), Russia needs to increase its investment in education, especially at the tertiary level. It also needs to invest in and promote research and development, both at the level of national research institutions and universities and at the corporate level. This entails fostering closer cooperation between public and private institutions. Indeed, Russia needs to make these investments today, for only then can it build the innovative capacity to allow it join the ranks of the world's most competitive economies.

This reform agenda is no doubt ambitious. But without making determined progress on all these fronts, it would appear questionable whether Russia's impressive economy recovery will actually launch the economy on a steeper and sustained growth path. That a number of important reforms have already been initiated is a positive sign. Broadening and deepening the reform process holds the key for the country's further transition to a market economy and its longer-term growth prospects.

References

Åslund, Anders. 1995. *How Russia Became a Market Economy* (Washington, DC: The Brookings Institution).

Berglöf, Erik and Ernst-Ludwig von Thadden. 2000. "The Changing Corporate Governance Paradigm: Implications for Developing and Transition Economies," in *Corporate Governance and Globalization: Long-Range Planning Issues*, ed. by Stephen S. Cohen and Gavin Boyd (Cheltenham: Edward Elgar), pp. 275–306.

Blanchard, Olivier, Simon Commander, and Fabrizio Coricelli. 1995. "Unemployment and Restructuring in Eastern Europe and Russia," in *Unemployment, Restructuring, and the Labor Market in Eastern Europe and Russia*, ed. by Simon Commander and Fabrizio Coricelli. EDI Development Studies (Washington, DC: The World Bank), pp. 289–330.

Economist Intelligence Unit. 2001. Russia Country Briefing (London: EIU).

European Bank for Reconstruction and Development. 2001. *Transition Report* (London: EBRD).

Fischer, Stanley. 1994. "Russia and the Soviet Union Then and Now," in *The Transition in Eastern Europe. Volume 1: Country Studies*, ed. by Olivier Jean Blanchard, Kenneth A. Froot, and Jeffrey D. Sachs. National Bureau of Economic Research (Chicago and London: University of Chicago Press), pp. 221–258.

International Monetary Fund. 1998. *World Economic Outlook and International Capital Markets: Interim Assessment: December 1998* (Washington, DC: International Monetary Fund).

International Monetary Fund. 1999. *World Economic Outlook: May 1999* (Washington, DC: International Monetary Fund).

Litwack, John M. 1995. "Corporate Governance, Banks, and Fiscal Reform in Russia," in *Corporate Governance in Transitional Economies: Insider Control and the Role of Banks*, ed. by Masahiko Aoki and Hyung-Ki Kim. EDI Development Studies (Washington, DC: The World Bank), pp. 99–120.

Lopez-Claros, Augusto and Mikhail M. Zadornov. 2001. "Economic Reforms: Steady as She Goes," *The Washington Quarterly*, 25(1): 105–116.

McArthur, John W. and Jeffrey D. Sachs. 2001. "The Growth Competitiveness Index: Measuring Technological Advancement and the Stages of Development," in *The Global Competitiveness Report 2001–2002*, The World Economic Forum (Oxford: Oxford University Press), pp. 28–51.

Porter, Michael E., Jeffrey D. Sachs, and Andrew M. Warner. 2000. "Executive Summary: Current Competitiveness and Growth Competitiveness," in *The Global Competitiveness Report 2000*. The World Economic Forum (Oxford: Oxford University Press), pp. 14–17.

Porter, Michael E., Jeffrey D. Sachs, and John W. McArthur. 2001. "Executive Summary: Competitiveness and Stages of Economic Development," in *The Global Competitiveness Report 2001–2002*, World Economic Forum (Oxford: Oxford University Press), pp. 16–25.

World Economic Forum. 2001. *The Global Competitiveness Report 2001–2002* (Oxford: Oxford University Press).

Notes

[i] For details, see IMF (1998) and IMF (1999).

[ii] Thorough discussions of Russia's early reform efforts are provided, for example, by Fischer (1994), Aslund (1995), and Blanchard et al. (1995). The more specific issue of enterprise restructuring and the role of banks in corporate governance is discussed in detail, for example, in Litwack (1995) and Berglöf and von Thadden (2000). A more recent assessment can be found in Lopez-Claros and Zadornov (2001).

[iii] There are a number of outliers, however, which may be explained by different reasons. For example, the level of per capita income can be misaligned with current competitiveness if a favorable growth environment (eg, high capital inflows) masks weaknesses in current competitiveness. Or the progress of an economy along various dimensions of current competitiveness may be uneven, with some areas becoming constraints that ultimately become binding.

[iv] For an explanation of the methodology used to make this calculation, consult "Changing Corporate Governance in Russia," The Corporate Governance Initiative of the World Economic Forum (in collaboration with Troika Dialog), January 2001.

[v] Gazprom, for example, sells its production domestically at prices on average up to four times below international prices. Based on last year's prices, this amounted to US$ 6.3 billion, or 3 percent of GDP.

The World Economic Forum would like to thank Troika Dialog Investment Company for their support in making this *Report* possible.

 **TROIKA DIALOG**

Troika Dialog is Russia's leading investment banking and securities company, providing a full range of investing, advisory, and financing services to a substantial and diversified client base, which includes corporations, financial institutions, governments, and high net worth individuals. The company's top-ranked research, along with path-breaking product origination and asset management, provide both individual and institutional clients with access to the most comprehensive array of high-quality products and services in the Russian financial services industry today. Founded in 1991 with the fall of the USSR, Troika Dialog is the oldest and largest investment bank in Russia. The Firm is headquartered in Moscow and maintains offices in the Russian regions as well as in New York.

Since the first days of Russia's market economy, Troika senior managers—Russian and foreign—have played a leading role in developing the infrastructure of Russian capital markets. In May 2001, *Fortune* magazine named Ruben Vardanian, President of Troika Dialog, one of the 25 "Next Generation of Global Leaders." Troika's dedication to upholding international standards and the implementation of corporate governance has been well recognized. At the Davos World Economic Forum, Troika was named as Emerging Market Leader. Furthermore, *Euromoney* cited Troika Dialog as Russia's best investment bank, and the American Chamber of Commerce awarded Troika's two senior partners a joint prize: Businessperson of the Year.